The Last Tax

The Last Tax

How Wealth Taxes Could Technically Work

Dan Shaffer

4D4 Labs Press
Cleveland, Ohio

Published by 4D4 Labs Press Cleveland, Ohio TheLastTax.com (calculator, errata, and updates)

First Edition, 2026

ISBN 979-8-9960017-1-2 (hardcover) ISBN 979-8-9960017-0-5 (paperback) ISBN 979-8-9960017-2-9 (ebook) ISBN 979-8-9960017-3-6 (audiobook)

Library of Congress Control Number: 2026911739

Printed in the United States of America

CONTENTS

DISCLAIMER

This book is intended for educational, civic, and policy discussion purposes only. It does not provide legal, tax, accounting, financial, investment, or professional advice. The examples, calculations, and policy designs discussed are illustrative unless otherwise stated. Anyone making legal, tax, financial, or investment decisions should consult qualified professionals.

PREFACE

I am a data engineer. For over fifteen years, my work has been to design systems that track and reconcile all types of data at scale. I have built automated systems for financial instruments, healthcare claims, payment transactions, and government records, each with their own protocols, statutes, and business requirements. The job is always the same: understand what the system needs to do, catalog the constraints it must live inside, and build something that actually works.

This is not the resume of a tax expert. It is a different angle on the same problem.

Tax policy in this country belongs to economists, lawyers, and politicians. Each profession brings real knowledge and reputational risks for going against the conventional wisdom. An economist who argues for a comprehensive wealth tax may risk a tenure track. A politician may risk an election. A tax attorney may risk their client list. The people closest to the problem are often the people most exposed to consequences for naming it plainly.

I have no tenure track. I have no political ambitions. I have no roster of wealthy clients to lose. That grants me a freedom that many in the field cannot afford to use. I can write down what the system could actually look like if we stopped pretending the obstacles are technical and started treating them as political.

Engineering is not a worldview. It is a discipline. You start with the goal. You catalog the constraints, statutory, physical, and behavioral. You design mechanisms that satisfy the goal within the constraints. Where a constraint conflicts with the goal, you flag the conflict honestly instead of redefining the goal until the conflict disappears.

That discipline is what this book brings to the question of wealth taxation.

The conventional wisdom holds that a comprehensive wealth tax is impossible or impractical at national scale. Assets cannot be tracked. Valuation is too hard. The Constitution forbids it. The rich will leave. Privacy will be destroyed.

So, we work the problem.

Examined as engineering problems, each of those objections turns out to have a solution either already in production somewhere or sitting in an adjacent field, waiting to be applied.

That is what this book is for.

CHAPTER 1

INTRODUCTION

What if tax evasion were structurally self-defeating, and the entire federal tax code fit on a cocktail napkin?

$$\text{Tax} = \frac{\text{Your Wealth}}{\text{National Wealth}} \times \text{Federal Spending}$$

Every dollar of wealth is as visible as every acre of land. The billionaire is unable to hide behind shell companies any more than a farmer can hide his fields. The tax you owe is calculated automatically against the share of national wealth you control. Paying taxes on wealth is the ultimate claim to ownership, because refusing to do so opens the claim to challengers who will. It is also what shields the claim once made: a duty-paying stake cannot be extinguished without due process and equitable compensation, whether the challenger is a private party or the government itself.

The technology exists. The precedents exist. The formula is right there. What is missing is the political will to build it, and the understanding that makes political will possible. That is what this book provides.

1.1 The Idea

What would it look like if we replaced all federal taxes with a single, proportional wealth tax?

No income tax. No payroll tax. No corporate tax, estate tax, capital gains tax, or any of the other federal levies. One tax. One rate. One ledger.

The design rests on four pillars:

One Tax. A single proportional wealth tax replaces every federal tax currently collected. The Internal Revenue Code, its Treasury regulations, and the seventy-thousand-page tax-research library built around them all become obsolete. In their place: a formula simple enough to fit on a napkin. Your tax equals your share of the nation's wealth multiplied by federal spending. That is it. All wealth is taxed annually, the same way property taxes work on land. The system does not distinguish between realized and unrealized gains, or between earned and unearned income. You control it, you pay on it.

One Ledger. A public record of all wealth, who controls it, and what they owe. Think of county land records, which have tracked property ownership for centuries. Now extend that principle to all forms of wealth: stocks, bonds, business equity, intellectual property, cryptocurrency, art, vehicles, and everything that can be exchanged, valued, and transferred. The ledger is the authoritative record. Registration is the strongest claim to ownership the system offers.

One Principle. Those who control wealth pay proportionally to what they control. Not based on income, which can be manipulated, deferred, and hidden, but on control. If you can direct an asset, benefit from it, exclude others from it, or transfer it, you bear the duty to pay your share. This is the "duty of control," and it follows the wealth wherever it goes, through whatever structures are placed around it.

One Consequence. The incentive structure inverts. Today, hiding wealth is advantageous: the concealed asset is off the tax rolls and still yours. Under this system, hiding wealth means risking that someone else registers it first and holds the superior claim. If you control wealth above the de minimis threshold, you register it. If you do not, anyone else with evidence of control can. Chapter 7 details how the ledger works, including thresholds and how competing claims are resolved.

This sounds radical. But is it?

Property taxes already work this way for real estate. You declare your property. The county assesses its value. You pay a percentage annually. If you do not pay, the county sells your property to someone who will. The wealth stays in the tax base; only the owner changes. Across the United States, counties routinely identify assets, assess their value, and collect taxes on them. The methods vary from state to state, but the capability is universal.

What this book describes is an extension of that proven principle to all forms of wealth. The technology to do so now exists. The question is whether we have the will to use it.

1.2 Why This Book, Why Now

Three developments make this idea timely in a way it has never been before.

The current system is broken beyond repair. The federal tax system nominally collects about $5.1 trillion per year,[1] but the "tax gap" (the difference between what is owed and what is collected) runs to $696 billion annually in gross terms, with roughly $606 billion never recovered even after enforcement.[2] That is not a bug; it is a feature. The system is designed to be gamed by those with the resources to game it.

The numbers are stark. ProPublica's analysis of leaked IRS data showed the 25 richest Americans paid a true tax rate of just 3.4% between 2014 and 2018 (Chapter 2 provides the individual figures).[3] Meanwhile, a nurse or a teacher earning $60,000 pays 20-30% when you include income and payroll taxes.

The system appears progressive when measured by income. The top 1% paid an average federal income tax rate of 23.1% on reported adjusted gross income.[4] But the wealthy do not have "income" in the legal sense. They have wealth appreciation. Their stocks go up. Their companies grow. Their real estate appreciates. None of this is taxed until they choose to sell, and many never need to sell a share in their lifetime. They borrow against their assets, live on the loans, and when they die, the gains disappear. This is the "buy-borrow-die" strategy (Chapter 2 details the mechanics), and it is perfectly legal.

The tax code is not failing. It is working exactly as designed, for those who designed it.

Technology accidentally solved the implementation problem. For most of history, a comprehensive wealth tax was impractical. How do you track all the wealth in a nation? How do you prevent people from hiding assets? How do you value things that are not publicly traded? The answer is blockchain.

Blockchain is unfamiliar to most people. Three things matter:

1. **Things have identities.** A traditional ledger tracks money moving between accounts. This person paid this amount for this thing, new balance, next line, repeat. Blockchain adds something new: the objects being exchanged have identities on the ledger too. That object could be a house, a share of stock, a piece of art, or a fraction of one. This makes it possible to trace the complete ownership history of anything, not just the flow of money.

2. **No single person controls it.** When ownership changes hands, the transaction is announced simultaneously to thousands of independent ledger-keepers. No single party can silently add to the ledger, because any change is immediately visible to everyone else.

3. **The past is arithmetically protected.** Each entry is mathematically linked to the one before it, like a chain. Change anything in the past and

> you corrupt every entry that follows, making it glaringly obvious which record was tampered with.

The result is a tamper-evident history of who owns what, verified by math rather than trust.

Blockchain idealists set out to circumvent the powerful. They wanted to create money and property systems outside government control. In the process, they built something unexpected: high-volume, tamper-evident, distributed ledger technology capable of tracking ownership at massive scale.

The technology built to escape government accountability can be repurposed to enable it. The tools exist, already processing millions of transactions daily with immutable records and cryptographic verification. The wealthy may have captured cryptocurrency as a means of banking in the dark (a way to hold assets beyond taxation and regulation), but in the process they created the very tools needed to track and tax the wealth they were trying to hide.

What was impossible in 1913, when the income tax amendment was ratified, is routine today.

The political window exists. Wealth inequality has reached levels not seen since the Gilded Age. The top 1% now controls roughly a third of all US wealth, more than twelve times what the bottom half of households hold combined.[5] Chapter 3 examines what this concentration means for republican government. Public frustration with a "rigged system" spans the political spectrum from progressive Democrats to populist Republicans. The sense that the rules are different for the powerful is widespread and accurate.

The 16th Amendment precedent (Chapter 2 tells the full story) proves that Americans can restructure federal taxation when the need is clear. Movements start with understanding. This book provides that understanding.

The government goes first. Before asking any citizen to declare their wealth on a public ledger, the system described in this book puts federal spending on the same kind of ledger. The Pentagon has failed its financial audit eight consecutive years, running 208 systems relevant to its financial audit that cannot be reconciled into a single audit trail.[6] A tamper-evident spending ledger solves that problem and proves the technology at scale. If the government will not submit to the transparency it asks of citizens, it has no standing to ask. Chapter 14 details how this works.

1.3 What This Book Will Show You

This book is organized into four parts.

Part I: The Problem (Chapters 2-4) traces how the current tax system evolved from simple tariffs to the labyrinthine code we have today. It explains why the system punishes work while rewarding wealth accumulation, and why incremental reforms to "close the loopholes," "raise the rates," "fund the IRS" keep running into structural problems.

Part II: The Design (Chapters 5-9) walks through each component of the system. What counts as wealth? Who bears the duty to pay? How would the ledger work? What is the formula? How is it enforced? Each chapter addresses one component with concrete mechanisms, not vague aspirations.

Part III: Hard Questions (Chapters 10-13) takes on the strongest objections. "It's unconstitutional." "You can't value everything." "The rich will just leave." "What about privacy?" These are serious concerns, and they deserve serious responses. You will find them here.

Part IV: Implementation & Action (Chapters 14-16) explains how we get from here to there. What is the transition plan? What does this mean for you personally? What would it take to make it happen?

You can read straight through, or jump to what interests you most. Skeptics might start with Part III. Numbers people will find detailed calculations in Chapter 8. If you want to know what this means for your own situation, Chapter 15 has worked examples at every wealth level.

1.4 The Core Question

Here is the question this book tries to answer:

Can we build a tax system where those who control the most wealth pay proportionally to support the civilization that makes that wealth possible, and where the technology exists to actually enforce it?

"Taxes are the maintenance fee for civilization." Roads, courts, police, contracts, property rights, national defense, public health, education: all require funding. Wealth itself only exists because society enforces it. Your ownership of a house means nothing without courts to adjudicate disputes, police to prevent theft, and a legal system that recognizes your title. Your ownership of stock means nothing without securities laws, contract enforcement, and a stable currency. Wealth is built inside a social infrastructure, and that infrastructure has to be maintained.

"Those who control the most should pay proportionally." The tax is proportional, not punitive. Whether the wealth is one million dollars or one billion, the rate is the same; only the dollar amount changes. Those who benefit most from the infrastructure of civilization and whose wealth depends most heavily on courts, contracts, and stability should contribute most to maintaining it. This is not redistribution; it is contribution.

"Technology now makes this enforceable." The practical objection to wealth taxation has always been enforcement. How do you know what people own? How do you prevent concealment? How do you value illiquid assets? These were genuine obstacles in 1913. They are not obstacles today. Distributed ledger technology can track hundreds of millions of assets. Cryptographic signatures can verify ownership. Tamper-evident records can prevent manipulation. The infrastructure exists; it needs only to be applied to civic purposes.

"The ledger captures wealth we cannot even see today." When this book refers to "national wealth," it uses the Federal Reserve's estimate of US household net worth: roughly $175 trillion. But that figure only counts what American households own. It excludes tens of trillions of dollars controlled by foreign individuals, foreign corporations, and foreign governments holding assets within US jurisdiction. The ledger does not care about passports. If you control wealth in the United States, you register it and bear the duty, or someone else can. When foreign-controlled wealth enters the ledger, the denominator grows substantially, and the effective tax rate falls. The 4% rate cited throughout this book is based on conservative assumptions; the true rate could be closer to 3%. Chapter 8 works through these numbers in detail.

1.5 A Note to the Reader

This book is written for anyone who pays taxes, which is to say, nearly everyone. It does not assume expertise in tax law, blockchain technology, or constitutional history. Where technical concepts are necessary, they are explained. Where numbers are used, they are sourced.

The author brings more than fifteen years of data engineering experience across private industry, ecommerce, and government. This is not an economist's thought experiment or a politician's platform; it is an engineer's design, built from the perspective of someone who has spent a career designing systems that track, value, and move data at scale. The question that drives this book is the same one that drives any engineering project: *Can we build this?*

If you are skeptical, good. Skepticism is the right response when someone describes replacing the entire federal tax system. Read the hard questions chapters. Check the sources. Do the math yourself. Chapter 8 gives you the formula.

If you are already convinced that the system is broken, this book offers something beyond outrage: a concrete alternative. Not "tax the rich" as a slogan, but a specific mechanism for how it could work in a way that cannot be evaded.

If you are wealthy, you may find this idea threatening. Or you may find it liberating. A system where everyone pays their share, including you, is also a system where no one can accuse you of cheating. The ledger is public. Your contribution is visible. The social contract is honored by all.

Whatever your starting point, the goal is the same: to understand what is possible, and to decide what to do about it.

1.6 What This Means in Practice

Consider one person.

Maria teaches fourth grade. She earns $58,000 a year and has $117,000 in total wealth: modest savings, a retirement account, a paid-off car. Under the current system, she pays approximately $13,700 in federal taxes, including income tax, her payroll tax, and the employer payroll tax that suppresses her wages before she ever sees a job offer (Chapter 2 explains this hidden cost). That is 24% of her income.

Under the wealth tax: $117,000 times 4% equals $4,680. Maria saves $9,020 per year. Not because anyone gave her a tax cut, but because the system stopped taxing what she earns and started taxing what people control.

At the other end: a billionaire controlling $8.3 billion currently pays about $25 million in federal taxes, an effective rate of 0.3% on his wealth. Under the same formula: $8.3 billion times 4% equals $332 million. The rate is identical. The amount differs because the wealth differs.

Chapter 15 walks through twelve detailed profiles at every wealth level, from a working family earning $48,000 to a billionaire, with full asset tables and side-by-side comparisons. The crossover point, where the wealth tax equals current federal taxes, falls at roughly $1.5-2 million. Below that, approximately 88-90% of American households pay less.

1.7 What Comes Next

The next chapter traces how we got here, how a nation founded on opposition to taxation developed the most complex tax code in the world, and how that code came to serve the interests of those it was meant to constrain.

But first, a preview of where we are going.

The system described in this book would:

- **Replace every federal tax (income, payroll, corporate, estate, and capital gains) with a single proportional wealth tax** (approximately 4% based on conservative estimates, potentially as low as 3% once all wealth is captured on the ledger)
- **Record all wealth on a public ledger** with tamper-evident verification
- **Make tax liability automatic and transparent**: no returns, no withholding, no quarterly estimates
- **Protect homeowners and retirees**: no one loses their home for lack of cash flow
- **Require a constitutional amendment** to implement (as the income tax did)
- **Build in 4-6 years at a cost of $2-5 billion** (a fraction of current IRS costs)
- **Generate revenue equivalent to the federal budget**, matching current levels, while closing the tax gap and distributing the burden proportionally

Every dollar of wealth as visible as every acre of land. Every citizen's contribution proportional, transparent, and automatic. That is the system this book describes. That is the system we could build.

1.8 Notes

1. Internal Revenue Service, *Internal Revenue Service Data Book, 2024*, Publication 55B (Washington, DC: U.S. Department of the Treasury, 2024), https://www.irs.gov/pub/irs-pdf/p55b.pdf.

2. Internal Revenue Service, "Tax Gap Projections for Tax Years 2021 and 2022," October 2024, https://www.irs.gov/newsroom/the-tax-gap.

3. Jesse Eisinger, Jeff Ernsthausen, and Paul Kiel, "The Secret IRS Files: Trove of Never-Before-Seen Records Reveal How the Wealthiest Avoid Income Tax," ProPublica, June 8, 2021, https://www.propublica.org/article/the-secret-irs-files-trove-of-never-before-seen-records-reveal-how-the-wealthiest-avoid-income-tax.

4. Internal Revenue Service, *Statistics of Income, Individual Income Tax Returns, Tax Year 2022* (Washington, DC: Internal Revenue Service, 2024), https://www.irs.gov/statistics.

5. Board of Governors of the Federal Reserve System, "Distributional Financial Accounts," Q3 2025 release, https://www.federalreserve.gov/releases/z1/dataviz/dfa/. Top 1% share: 31.7%; bottom 50% share: approximately 2.5%; ratio ≈ 12.7x.

6. U.S. Government Accountability Office, *Financial Management: DOD Needs to Improve System Oversight*, GAO-23-104539, March 2023, https://www.gao.gov/products/gao-23-104539.

CHAPTER 2

HOW WE GOT HERE, A BRIEF HISTORY OF AMERICAN TAXATION

The story of American taxation begins with a constitutional provision designed to protect slaveholders. The "direct tax" clause, born of the original compromise over slavery, became the legal barrier to taxing accumulated wealth. Tracing how we arrived at this inheritance helps explain why incremental reform keeps stalling and why fundamental redesign deserves serious consideration.

The tax code is not the product of a single design session. It is the accumulated result of two centuries of legislation, each provision added by someone, for someone. The pattern across that history is consistent: each reform creates new opportunities for avoidance, each loophole gets exploited, and the system grows more complex while becoming less effective at its stated purpose.

2.1 The Original Design (1789-1913)

The Founders deliberately avoided direct taxation. The federal government was funded primarily through tariffs, taxes on imported goods, and excise taxes on specific products like whiskey and tobacco. This worked for a small agrarian nation with limited federal responsibilities, but it couldn't scale.

The Constitution's treatment of direct taxes reflects an ugly compromise. Article I requires that direct taxes be apportioned among the states according to population. This provision was linked to the Three-Fifths Compromise: Southern states wanted enslaved people counted for congressional representation, and the apportionment requirement was part of the deal. If direct taxes were apportioned by population, states with large enslaved populations would bear higher tax burdens, theoretically offsetting their increased representation.

The federal government's first attempt at income taxation came during the Civil War. The Revenue Act of 1861 imposed a flat 3% tax on incomes over $800. By 1865, the rates had risen to 10% on incomes over $10,000. The tax was administratively successful, raising significant revenue for the Union war effort. After the war ended, it was gradually phased out and repealed entirely in 1872.

The Civil War income tax proved something important: income taxation was administratively possible. The federal government could identify taxpayers, assess their incomes, and collect what was owed. The question was whether it was constitutional.

In 1894, Congress passed a new income tax: a 2% tax on incomes over $4,000. The following year, the Supreme Court struck it down in *Pollock v. Farmers' Loan & Trust Co.* The Court ruled that taxes on income from property were "direct taxes" requiring apportionment by state population. Since apportionment was unworkable for an income tax (it would mean different rates in different states based on population, not income) the decision effectively prohibited federal income taxation.

Justice John Marshall Harlan dissented vigorously, warning that the decision would make it impossible to tax accumulated wealth. He was right, until the Constitution was changed.

2.2 The Income Tax Amendment (1913)

The Pollock decision created a constitutional crisis. But the years that followed weren't spent building support for an amendment. They were spent trying to work around the Court's ruling, hoping the problem would solve itself.

Once reformers committed to the amendment path, momentum built quickly. Progressive Era reformers, populists, and labor unions organized. The campaign built pressure state by state. Legislatures passed resolutions calling for an amendment. Politicians who opposed it faced electoral consequences.

By 1909, the political moment had arrived. President William Howard Taft, a Republican, supported the amendment. Congress proposed it with near-unanimous votes: 77-0 in the Senate, 318-14 in the House. When the political will was clear, the constitutional barrier fell.

Ratification took less than four years. Forty-two states ratified, well above the thirty-six required. The Sixteenth Amendment became law on February 3, 1913:

> "The Congress shall have power to lay and collect taxes on incomes, from whatever source derived, without apportionment among the several States, and without regard to any census or enumeration."

The original income tax was modest by today's standards. It imposed a 1% tax on incomes over $3,000, equivalent to roughly $98,000 today. Rates graduated up to 7% on incomes over $500,000. Only about 2% of the population paid any income tax at all.

The original intent was clear: tax the wealthy, spare the workers. The income tax was designed as a levy on accumulating capital wealth, not on wages. It took decades for that intent to be inverted.

The 16th Amendment did not emerge from nowhere. It was the culmination of a tradition that runs through American politics like a fault line. Henry George's *Progress and Poverty* (1879) argued that the fruits of civilization belong to the civilization that produced them, and sold three million copies in a country of sixty million. The Populist movement of the 1890s organized farmers and workers around the same principle: that concentrated wealth owed a duty to the commonwealth. The Progressive reformers who pushed the amendment through Congress were heirs to that tradition, not its inventors. The idea that wealth should be visible and accountable is not new. It is unfinished.

The lesson for today is worth noting: constitutional barriers to taxation can be overcome, and faster than most people expect. Once Congress proposed the amendment, ratification took less than four years. It takes organization, sustained advocacy, and political will. But when the moment arrives, change happens fast.

2.3 The Growth of Complexity (1913-1980)

The income tax started simple. It did not stay that way.

World War I transformed the tax system. Rates rose dramatically to fund the war effort and the top marginal rate reached 77% by 1918. More importantly, the tax base expanded. Exemptions were lowered, bringing more Americans into the system. And the first major deductions and exemptions were created, planting the seeds of future complexity.

The 1920s brought rollback. Top rates were cut to 25%. Wealth concentrated rapidly during the "Roaring Twenties." The crash of 1929 and the Great Depression followed, a pattern that would repeat.

The New Deal and World War II transformed the income tax into a mass levy. Top rates rose to 94% by 1944. More significantly, withholding was introduced in 1943. For the first time, taxes were deducted from paychecks before workers ever saw the money. This was administratively efficient, and it created a fundamental asymmetry. Workers paid immediately and automatically. The wealthy, whose income came from investments rather than wages, retained control over when and whether to realize taxable income.

The post-war period saw an explosion of complexity. Each new provision in the tax code created new avoidance strategies. Tax lawyers and accountants became essential for anyone with significant wealth. The code grew from a few dozen pages to thousands, then tens of thousands.

A cycle established itself: reform, capture, new loopholes. Congress would pass legislation to close one avenue of avoidance, and the tax planning industry would find three more. Complexity became a feature of the system itself.

By 1980, the tax code was already labyrinthine. But the most consequential changes were still ahead.

2.4 The Capture (1980-Present)

Over the last four decades, a series of policy changes have reshaped the tax system in ways that consistently favor wealth over work. Each round of "reform" created new avoidance routes for the wealthy while ordinary workers continued to pay.

Declining top marginal rates. In 1980, the top marginal income tax rate was 70%. By 1988, after the Reagan tax cuts, it had fallen to 28%. Today it stands at 37% nominally. But the nominal rate tells only part of the story.

Capital gains preferences. Long-term capital gains, profits from selling assets held more than a year, are taxed at a maximum rate of 20%, compared to 37% for ordinary income like wages. This preference is justified as encouraging investment, but its primary effect is to ensure that the wealthy pay lower rates than workers.

The "carried interest" loophole allows hedge fund and private equity managers to treat their compensation as capital gains rather than ordinary income. A fund manager earning $50 million pays a 20% rate while a surgeon earning $500,000 pays 37%. Warren Buffett famously noted that he pays a lower tax rate than his secretary.

Corporate tax avoidance goes global. Multinational corporations developed sophisticated strategies to shift profits to low-tax jurisdictions. Transfer pricing, charging artificially high or low prices for transactions between subsidiaries, moves income to tax havens. Intellectual property is held in Ireland or the Netherlands, where royalty payments reduce taxable income in the United States.

The statutory corporate tax rate has fallen from 46% in 1980 to 21% today. But effective rates, what corporations actually pay, are often far lower. Some of the most profitable companies in the world pay little or no federal income tax in many years.

The "buy-borrow-die" strategy. This is the ultimate tax avoidance technique, available only to the very wealthy. It works in three steps:

First, don't sell appreciated assets. If you own stock that has increased in value, you owe no tax until you sell. So don't sell. Your wealth grows, but you have no taxable income.

Second, borrow against your assets. Banks are happy to lend against a portfolio worth billions. Loans are not income, you're not selling anything, just borrowing. You can live lavishly on borrowed money, paying low interest rates, while your assets continue to appreciate tax-free.

Third, die. When you die, your heirs receive your assets with a "stepped-up basis," meaning their cost basis resets to the current market value. All the appreciation that occurred during your lifetime is never taxed. The gains simply disappear.

This is the logical result of a system that taxes income rather than wealth, that preferences capital gains over wages, and that resets basis at death. In 2022, Elon Musk acquired Twitter for $44 billion. His original financing plan included a $12.5 billion margin loan secured by his Tesla stock: unrealized, untaxed wealth deployed as purchasing power. Banks were happy to lend against it; they could value Tesla shares to the penny every second of every trading day. In that structure, Musk could have spent $12.5 billion of his wealth without selling a single share and without triggering a single dollar of tax. Loans are not income. The man whose "true tax rate" was 3.27% was prepared to deploy $44 billion in a single transaction. If the banks can value it precisely enough to lend billions against it, the wealth is real.

IRS defunding. Even the rules that exist are barely enforced. The IRS has been systematically defunded, with consequences Chapter 4 examines in detail. The result: an estimated $696 billion gross tax gap goes uncollected each year.[1] Wealthy taxpayers and their representatives in Congress have systematically weakened the agency responsible for enforcing tax laws. An underfunded IRS cannot close the gap.

2.5 Where We Are Now

The current system produces predictable results. It was built through decades of incremental decisions, each one rational from someone's perspective, and the cumulative effect is a structure that treats work and wealth very differently.

Workers pay immediately. Wages are subject to withholding, taxes are deducted before you ever see the money. Payroll taxes (Social Security and Medicare) take another 15.3% off the top, split between employee and employer. A worker earning $60,000 might pay an effective federal rate of 20-25% when all taxes are included.

That "split between employee and employer" deserves scrutiny. It is an accounting fiction. The Congressional Budget Office and the Joint Committee on Taxation both treat the employer's share of payroll taxes as part of the worker's total compensation cost. Mainstream economists agree: the employer's 7.65% comes out of what the employer would otherwise pay the worker in wages.[2]

Here is how it works. An employer budgets $65,000 for a position. Before the worker sees an offer letter, $4,973 is set aside for the employer's share of Social Security and Medicare. The job listing says $60,027. The worker never knows the position's real compensation capacity. She negotiates from $60,027, not from $65,000. Her own payroll taxes and income tax withholding then reduce her take-home pay further. She sees roughly $45,000 in her bank account and believes that is what the job pays.

The effect is wage suppression. The employer's payroll tax is invisible to the worker, but it is real in its effect. It does not appear on any pay stub. It is not discussed in any job interview. It depresses every wage offer in the economy by 7.65% before the first dollar is negotiated.

The implication for reform is a double dividend. Eliminating payroll taxes does not just end the tax on the worker's paycheck. It ends the invisible tax on the worker's job offer. The worker's taxes disappear, and the employer's cost of employing her drops by 7.65%, creating room for wages to rise. For a worker earning $60,000, that is nearly $10,000 in combined benefit: roughly $4,600 in eliminated employee payroll taxes plus $4,600 in freed employer capacity that market competition pushes toward higher wages. The benefit is larger than most people calculate, because most people do not know the hidden half of the tax exists.

Wealth pays never, or at least not until the owner chooses. Investment gains are not taxed until realized. Borrowing against assets is not taxed at all. And death resets the basis, erasing a lifetime of untaxed appreciation.

The results are stark. ProPublica's analysis of leaked IRS data revealed the "true tax rates" of the wealthiest Americans (the taxes they actually paid divided by the growth in their wealth):[3]

- Warren Buffett: 0.10%
- Jeff Bezos: 0.98%

- Elon Musk: 3.27% (the same man who deployed $44 billion to acquire Twitter)
- Michael Bloomberg: 1.30%

Meanwhile, a teacher or nurse earning $60,000 pays 20-30% in federal taxes. The system is regressive in the truest sense: those with the most pay the least.

Incremental reform has not changed this trajectory. Every loophole closed creates two more. Every rate increase is offset by new avoidance strategies. The complexity itself creates infinite opportunities for those with resources to exploit it.

Understanding why gets us to the central question: what would it take to build something that actually works?

2.6 The Structure Is the Problem

Two centuries trace the same cycle. Crisis forces change. Change brings complexity. Complexity rewards whoever can afford to navigate it. The wealthy fund the politicians who protect the complexity. Incremental fixes get absorbed. The cycle resumes.

This cycle has been broken exactly once. The 1913 income tax took eighteen years, a constitutional amendment, and a generation of organizing. It happened because reformers stopped trying to patch the existing system and recognized that no amount of patching would be enough. The structure had to be replaced.

We are at the same moment. The income tax began as a levy on the wealthy. Decade by decade, it has been reshaped into a levy on work.

2.7 Notes

1. Internal Revenue Service, "Tax Gap Projections for Tax Years 2021 and 2022," October 2024, https://www.irs.gov/newsroom/the-tax-gap.

2. Congressional Budget Office, "Revisiting the Extent to Which Payroll Taxes Are Passed Through to Employees," Working Paper 2021-06, June 2021, https://www.cbo.gov/publication/57089.

3. Jesse Eisinger, Jeff Ernsthausen, and Paul Kiel, "The Secret IRS Files: Trove of Never-Before-Seen Records Reveal How the Wealthiest Avoid Income Tax," ProPublica, June 8, 2021, https://www.propublica.org/article/the-secret-irs-files-trove-of-never-before-seen-records-reveal-how-the-wealthiest-avoid-income-tax.

CHAPTER 3

THE RETURN OF FEUDALISM

The Sackler family, through Purdue Pharma, aggressively marketed OxyContin while knowing it was fueling an addiction crisis. Hundreds of thousands of Americans died in the epidemic that followed.[1] The family extracted approximately $11 billion from the company,[2] moving wealth through a maze of trusts and corporate entities before it declared bankruptcy. By the time courts intervened, the money had been dispersed into structures designed to be invisible. No one could trace where it went until it was gone.

It looks familiar. The word "feudalism" conjures images of castles and serfs, but feudalism was never primarily about castles. It was about extraction in darkness: a class of people that takes from society while operating beyond public sight, that benefits from courts, contracts, infrastructure, and peace while bearing no corresponding duty. Through legal innovation, modern law has reassembled feudal power structures without feudal titles. The mechanisms are different. The structural result is remarkably similar.

3.1 What Feudalism Actually Was

Feudalism was not simply "kings and peasants." It was a specific system of social organization with distinctive characteristics that are worth understanding before examining their modern counterparts.

In theory, feudalism was a system of mutual obligation. The lord provided protection and justice. The peasants provided labor and tribute. Each party owed duties to the other. The lord who failed to protect his tenants violated the feudal bargain as surely as the peasant who failed to pay his dues.

In practice, the obligations flowed one way. The lord extracted from those who worked the land: a portion of the harvest, days of labor, fees for using the mill or the oven. The peasant had no way to see the lord's ledgers, no mechanism to verify what was taken or where it went. Legal structures shielded the holder from scrutiny. The books did not open, and no one could make them open.

Feudal power had four defining characteristics:

Hereditary. Power passed through bloodlines, not merit. The son of a lord was a lord; the son of a peasant was a peasant. Birth determined destiny.

Extractive. The holders of the estate took from producers without proportional contribution. The lord did not create the harvest; he claimed a share of it. The contribution he returned, "protection," was in many cases protection from threats he himself posed.

Opaque. The lord's holdings, dealings, and extractions were invisible to those he ruled. No public record. No right of inspection. No mechanism for the governed to see what was being taken or where it went. The feudal estate was a black box. The lord's wealth was whatever he said it was.

Perpetual. Feudal estates outlived individuals. The lordship passed from father to son indefinitely. Wealth and power compounded across generations without natural endpoint.

The American Revolution was explicitly a rejection of this system. The Founders had lived under hereditary privilege and opaque power. They designed a republic to prevent its return.

3.2 The American Rejection of Feudalism

The Constitution contains provisions specifically designed to prevent the emergence of a new aristocracy.

Article I, Section 9 prohibits the federal government from granting titles of nobility. Article I, Section 10 extends this prohibition to the states. No American can be made a duke or an earl. There are no hereditary offices, no permanent claims to power based on bloodline.

The Founders also feared concentrated, invisible power in non-governmental forms. Early American corporations were tightly controlled. They required specific legislative charters that defined their purpose and duration. A corporation chartered to build a bridge could not pivot to banking. Charters expired and had to be renewed. Corporations that abused their privileges could be dissolved.

The Founders recognized that concentrated power threatens liberty regardless of whether it wears a crown or a logo. A republic requires rough equality of power among citizens; permanent concentrations of wealth and influence inevitably corrupt democratic governance. Power derives from the people, and the dealings of the powerful are visible to the people. No permanent overclass. Equal duty under law. Citizens, not subjects.

What went wrong?

3.3 How Feudalism Returned

Through a series of legal innovations over two centuries, American law reassembled the four structural features of feudal wealth (hereditary, extractive, opaque, perpetual) out of modern parts. The mechanisms look nothing like castles or charters. The shape they produce is older than either.

Corporate "personhood" became a shield. The legal fiction that corporations are "persons" was originally a convenience, allowing corporations to enter contracts and be sued. But it evolved into something else: a way for human controllers to disappear from view.

Corporations gained rights (free speech, religious exercise under *Burwell v. Hobby Lobby Stores, Inc.*, 573 U.S. 682 (2014), due process) without proportional duties. Human controllers disappear behind corporate liability. When a corporation pollutes, defrauds, or kills, the response is "the corporation did it." But corporations are not people. They are abstractions. The humans who made the decisions, who profited from the harm, vanish from view.

"The corporation did it" has become the modern equivalent of the feudal black box. The human controller is invisible. The system proposed in this book reverses that fiction. On the public ledger, no corporation signs. Only the humans behind it do.

Limited liability inverted risk. The principle of limited liability means that investors can only lose what they invested. If a corporation causes harm exceeding its assets, victims go uncompensated. The investors keep their other wealth.

This was justified as encouraging investment and entrepreneurship. But it also means that risk is socialized while profit is privatized. The corporation takes chances with other people's lives and livelihoods. If the gamble pays off, shareholders profit. If it doesn't, the losses fall on workers, communities, and the public.

The same asymmetry, extraction without proportional exposure, is what modern limited liability reconstructs in statute.

Immortal entities extend the perpetuity feature. Feudal estates already outlived their holders. The estate passed from father to son indefinitely.

Modern corporations and trusts do the same thing with greater efficiency. A dynasty trust compounds wealth across generations while avoiding estate taxes entirely. In states that have abolished the rule against perpetuities, these trusts can last forever. The old estate at least needed an heir; the modern trust doesn't even need that.

The labyrinth of shells and trusts obscures control. Consider the structure revealed in the Trump fraud case: dozens of entities (LLCs, corporations, and trusts layered on top of each other). Assets nominally owned by one entity, controlled by another, benefiting a third. When the question "who is responsible?" is asked, the answer disappears into the fog.

The obscurity is intentional. The beneficial owner, the human who actually controls and benefits from the wealth, is hidden behind layers of legal abstraction. Trustees claim they're just following instructions. Grantors claim they've given up control. Nominee directors claim they're just lending their names.

The result is concentrated, inheritable, opaque control: the same four structural features the Founders thought they had abolished, rebuilt out of different legal parts. The people who exercise that control benefit from society's protections and wield enormous influence, but their existence as controllers is hidden from public sight.

3.4 The Racial Architecture of Neo-Feudalism

The mechanisms described above (corporate personhood, limited liability, immortal entities, layered shells) are the general architecture of modern feudalism. But America has a specific architecture as well, and it is racial.

Slavery was the original American feudalism. It was labor extraction without compensation, wealth accumulation beyond public scrutiny, hereditary power maintained by law. The slaveholder controlled people as assets, extracted their labor, and passed the accumulated wealth to his heirs. This was not a metaphor for feudalism. It was feudalism, stripped of even the feudal lord's nominal obligations to his serfs.

Emancipation ended legal ownership of human beings. It did not end the extraction. Black Codes criminalized Black autonomy. Sharecropping replaced slavery with debt peonage. Convict leasing sold imprisoned Black men's labor to the same plantations they had worked as slaves. Each new system preserved the feudal relationship under a different legal name.

The twentieth century refined the mechanism. When the federal government created the modern middle class through the New Deal, the GI Bill, and the FHA mortgage system, it did so on racially exclusive terms. FHA underwriting manuals explicitly designated Black neighborhoods as ineligible for federally backed mortgages. The practice, known as redlining, locked Black families out of homeownership during the decades when home values were rising fastest.[3] GI Bill benefits were administered by state agencies that routinely denied Black veterans access to subsidized education and housing, particularly in the South. Discriminatory lending practices continued long after formal redlining ended, through steering, predatory subprime targeting, and appraisal bias.

The results are measurable. As of 2022, the median white household controls approximately $284,310 in wealth. The median Black household controls $44,100. The median Hispanic household controls $62,120.[4] Nearly 20% of Black households have zero or negative net worth. Black household wealth is approximately 50% concentrated in home equity, compared to roughly 20% for white households, meaning Black families are disproportionately dependent on a single asset class they were systematically excluded from acquiring.

These gaps are the direct products of specific policy decisions, many within living memory, that built wealth for white families while extracting from or excluding Black and Latino families. The feudal pattern is unmistakable: one class accumulates across generations while another labors without accumulating.

The current tax system compounds the disparity. It taxes income, which these communities earn through labor, while exempting wealth, which they were systematically prevented from building. Capital gains preferences deliver 92% of their benefits to white families.[5] The stepped-up basis erases appreciation at death, but only for those who have assets that appreciate. The mortgage interest deduction subsidizes homeownership, but primarily for those who could get mortgages in the first place. Payroll taxes, the most regressive element of the federal tax system, fall hardest on low-wage service workers, who are disproportionately Black and Hispanic.

The feudal structure has a racial architecture. Any reform that ignores it is incomplete. Chapter 15 examines specifically how shifting from income to wealth taxation changes the equation for these communities.

3.5 Feudalism in Modern Dress

The racial architecture above is the sharpest expression of the feudal pattern, not a separate one. Today's largest fortunes sit inside the same four-feature architecture. They extract from the economy while contributing less than their proportional share. They benefit from the infrastructure of civilization while paying effective tax rates that are, by the numbers, lower than what a medieval peasant owed: under the feudal bargain, a peasant owed roughly a tenth of their harvest to the estate and a tenth to the church, a combined nominal rate vastly higher than what the ultra-wealthy pay on wealth growth today.

Wealth perpetuates untaxed. The stepped-up basis rule (described in Chapter 2) eliminates capital gains at death. If you buy stock for $1 million and it grows to $100 million, you owe no tax until you sell. If you never sell, you never pay. When you die, your heirs inherit the stock with the gains erased.

Dynasty trusts compound this advantage. Properly structured, wealth can pass from generation to generation without ever triggering estate taxes. The Walton family, heirs to the Walmart fortune, are worth more than $500 billion as of 2025, per Bloomberg's Richest Families ranking. Through dynasty trusts and careful estate planning, they have structured their holdings to minimize estate taxes on virtually all of it.

Medieval estates passed intact to heirs. Modern dynasty trusts achieve the same continuity, and do so without the inheritance taxes that once provided at least some check on dynastic accumulation.

Controllers benefit without contributing proportionally. The ultra-wealthy use courts to enforce their contracts, police to protect their property, infrastructure to move their goods, and the entire apparatus of civilization to make their wealth meaningful. A stock certificate is just paper without a legal system to enforce ownership rights.

Yet as Chapter 2 documented, they pay effective rates near zero on their wealth growth. For the ultra-wealthy, that is the norm.

The social contract is supposed to be reciprocal. You benefit from society; you contribute to society. At the top of the current distribution, the relationship has become lopsided.

Political influence operates through obscured channels. Dark money floods elections. Lobbying armies shape legislation. Regulatory agencies are captured by the industries they're supposed to regulate. The rules are written by those they're supposed to constrain.

This is not corruption in the crude sense of briefcases full of cash. It is structural capture, and it follows naturally from the incentives. A tax system built on income rather than wealth creates, by design, a class with the concentrated resources to influence the rulemaking process. You do not need a conspiracy theory. You just need a system where one class accumulates without visibility. The wealthy fund think tanks that produce research supporting their interests. They endow university chairs that train the next generation of policymakers. They own media outlets that shape public opinion. They hire the lawyers who become judges and the staffers who become regulators.

The rules that maintain their invisibility are the rules they are best positioned to protect.

A class operates beyond the reach of the rules. When corporations commit fraud, executives pay civil fines, often covered by insurance or the corporation itself. When wealthy individuals evade taxes, they negotiate settlements. When they cause harm, they write checks. A poor person who steals $100 goes to jail. A wealthy person who steals $100 million pays a fine and admits no wrongdoing.

You cannot regulate what you cannot see. You cannot tax what you cannot measure. A system that taxes labor but not wealth creates, by design, a class whose economic life takes place entirely off the books. The enforcement failures are a downstream symptom: the system was never built to make these people visible.

The titles are different. The legal vocabulary is different. A class operates beyond the sight of the system that binds everyone else.

3.6 The Architecture of Invisibility

The defining feature of neo-feudalism is not that the powerful escape punishment. It is that the powerful escape sight. What looks like a gap in justice is actually a gap in information. The system cannot hold anyone responsible because the system cannot see anyone.

The BP Deepwater Horizon disaster killed eleven workers and ultimately cost BP more than $65 billion in cleanup, settlements, and fines.[6] The corporation paid fines. But who made the decisions that led to the disaster? The corporate structure diffuses control across boards, committees, subsidiaries, and contractors until the human being who chose to cut costs on safety disappears into the fog.

Wells Fargo employees created millions of fake accounts to meet sales quotas. The fraud was systematic and directed from above. The corporation paid billions in fines, ultimately borne by shareholders, many of them pension funds and ordinary investors. The executives who created the pressure and ignored the warnings? The corporate structure was not designed to make them visible. It was designed to make them disappear.

The Sackler case follows the same arc: the system fails to identify long before it fails to punish. Corporate boards, bylaws, committees, and "internal reviews" create layers of abstraction between the human controller and the public. "We've conducted an internal investigation and taken appropriate action." What action? Against whom? The public rarely learns. A duty of control, the principle that whoever can direct an asset is responsible for it, would collapse this labyrinth. It requires a system built to track control in the first place.

No amount of political will alone fixes this. The fog is a structural consequence of how the system was built. Every layer of corporate abstraction, every shell entity, every trust with a nominee director exists because our tax code never required wealth to be declared, tracked, or attributed to natural persons. A tax system built on wages and not on wealth produces exactly the opacity its architecture permits.

3.7 The Stakes

Here is what is at risk.

A republic requires rough equality of power among citizens. When wealth concentrates, political power concentrates with it. The wealthy fund campaigns, hire lobbyists, and shape the information environment. Their preferences become policy; everyone else's preferences become irrelevant.

Every republic in history that tolerated oligarchy eventually fell. Rome's republic gave way to empire as wealth concentrated in fewer hands. The Italian city-states were absorbed by monarchies. The arc is consistent: concentrated wealth corrupts democratic institutions until they become hollow shells, maintaining the forms of self-government while the substance belongs to the few.

We are on this trajectory. Wealth inequality has reached levels not seen since the Gilded Age. The top 1% now controls more wealth than the entire middle class. Political scientists have documented that policy outcomes correlate with the preferences of the wealthy and show no correlation with the preferences of average citizens.

The current trajectory leads toward permanent aristocracy. Technology accelerates concentration; network effects create winner-take-all markets; automation displaces workers while enriching owners; artificial intelligence promises to concentrate power further. The window for meaningful reform narrows with each passing year.

Working-class conservatives and progressives share this interest. The division is not between Democrats and Republicans but between those who play by the rules and those who write them. Between citizens whose tax liability is calculated for them and fortunes whose liability is negotiated. Between those whose economic lives are visible and those who operate in darkness.

Visibility is paramount for the long term stability of a Republic. The Founders of the American experiment wrote the Constitution specifically to prevent this kind of power asymmetry.

3.8 Notes

1. Centers for Disease Control and Prevention, "Drug Overdose Deaths," https://www.cdc.gov/overdose-prevention/data-research/facts-stats/. CDC counts approximately 500,000 opioid overdose deaths from 1999 through 2020; subsequent estimates exceed 700,000.

2. NPR, "Purdue Pharma, Sacklers Reach New $7.4 Billion Opioid Settlement," June 16, 2025, https://www.npr.org/2025/06/16/nx-s1-5435318/purdue-pharma-sacklers-reach-new-7-4-billion-opioid-settlement; multistate attorney general press releases on the settlement's May 1, 2026 effective date reference the approximately $11 billion the Sackler family withdrew from Purdue Pharma prior to its bankruptcy filing.

3. Richard Rothstein, *The Color of Law: A Forgotten History of How Our Government Segregated America* (New York: Liveright, 2017).

4. Aditya Aladangady, Jesse Bricker, Andrew C. Chang, Sarena Goodman, Jacob Krimmel, Kevin B. Moore, Sarah Reber, Alice Henriques Volz, and Richard A. Windle, "Changes in U.S. Family Finances from 2019 to 2022: Evidence from the Survey of Consumer Finances," *Federal Reserve Bulletin* 109, no. 6 (October 2023), https://www.federalreserve.gov/publications/files/scf23.pdf.

5. U.S. Department of the Treasury, Office of Tax Analysis, "Disparities in the Benefits of Tax Expenditures by Race and Ethnicity," January 2023, https://home.treasury.gov/news/featured-stories/disparities-in-the-benefits-of-tax-expenditures-by-race-and-ethnicity.

6. Wikipedia, "Deepwater Horizon oil spill," https://en.wikipedia.org/wiki/Deepwater_Horizon_oil_spill, summarizing BP's cumulative cleanup costs, charges, settlements, and penalties through 2018. The 2016 environmental settlement alone was $20.8 billion.

CHAPTER 4

WHY CURRENT REFORMS WON'T WORK

Every few years, a new wave of reformers promises to fix the tax system. Close the loopholes. Raise the rates. Fund the IRS. The proposals are well-intentioned, the advocates sincere, and the results have been consistently disappointing.

Here is why the usual fixes haven't worked. The answer has three parts, each developed in this chapter. The first is that the wealthy do not have the kind of economic thing the current system knows how to tax, so every standard reform aims at a target that is not there. The second is that the tax code's complexity is not a bug to be patched but a product sold to the people the reforms would touch, and every round of reform extends the product line. The third is that the political system that writes tax law is the same political system influenced by the wealth the law is supposed to reach, which means any reform serious enough to threaten concentrated wealth tends to get bent back into harmlessness before it takes effect.

The three familiar proposals, close the loopholes, raise the rates, and fund the IRS, each run into one or more of these structural barriers. Understanding why helps clarify what a workable alternative would need to look like.

4.1 The Inequality Data

Workers have income. They receive wages, reported by their employers, subject to withholding, taxed immediately. There is no escape. The visible burden understates the real one, because the employer's share of payroll tax ultimately suppresses wages (Chapter 2).

The wealthy have wealth. They own stocks, real estate, businesses, and art that appreciate in value. Under current tax law, appreciation is not "income" until the asset is sold, and the wealthy do not need to sell. They hold appreciating assets indefinitely and report minimal taxable income while their fortunes grow.

Jeff Bezos's wealth increased by $99 billion between 2014 and 2018. His reported income during that period was $4.2 billion, less than 5% of his wealth growth. He paid $973 million in taxes, an effective rate of 0.98% on his true economic gains. Raising the top income tax rate from 37% to 50% would not have touched the other 95%. It would not have touched any of it, because the gains never became income in the first place.

This is what makes the "raise the rates" approach ineffective against the largest fortunes. You can move the rate wherever you want. You are multiplying it by zero. The buy-borrow-die strategy from Chapter 2 is the structural expression of the same fact: the wealthy live off loans collateralized by unsold assets, pass those assets at death with stepped-up basis, and pay nothing on the appreciation, ever. No income tax rate increase reaches this strategy because no income is ever recognized.

The size of the gap between what the wealthy hold and what the tax system can see is the first structural barrier.

4.2 The Avoidance Machine

The second reform proposal is to close the loopholes. Identify the provisions that let the wealthy escape, eliminate them, and the system will work as intended. The historical record shows why this hasn't worked, and the mechanism of failure is visible in the page count.

The tax code was 400 pages in 1913. Today it exceeds 70,000. Each page represents someone's successful effort to carve out an exception, create a preference, or obscure a benefit. The code grows with each "reform," because reform itself becomes an opportunity for new complexity. Congress identifies an abusive shelter. Hearings are held. Legislation is drafted. The old shelter closes. The new legislation contains new provisions with new ambiguities, and tax lawyers study the new rules and find the gaps. New shelters emerge. The cycle repeats.

The Tax Reform Act of 1986 is the canonical case. Bipartisan, Reagan-supported, it lowered rates, broadened the base, and eliminated a pile of deductions. It was sold as simplification. Within a decade the complexity had returned and exceeded pre-reform levels.[1] The industry that sells complexity had absorbed the reform and produced the next version.

Complexity is the enemy of enforcement. A simple rule is hard to evade. "Pay 4% of your wealth" leaves little room for creative interpretation. "Pay X% of income as defined in Section 61, minus deductions allowed under Sections 162 through 199A, subject to limitations in Section 469, with credits available under Sections 21 through 54AA" leaves room for everything. The wealthy can afford the expertise to exploit that room. They hire teams of accountants whose full-time job is finding the gaps. Ordinary taxpayers pay what they are told. The wealthy pay what they choose.

The rate-raising and loophole-closing reforms interact in a way their advocates rarely acknowledge. Higher rates mean higher payoffs for avoidance. Avoiding $1 million in taxes saves $200,000 at a 20% rate and $400,000 at 40%. The return on hiring a tax planner doubles. When rates rise, the wealthy devote more resources to avoidance, and the complexity the loophole-closers are trying to drain deepens instead.

Complexity is not a bug. It is the product the tax-services industry sells. Seventy thousand pages is the product specification.

4.3 Political Capture

The third reform proposal is to fund the IRS and enforce the rules the system already has. This runs into a structural problem: the people writing the IRS's budget are the same people whose donors the IRS would need to audit.

The IRS budget was cut by roughly 24% in real terms between 2010 and 2022. Between 2010 and 2018, the agency lost more than a fifth of its workforce. Revenue agents, the specialists who audit complex returns, fell 35%. Revenue officers fell nearly 50%. Audit rates for millionaires plummeted. In some recent years, taxpayers claiming the Earned Income Tax Credit, with average incomes around $20,000, were audited at higher rates than millionaires, because auditing the poor is cheap and auditing the wealthy is slow.

Each budget cut, each hiring freeze, each restriction on enforcement authority was a deliberate choice. Wealthy taxpayers and their representatives in Congress have systematically weakened the agency responsible for enforcing tax laws, and they have done it in the open, in appropriations bills, under the rhetorical cover of protecting citizens from "IRS abuse." Every high-profile case against a powerful taxpayer triggers the same backlash. Congressional hearings. Accusations of overreach. Threats to next year's budget. The message to future commissioners is clear.

Even a fully funded IRS would face significant challenges. A wage-earner audit takes hours. The return is simple: W-2 income, standard deduction, done. A wealthy-taxpayer audit takes years and involves partnerships, trusts, foreign accounts, and aggressive positions defended by teams of lawyers. Each audit requires specialized expertise the IRS cannot retain, because private firms pay three times as much. When resources are scarce, the easy cases win.

Underneath all of it is a structural fact the "better enforcement" approach cannot address: the income tax relies on voluntary compliance. Taxpayers calculate their own liability and submit their own returns. This works when the rules are simple. It fails when complexity makes compliance a matter of interpretation.

For wage earners, compliance is automatic, because employers report and the IRS knows. For the wealthy, compliance is optional, because complex structures and aggressive positions make the "correct" tax liability a matter of negotiation.

The political economy does not reward the commissioner who changes this. It punishes them. That is the third structural barrier.

4.4 The Tax Code as Hidden Welfare

The tax code is a welfare system disguised as a revenue system.

Approximately 40% of American households pay zero or negative federal income tax.[2] This is the data point opponents of any reform inevitably cite. "Half the country doesn't even pay taxes!" The implication is that these households are free riders.

Most of these households pay plenty of taxes. They pay payroll taxes on every dollar of wages, at a combined rate of 15.3% including the employer's share that suppresses their wages (see Chapter 2). They pay sales taxes, property taxes, excise taxes, and state income taxes. What they don't pay is *federal income tax*, because a series of credits and deductions reduce their income tax liability to zero or below.

The largest of these is the Earned Income Tax Credit. The EITC delivers approximately $64 billion per year to 23 million working families.[3] It is *refundable*: if the credit exceeds the household's income tax liability, the government pays the difference as a cash refund. A family of four earning $30,000 might owe $500 in income tax but receive a $5,800 EITC plus $4,000 in partially refundable Child Tax Credits, for a net federal income tax position of negative $9,300. This family is a net recipient of federal funds through the tax code.

In 2024, the EITC lifted an estimated 4.4 million people above the poverty line. Combined with the Child Tax Credit, the two programs lifted 8.2 million out of poverty.[3]

But there is a cost to running welfare programs through the tax code. The IRS becomes simultaneously a revenue collector and a benefits administrator. Low-income families must file tax returns not because they owe taxes, but because filing is the only way to receive benefits they are entitled to. This forces the poorest Americans into a system designed for revenue collection, where they face the same complexity, the same audit risk, and the same bureaucratic friction as everyone else.

Congress runs anti-poverty programs through the tax code because direct spending is politically toxic. "Welfare" is demonized. "Tax credits" are acceptable.

The money is the same. The label is different. The result is a system that hides its most important function behind 70,000 pages of complexity and forces its neediest beneficiaries to navigate that complexity to receive what they are owed.

This matters for the proposal in this book, because if we eliminate all federal income taxes, these transfer payments disappear with them. Twenty-three million families currently receive net payments from the federal government through the tax code. Any honest proposal to replace the income tax must account for them. Pretending they do not exist, or hoping the question does not come up, is not a strategy. It is negligence.

The wealth tax replaces the revenue mechanism. It does not abandon the anti-poverty commitment. The $64 billion the EITC delivers and the billions more from the Child Tax Credit can be funded from wealth tax revenue through direct transfer programs that do not require filing tax returns, route benefits through the IRS, or subject the working poor to audit risk. Chapters 14 and 15 detail the transition and show the math for a representative household, including eliminated payroll taxes, negligible wealth tax liability, and direct transfers.

4.5 Adding a Wealth Tax to What We Already Have

Some reformers propose keeping the income tax and stapling a wealth tax on top of it. Senators Warren and Sanders have each put versions of this proposal into legislation. The approach inherits every problem this chapter has described and adds new ones.

Two systems mean two sets of avoidance strategies. The wealthy already have sophisticated techniques for minimizing income tax liability. Give them a wealth tax to minimize and they will develop equally sophisticated techniques for it, then exploit the interactions between the two. Shift wealth into forms that are hard to value under the new rules. Create structures that obscure beneficial ownership for the wealth tax while preserving it for the income tax. The complexity multiplies. The avoidance machine scales with it.

Germany learned this in 1995. Its constitutional court ruled that layering a wealth tax on top of income taxes pushed combined burdens past the constitutional ceiling of half a taxpayer's income.[4] The legislature failed to reform the tax by the court's deadline, and the wealth tax was suspended from 1997. The government abandoned it rather than redesign it, because stacking a new tax on a broken system had no incremental fix.

Chapter 12 examines the broader international experience with wealth taxes in detail, and Appendix F catalogues each country's attempt. The short version is that every country that tried made one of two mistakes: taxing persons instead of wealth, or stapling a wealth tax on top of a flawed income tax. The United States cannot reform its way to a working wealth tax. It cannot add exemptions and expect compliance. It cannot layer a wealth tax on top of an income tax and expect the structure to hold.

You cannot stabilize a failing foundation by adding floors to it. You have to rebuild the foundation first. What gets built on top of a sound foundation, and when, and for what purpose, is a separate question for a separate chapter.

4.6 The Government That Cannot Account for Itself

If you want to see how deep the structural challenges run, look at the institution that is supposed to be enforcing accountability: the federal government itself.

The Pentagon has failed its financial audit eight years in a row. In 1990, Congress passed the Chief Financial Officers Act, requiring annual audits of all 24 major federal agencies. Most complied within a few years. The Department of Defense did not attempt its first full audit until 2018, twenty-eight years late. It failed. It has failed every year since.

Each year, auditors issue a "disclaimer of opinion," the worst possible outcome: they cannot even gather enough evidence to form an opinion about whether the financial statements are accurate. Between fiscal years 2017 and 2019, DOD accountants made $94.7 trillion in accounting adjustments, $29 trillion in 2017, $30.7 trillion in 2018, and $35 trillion in 2019.[5] That figure does not represent missing money. It represents the gross volume of journal-voucher entries the Pentagon's financial systems had to make to reconcile themselves, year after year, because those systems cannot talk to each other. The Government Accountability Office found that 96% of these adjustments lacked adequate supporting documentation. The Pentagon's own explanation was that the adjustments were necessary "due to a lack of system capabilities or interfaces." In plain English, the largest bureaucracy on earth is held together with hand-keyed corrections nobody can show their work for. This is not a scandal of theft. It is a scandal of architecture.

The specifics are staggering. Over nearly five years, more than one million F-35 spare parts were lost, damaged, or destroyed.[6] Confirmed losses exceeded $85 million, but an estimated $18.63 billion in taxpayer-funded parts remain unaccounted for. The government had visibility into less than 2% of the losses, because it relied on contractors to self-report what they held. During one Navy audit, investigators discovered an entire warehouse, containing $126 million in aircraft parts, that had simply disappeared from the records. The warehouse existed. The parts existed. The Navy had just forgotten they were there.

The Department of Defense operates more than 208 business and financial systems relevant to its audit, built over decades by different branches using different standards. They do not communicate with each other effectively. The Pentagon spends approximately $1 billion per year on its audit process, deploying 1,600 auditors to over 600 sites worldwide. The result, year after year, is a disclaimer. A billion dollars spent to confirm that the books are unknowable.

And the DOD is the most dramatic case, not the only one. The federal government made an estimated $162 billion in improper payments in fiscal year 2024 alone. The GAO estimates the government loses between $233 billion and $521 billion to fraud every year.

The usual response to an audit failure is "spend more on auditors." The Pentagon already spends a billion dollars a year on its audit process and deploys 1,600 auditors across 600 sites to confirm that the books are unknowable. The problem is not that nobody is checking. The problem is that 208 financial systems built on different standards cannot be reconciled by checking. The only thing that can reconcile them is a single ledger with a single schema, written once, readable by anyone with authority, where every transaction posts against a shared record the moment it happens. That is what the accountability architecture of Chapters 7 through 9 is designed to deliver. A tax system built on that architecture does not have a 96%-undocumented-adjustments problem, because it does not have 208 systems to reconcile. It has one.

4.7 The Case for Fundamental Redesign

The current system's failures are structural. The complexity serves those who can afford to work it. The loopholes benefit those who can afford to exploit them. The weak enforcement protects those who can afford to fight back. These are not accidents; they are the predictable consequences of how the system was built.

Every generation has tried to fix this system. The Progressive Era reformers. The New Deal legislators. The 1986 tax reformers. Each generation's fixes have been absorbed and redirected over time. The historical pattern suggests that incremental reform fails because the system's structure lends itself to absorbing and neutralizing reform.

Here is what a redesign would need to accomplish:

Simplicity. One tax, one rate, one formula. No deductions, no exemptions, no special provisions to be lobbied for and exploited. A system simple enough that compliance is straightforward and evasion is obvious.

Verifiability. Every claim of control and every transfer of control written against a distributed ledger. The ledger is the authoritative record of ownership. Register your wealth, and your claim of ownership is the strongest the system offers.

Enforcement that follows control. Tax liability based on who actually controls wealth, not on whose name appears on paperwork. Pierce the corporate veil, the trust structure, the nominee arrangement. Find the human who benefits and hold them responsible.

This is what Part II of this book describes: a system designed for accountability from the ground up. Not a patch on the existing system but a replacement for it. Not another reform to be absorbed but a structure designed to resist capture.

An ordinary statute would be consumed and corrupted by the same system that produced these problems. A constitutional amendment does not. Chapter 10 makes that case.

The income tax system has had over a century to prove itself. It has proven that it cannot be made to work fairly. We have the technology and the skills to build something better, we just have to decide to do it.

4.8 What Comes Next

Part I has laid out the structural barriers. Complexity breeds avoidance. Avoidance breeds more complexity. The cycle has not been broken from within.

Part II presents an alternative: a complete redesign built on three principles.

First, we must define what counts as taxable wealth with precision that leaves no room for creative interpretation. Chapter 5 introduces the **Wealth Test**, three criteria that together determine what should be taxed.

Second, we must determine who bears the duty to pay, not based on legal fictions but on actual control. Chapter 6 explains the **Duty of Control**, the principle that tax liability follows whoever can legally seize control of an asset.

Third, we must create an enforcement mechanism that makes evasion structurally self-defeating rather than merely illegal. Chapters 7-9 describe the **Public Ledger** and the proportional tax formula that together create a system where the ledger is the authoritative record, and hiding wealth means leaving your claim vulnerable to anyone willing to register it.

The shift from Part I to Part II is a shift from diagnosis to design. We have seen why the current system fails. Now we build what could replace it.

4.9 Notes

1. See W. Elliot Brownlee, *Federal Taxation in America: A History*, 3rd ed. (Cambridge: Cambridge University Press, 2016).

2. Tax Policy Center, "Who Will Pay No Federal Individual Income Tax in 2025?," Urban-Brookings Tax Policy Center, 2025, https://taxpolicycenter.org/fiscal-facts/who-will-pay-no-federal-individual-income-tax-2025.

3. Center on Budget and Policy Priorities, "Policy Basics: The Earned Income Tax Credit," 2024, https://www.cbpp.org/research/policy-basics-the-earned-income-tax-credit.

4. Bundesverfassungsgericht, 2 BvL 37/91 (June 22, 1995).

5. Anthony Capaccio, "Pentagon Racks Up $35 Trillion in Accounting Changes in One Year," Bloomberg, January 22, 2020, https://www.bloomberg.com/news/articles/2020-01-22/pentagon-racks-up-35-trillion-in-accounting-changes-in-one-year. The underlying audit data is from U.S. Government Accountability Office, GAO-20-96, *Department of Defense: Actions Needed to Reduce Accounting Adjustments* (January 2020), https://www.gao.gov/products/gao-20-96.

6. U.S. Government Accountability Office, GAO-23-106098, *F-35 Program: DOD Needs Better Accountability for Global Spare Parts and Reporting of Losses Worth Millions* (May 2023), https://www.gao.gov/products/gao-23-106098. Loss period: May 2018 through October 2022. The $85M+ confirmed-loss figure refers to the subcontractor sample examined in the audit. The $18.63 billion figure is the F-35 program officials' own estimate

of the total value of taxpayer-funded F-35 property held in over 50 domestic and international non-prime-contractor facilities and not properly accounted for, based on the cumulative value of nearly 20 years of contracts.

End of Part I

CHAPTER 5

THE WEALTH TEST, WHAT SHOULD BE TAXED

How would you decide what counts as wealth?

A billionaire's lawyers will tell you his superyacht is "personal use," not taxable wealth. His art collection is "priceless," meaning unvaluable. His charitable trust "belongs to the foundation," not to him. His stock options "haven't vested yet." Every asset in a billionaire's portfolio has a lawyer ready to reclassify it as something other than wealth.

So before designing anything else, a wealth tax has to answer a question most proposals skip: what, precisely, counts as wealth?

5.1 Why Definition Matters

"Tax the rich." It's a popular slogan. But what counts as "rich"? Income? Net worth? Lifestyle? Vague definitions create room for argument, and argument creates room for escape.

"Tax wealth." Better, but still unclear. Does wealth include your house? Your retirement account? Your skills and education? The value of your professional license? Your social media following? Without a clear definition, every edge case becomes a battleground, and the wealthy have more resources to fight those battles.

If the definition of "wealth" is unclear, taxpayers will argue that their particular holdings don't qualify. Lawyers will find the gaps. Accountants will exploit the uncertainties. The system will fail not through direct evasion but through definitional erosion.

A clear definition also serves a moral purpose: it distinguishes property from personhood. A wealth tax taxes what you *have*, not what you *are*. Your labor, your skills, your health, your relationships: none of these are taxable. They are you. The line between property and personhood must be bright and inviolable.

Finally, a good definition must be future-proof. Cryptocurrency didn't exist in 1913 when the income tax was established. Neither did software patents, carbon credits, or NFTs. New forms of wealth will continue to emerge. The definition must be principled enough to handle assets we haven't invented yet.

What follows is a framework called the Wealth Test. It consists of three criteria: Exchange, Assessment, and Separation. An asset must pass all three to be considered taxable wealth.

5.2 The Three Tests

Test 1: Exchange. Can It Be Traded or Pledged?

The first question is whether something can be exchanged in a lawful market. If it can command labor, goods, services, or influence through trade, it's a candidate for wealth. Exchangeability is the mark of social power.

Money obviously passes. It can buy anything. Stocks and bonds pass because they're traded on markets. Real estate passes because it can be bought, sold, or mortgaged. Business equity passes because ownership stakes can be transferred. Cryptocurrency passes because it's traded on exchanges. Intellectual property passes because patents and copyrights can be licensed, sold, or pledged as collateral.

What fails? Voting rights, because you cannot legally sell your vote. Job titles, because you cannot sell your position as Vice President of Marketing. Security clearances, because they're personal and non-transferable. Personal promises, because "I owe you a favor" is not enforceable in markets.

The exchange test captures the essence of economic power. If you can use something to command resources in the marketplace, it gives you power over others.

Test 2: Assessment. Can It Be Valued?

The second question is whether something can be measured in monetary terms. You cannot tax what you cannot measure. If an asset can be exchanged, pledged, or insured, it can be valued.

Public stocks are trivially easy to value: multiply the share price by the number of shares. Real estate is valued through comparable sales and professional appraisal, methods that have worked for centuries. Private businesses can be valued through revenue multiples, EBITDA (earnings before interest, taxes, depreciation, and amortization) multiples, or book value. Art and collectibles are valued through insurance appraisals and auction records. Cryptocurrency has real-time exchange prices.

What fails? Sentimental value, because your grandmother's ring may be priceless to you, but its market value is what matters. Handshake deals with no enforceable terms or market prices. Social standing, because being well-connected is valuable but unmeasurable. Rumors and speculation, because potential future value is not current wealth.

If you can pledge it as collateral, you can value it. Banks value assets every day when deciding whether to lend against them. Insurance companies value assets when writing policies. The mechanisms exist.

Test 3: Separation. Can It Be Transferred Without Destroying Its Nature?

The third question is whether something can change hands while remaining what it is. This is the test that distinguishes property from personhood.

Land passes. When you sell your farm, the new owner gets the same land: the same acres, the same soil, the same location. The land's nature is unchanged by the transfer. Shares pass because transferring stock doesn't change the underlying company. Patents pass because assigning a patent to a new owner doesn't change the invention. Vehicles pass because title transfer doesn't change the car. Art passes because selling a painting doesn't alter the painting.

What fails? Labor, because you cannot transfer your capacity to work. If you're a skilled surgeon, you cannot give someone else your surgical abilities. Skills fail for the same reason: expertise is inherent to the person. Health is inherently personal. Reputation is attached to the individual. Citizenship cannot be transferred.

The separation test establishes a moral boundary. A wealth tax does not tax people; it taxes what people control. Your skills, your health, your labor: these are you. They cannot be separated from you without destroying what they are. Property, by contrast, can change hands while remaining itself. That's what makes it property rather than personhood.

Inheritance is the clean version of the test. Your children inherit your house, your stocks, your business. They do not inherit your skills, your health, or your reputation.

5.3 Why All Three Tests Matter

Each test alone is insufficient. Together, they create a complete and principled definition.

Exchange & Assessment without Separation collapses into slavery. Labor has value, but it cannot be separated from the person who controls it. The only way to transfer labor itself would be to transfer the laborer, and that is slavery. There is no lawful market for slavery, which is exactly why labor is not taxable property. The separation test protects the boundary between assets that can be owned and traded, and human beings who cannot.

Assessment & Separation without Exchange validates black markets. A kidney has medical value and can be surgically removed, but it cannot be sold in a lawful market. There is no lawful market for the trade in organs, which is exactly why a kidney is not taxable property. The exchange test protects the boundary between what the lawful economy recognizes and what it refuses to.

Separation & Exchange without Assessment equals uncertainty. A treasure map can be transferred without ceasing to be the same map, and it can be sold in a speculative market. It may lead to fortune. It may lead to nothing. The assessment test exists to stop the tax base from being built on hidden outcomes and hopeful guesses.

All three together define wealth. Something that can be traded, can be valued, and can be transferred while retaining its nature: that is wealth. That is what gets taxed.

The three tests work together as a system. Remove any one, and the definition becomes either too broad (capturing personhood) or too narrow (missing real wealth) or too vague (inviting endless argument).

5.4 Edge Cases and How to Handle Them

The power of the three-test framework is that it handles edge cases clearly. When in doubt, apply the tests.

Cryptocurrency. Can it be exchanged? Yes, on numerous exchanges worldwide. Can it be valued? Yes, real-time prices are available. Can it be separated? Yes, wallet transfers move ownership without changing the asset. Cryptocurrency clearly passes all three tests. It's taxable wealth.

Personal residence. Can your home be exchanged? Yes. Can it be valued? Yes. Can it be separated from you? Yes, you can sell it and move. Your home passes all three tests. It's taxable wealth. (Chapter 15 discusses how the system might treat primary residences, but the definitional question is clear.)

Human capital. Can your education and skills be exchanged? No, you cannot sell your medical degree. Can they be valued? Not meaningfully; the "value" of an education is speculative. Can they be separated? No, your skills are inherent to you. Human capital fails all three tests. It's not taxable. Your skills are you, not your property.

Contingent inheritance. Can an expected inheritance be exchanged? No, you don't own it yet. Can it be valued? No, you might be disinherited. Can it be separated? No, it doesn't exist as your property. A contingent inheritance fails all three tests. It's not taxable until received. Once you inherit, the inherited assets are subject to the tests individually.

5.5 How the Test Protects the Republic

The Wealth Test serves two purposes that work in tandem: it prevents government overreach while closing evasion routes.

Clear boundaries prevent overreach. The government cannot tax your skills, your labor, your health, or your personhood. The separation test is a constitutional firewall. Citizens know exactly what's taxable and what isn't. The line between property and personhood is bright and inviolable.

The test adapts to new forms of wealth. When cryptocurrency emerged, there was confusion about how to treat it. Apply the three tests: Can it be exchanged? Yes. Can it be valued? Yes. Can it be separated? Yes. It's wealth. The same analysis works for whatever comes next: tokenized real estate, AI-generated intellectual property, carbon credits, digital collectibles. The tests don't depend on the specific form of the asset. They depend on its fundamental characteristics.

The test closes evasion routes before they open. Under the current system, wealthy taxpayers argue endlessly about whether their particular holdings count as "income" or qualify for various exemptions. Under the Wealth Test, the argument is simple: Does it pass the three tests? If yes, it's taxable. If no, it's not. There's no room for special pleading, no carve-outs to be lobbied for, no ambiguities to exploit.

5.6 Summary

Wealth, for purposes of this system, is anything that passes three tests:

1. **Exchange:** It can be traded or pledged in a lawful market.
2. **Assessment:** It can be valued in monetary terms.
3. **Separation:** It can be transferred without destroying its nature.

If an asset passes all three tests, it's wealth and it's taxable. If it fails any one of them, it's not.

CHAPTER 6

THE DUTY OF CONTROL, WHO SHOULD PAY

Here is the simplest version of the idea: follow the power, find the person who pays.

Not the "owner," because ownership is a legal fiction that can be manipulated endlessly. Not whoever *uses* the wealth, and not whoever *benefits* from it. The person who holds the ultimate power to reclaim, revoke, or dispose of it. That is the controller, and the controller bears the duty.

Consider a house titled in the name of an LLC. The LLC is owned by a trust. The trust is administered by a trustee in Delaware. On paper, the "owner" is a legal abstraction several layers removed from any human being. But someone lives in that house, or collects rent from it, or decides whether to sell it. Someone controls it. That person bears the duty.

The rest of this chapter explains how to identify that person in every case, from a family farm to a multinational holding company.

6.1 Indicators of Control

Four indicators serve as evidence that someone might be the controller of an asset:

Use: The power to manage or employ the asset. If you decide how it is used, whether to rent the house, which stocks to buy, how to run the business, you exhibit use-based control.

Benefit: The power to receive income or value from the asset. If the dividends come to you, if the rent checks are deposited in your account, if you enjoy the use of the property, you exhibit benefit-based control.

Exclusion: The power to prevent others from accessing the asset. If you can lock the door, revoke access, or deny others the use of what you hold, you exhibit exclusionary control.

Transfer: The power to sell, gift, or assign the asset. If you can decide to whom the asset goes next, you exhibit transfer control.

These indicators raise the question of who controls an asset, but they do not settle it alone. A tenant exercises three of four, yet controls nothing. An employee using a company laptop exercises three of four, yet controls nothing.

What distinguishes a controller from a user is the power to seize: the ability to reclaim the asset, terminate the other party's access, and ultimately dispose of it. Indicators identify candidates for control. Seizure power identifies the controller.

Quick Reference: The Control Hierarchy

Layer	Question	What It Tells You
Indicators (Use, Benefit, Exclusion, Transfer)	Who interacts with the asset?	Identifies *candidates* for control
Seizure Power	Who can reclaim, revoke, or override?	Identifies the *controller*
Terms of Seizure	Must the seizing party compensate the other's stake?	Determines *proportional* vs. *total* control

Once the controller is identified, duty is proportional to time: control for one day means one day's share of the annual duty. Control for six months means half. The ledger tracks control continuously, and liability follows.

6.2 The Power to Seize Is the Power to Control

This is the principle that pierces every shell game: *if someone else can revoke your control, that someone else is the real controller.*

If you can take it back, you are responsible for it.

A revocable trust is nominally controlled by a trustee. But the grantor, the person who created the trust, can revoke it at any time, reclaiming the assets. The trustee is just a custodian. The grantor has superior authority. The grantor bears the duty.

A subsidiary corporation is nominally a separate legal entity. But the parent company controls its board, directs its operations, and can dissolve it at will. The subsidiary is just a legal wrapper. The parent has superior authority. The parent bears the duty.

A lender will argue it has no seizure power until the borrower defaults, and so the borrower should bear the full duty. But retaining the legal authority to seize wealth, even under specific circumstances, means it has not relinquished the power to seize, nor its duty of control.

How the Terms of Seizure Divide Responsibility

Not all seizure power is absolute. Sometimes two parties each hold a genuine stake in the same asset, and the terms of their agreement determine who controls what. The question is: *when the seizing party acts, must they compensate the other party's stake?*

A standard mortgage illustrates this. You have a $500,000 house with a $200,000 mortgage. The bank can seize the house upon default, but it must sell at fair market value and return any surplus above the debt to you. Your $300,000 equity stake is protected even during seizure. Both parties have genuine control over their respective portions: you control your equity, the bank controls its lien. Both bear proportional duty.

Now consider a predatory car title loan. The lender can repossess the car and sell it at any price, keeping all proceeds, even if the car is worth far more than the outstanding debt. The borrower's "equity" vanishes upon seizure. The lender had full control all along and bears full duty.

The distinction is structural: where seizure requires compensating the other party's stake, control is genuinely shared. Where the seizing party can take everything without obligation, the other party never truly controlled the wealth.

The same structural rule shields every duty-paying stake against parties that would extinguish it. A recognized claim cannot be wiped out without equitable compensation through due process, whether the party seeking to take is a private lienholder, a competing claimant on the ledger, or the government acting for a public purpose. Non-payment is the one path that puts a stake outside this protection, the same way an unpaid property tax exposes a parcel to a tax lien today. Chapter 10 develops the constitutional grounding.

This principle eliminates the fundamental trick of tax avoidance: creating nominal ownership structures that obscure who really controls the wealth. It doesn't matter how many layers of LLCs, trusts, and offshore entities you stack. The question is always the same: *Who has the power to seize, revoke, or override? And when they seize, must they compensate?* Follow that chain upward, and you find a human being. That human bears the duty.

6.3 Common Patterns: Users vs. Controllers

A few everyday examples show how this works in practice.

The tenant. A residential tenant manages the space, benefits from living there, and can lock the door against the world. Three of four indicators. But the landlord can terminate the lease, reclaim possession, sell the building, and encumber it with a mortgage. The tenant has no transferable stake, no power to dispose of the property, and no claim to its value upon departure. The landlord bears the full duty on the property's value.

The employee. An employee uses a company laptop every day. They benefit from it, exercise direct control over it, and can exclude others from it (it has their password, their files, their workflow). Three of four indicators. But the employer can reclaim the laptop at any time: upon termination, upon reassignment, or simply because they choose to. The employee never controlled the wealth represented by that device. The employer did.

The lending spectrum. At one end, a standard mortgage where the bank must sell at market value and return the borrower's surplus. Both parties bear proportional duty. A margin loan on a brokerage account works the same way: the broker can liquidate shares to cover the loan, but must return any proceeds above the debt. At the other end, an equipment lease where the lessor retains title and can reclaim the machinery at any time with no obligation to compensate the lessee. The lessor bears the duty.

The pattern is consistent: indicators tell you where to look, but seizure power tells you who pays.

Borrowers and lenders both have skin in the game when structuring deals. A lender who wants to avoid bearing the full wealth tax on a collateralized asset must structure the loan to protect the borrower's equity stake. A borrower who wants to bear duty on their equity (and therefore claim legal protection for it) needs loan terms that preserve that equity upon default. The framework rewards responsible lending and penalizes predatory terms, not through regulation, but through the natural consequence of how control is assigned.

6.4 Types of Control

Control takes different forms, but the principle stays the same: whoever can revoke, override, or reclaim bears the duty.

Direct and Delegated Control

Direct control is the simplest case: you own your house, manage your portfolio, run your business. You bear the duty directly.

Delegation does not transfer duty. You can hire a financial advisor, employ a property manager, or appoint a CEO. But you can fire them. The power to revoke is the power to control. The delegate acts under your authority; their control is derivative of yours. You still bear the duty.

Shared and Conditional Control

When multiple people control the same assets (partnerships, corporate boards, marital co-ownership), duty divides proportionally. A 50/50 partnership means each partner bears 50% of the duty. Joint and several liability applies where control is mutual: if either spouse can withdraw from a joint account, both bear duty for the full amount. You cannot escape duty by sharing control; you can only share the burden.

Some control is contingent on future events: unvested stock options, pending inheritances, escrowed funds. The principle is that duty stays with the current controller until transfer completes. Your employer bears the duty on unvested options. The estate bears the duty until distribution. Once the condition is satisfied, duty transfers with control.

Automated and Institutional Control

What about algorithmic trading funds, AI-managed enterprises, and DAOs (decentralized autonomous organizations)? The principle remains unchanged: **humans who authorize the system bear the duty.** Someone designed the algorithm, deployed it, and can shut it down. That person bears the duty.

DAOs are the hardest case: decisions made by token holders through smart contracts (self-executing programs that run automatically when conditions are met), with no single controller. The rule is the same as for every other entity. Token holders who can be identified as humans bear proportional duty based on their governance stake. A DAO governing $500 million in US-jurisdiction assets distributes that duty across whichever holders are traceable. Any share whose holders cannot be identified sits on the ledger with no registered controller, open to claim by anyone who can demonstrate control. The "no one controls it" defense proves too much: if no human controls it, any human who steps up to the ledger can assert that they do.

6.5 Entities: From Family Farms to Foundations

Most Americans encounter wealth not as cash in a vault but through entities: shares of stock in a public company, equity in a family business or farm, a seat on the board of a church or charity. Each raises the same question: if wealth sits inside an entity, who bears the duty?

The answer follows directly from everything above. Entities do not bear duty. Humans do. Every dollar of wealth inside an entity traces to the humans who control it: through equity ownership, through debt claims, or through the power to direct the entity's resources. The entity is a pass-through. The humans are the taxpayers.

The Family Farm

Consider a family farm organized as an LLC. The farm's assets (land, equipment, livestock, crops) total $2 million. The farm carries a $500,000 mortgage. Who pays?

The farmer who owns 100% of the LLC controls $1.5 million in equity (assets minus debt). The farmer bears the duty on that $1.5 million. The bank holds a $500,000 lien and bears the duty on that. The farm itself, the LLC, pays nothing separately. It is a pass-through. No double-counting: equity plus lien equals total value, each dollar traced to a human controller.

If two siblings co-own the farm 60/40, the duty splits accordingly. If employees use the tractors and work the land, they exhibit indicators of control but have no seizure power. The owners bear the duty. Private businesses and partnerships follow the same logic: owners pay on equity, lenders pay on liens, and the entity's legal structure (LLC, S-Corp, C-Corp, partnership) is irrelevant.

The Small Business

The duty of control can sound alarming to a small business owner. It should not. Four things to know.

No double taxation. Your LLC is not taxed separately. You are taxed on what you own in it, minus what you owe on it. Same rule as every other form of wealth.

Debts under standard commercial terms stay with the lender. A truck loan where the bank can repossess and sell at market value (returning any surplus) is proportional control. The bank bears duty on the loan balance. You bear duty only on your equity. The same applies to equipment loans, building mortgages, and lines of credit with standard terms.

Your home has a safety valve. The primary-residence deferral (Chapter 15) lets you defer wealth tax on the first $500,000 of home equity at the Treasury rate plus one percent, with the lien and interest settling out of sale proceeds when you transfer the asset. This is a backstop for cash-tight years, not a long-term strategy.

Seizure power still decides upstream. If a franchisor can terminate your business, or a corporate parent controls the operating agreement, duty passes to whoever holds the power to seize. You are taxed on what you genuinely control.

Chapter 15 walks two small-business households (Jake the plumber at $280,000 of household wealth and Maya the contractor at $2.5 million) through the math from registration to annual payment, including how each chooses a valuation method from the menu in Chapter 11.

Public Companies and Shareholders

You own 100 shares of a publicly traded company. The share price reflects the market's assessment of the company's net assets minus its debts. When you pay 4% on your shares' market value, you are already paying on your proportional claim on those corporate assets. No separate entity-level tax exists. No double-counting occurs. The company's creditors (bondholders, banks) bear the duty on the debt instruments they hold. Every dollar traced to a human.

What about stock buybacks? No wealth disappears. The cash goes to selling shareholders, and remaining shareholders' per-share claim increases. The wealth is accounted for at every moment.

What about holding companies? When Berkshire Hathaway holds Apple shares, those holdings are assets on Berkshire's balance sheet, attributable to Berkshire's shareholders through the same pass-through principle. The chain always terminates at humans.

Banks and Other Lenders

A bank's primary asset is other people's debt, which makes its wealth chain less obvious than a manufacturer's or a retailer's. The principle is the same. The bank is an entity, and its net wealth traces through humans through one of three channels. **Equity-owned banks** (commercial, investment, foreign-operating-in-US, and bank holding companies) trace through shareholders the same way any other company does. **Member-controlled cooperatives** (mutual savings banks, credit unions) have no tradable equity, so duty on the institution's net wealth falls on the elected board the same way it does for non-profit endowments. **Government-controlled entities** (Federal Reserve banks, Fannie Mae and Freddie Mac in conservatorship) fall under the government-as-controller exception with no duty owed. In every case, the borrower bears duty on their equity in the financed asset and the lender bears duty on the debt. The bank's loan portfolio is the lender side of that split, not a second layer.

Non-Profits, Charities, and Churches

Non-profit entities have no shareholders, but they have controllers. The board members, directors, and trustees who decide how a charity's endowment is invested, when a foundation's assets are disbursed, and whether a church's building is sold hold collective seizure power. They bear the duty. It is paid from the entity's resources (donations, endowment returns, tithes), not the controllers' personal savings, the same way those funds already cover insurance and utilities. Appendix C provides worked calculations for institutions at various asset levels.

An exemption for non-profits would create the largest wealth shelter in the system. The humans who control $2 million in church or foundation wealth bear the same duty as every other human who controls $2 million. Without the rule, the wealthiest Americans could shield unlimited assets inside foundations they control. A university sitting on a $40 billion endowment while raising tuition faces a real cost for hoarding assets instead of deploying them toward its mission. (The First Amendment objection has been worked through by the courts and by 250 years of American history; Appendix I develops the legal case in full.)

The small-church case. Most churches in America are small. A congregation of 150 in a rural community is not the same institution as a university sitting on a $40 billion endowment. The system handles them differently, not through an exemption (which would reopen every loophole this chapter just closed) but through three mechanisms it already provides.

Use-value assessment. Chapter 11's principle that some property is worth what it does, not what a speculator might pay for the land, applies directly. A rural church building in a depressed real estate market, with no commercial buyer in sight, has a use value well below its replacement cost. The ledger value reflects the economic function the building performs for the congregation, not a hypothetical market price that cannot be realized.

The power to seize still decides. Many churches do not own their buildings outright. Catholic parishes hold under diocesan authority. Methodist congregations hold under conference trust clauses. Episcopal parishes hold under the Dennis Canon. Where an upstream religious authority has the power to seize, reassign, or dissolve the local property, the duty passes upward to that authority. The diocese pays on parishes it can take. The denomination pays on properties its charter lets it reclaim. This is the same seizure-power rule that governs corporate parents and revocable trusts elsewhere in this chapter.

Distributed control. For congregational churches with no upstream authority (independent Baptists, nondenominational congregations), a multi-person board is a design choice, not a constraint. A congregation whose members actively participate through voting membership, regular tithing, or documented shared authority is the de facto controller, and the duty distributes across the congregation accordingly. A 150-member congregation bearing collective duty on a $500,000 use-value building owes about $133 per member per year. For a congregation whose median household income is $48,000, that is about $11 per month, and remember those families are no longer paying federal income or payroll taxes on their wages. Larger congregations with strong tithe revenue or endowment income cover the duty from existing cashflow without needing to democratize at all.

The Ledger Rule: Only Humans Sign

This principle is an intentional design constraint. The public ledger accepts exactly two kinds of controllers: natural persons and governments. Nothing else.

No corporation opens a ledger account. No trust declares assets. No LLC, no foundation, no partnership, no algorithm, no DAO puts its name on the line. The human who controls the entity declares those assets under their own name. The entity can appear in the asset description. But the controller field is always a human name.

If duty always traces to a human, the ledger demands the human up front. It does not accept layers of abstraction and promise to sort them out later. It does not allow a Cayman Islands LLC to register as the controller of a Manhattan penthouse while the actual human controller hides behind it. Somebody has to put their name on the line. Hard stop.

Why this matters. Rights and duties are two sides of the same coin. To claim ownership in court, to have property rights enforced, to sue for theft or breach of contract, you must be someone courts can hold accountable in return. An entity that bears no duty has no standing to assert control on the ledger. If no human is on the line, any human who steps up and registers the asset, bearing the duty, holds the superior claim (Chapter 9 develops this into a full enforcement mechanism).

Liens, auctions, and tax certificates enforce against assets. But fraud, perjury, and evasion are crimes, and crimes require a defendant with a pulse. A corporation cannot be imprisoned. A shell company cannot be extradited. Without a human name on the ledger, deterrence collapses to asset-level remedies only, forfeiting the personal consequences that make deliberate fraud costly (Chapter 9 details the criminal penalty structure).

Most fundamentally: wealth is power, and in a democracy, power must be traceable to an accountable person. Allowing entities to wield wealth without a named human controller recreates the feudal opacity that Chapter 3 documented: extraction in darkness, power without a face. Any system that permits this will be exploited by the powerful to widen the accountability gap. The duty of control closes that door. If you wield the power, your name is on the line.

Why governments are the exception. Sovereign authority terminates at collective democratic accountability, not at a private individual who can pocket the value. For US governments, taxing their own assets is circular, so they appear on the ledger as controllers but bear no duty. The ledger's transparency ensures democratic accountability over what they hold. Foreign sovereigns holding US-jurisdiction assets bear the same duty as any other controller (the circular-taxation rationale applies only to the government collecting the tax). The classification question for sovereign wealth funds, when a fund is genuinely governmental versus a vehicle for private enrichment, is addressed in the International Control Chains section below.

What this means in practice. An asset held through a trust lists the trust's name in its description: "residential property held by the Rodriguez Family Trust." But the controller field reads "Jane Rodriguez." The structure is metadata. The human is the controller. A thousand shell companies deep, someone is making the decisions. That someone signs.

6.6 Vacant or Disputed Control

Even edge cases have clear rules.

Abandoned accounts. Sometimes assets have no active controller, such as a bank account whose owner died without heirs, or a property whose owner disappeared. These assets are held in trust until claimed. After a statutory period, they escheat to the government. During the interim, no duty accrues because no one controls them.

Disputed inheritance. When multiple parties claim the same assets, duty is deferred until the dispute resolves. Courts determine who controls; duty follows the determination. The assets aren't in limbo; they're under the court's control until allocated.

Unregistered wealth. Assets that appear on no one's ledger declaration have no registered controller. Any person who can demonstrate control may file to register them, bear the corresponding duty, and hold the authoritative claim. After due process, assets with no claimant may be auctioned to satisfy outstanding tax obligations. This is the enforcement mechanism: the ledger is the authoritative record of control, and anyone willing to bear the duty can assert it.

Mutually revocable control. Joint accounts where any party can withdraw, partnerships where either party can dissolve: these create joint and several liability. All parties bear the cumulative duty because any party has full control. You cannot hide behind your partners; you are equally responsible.

6.7 Lessons From Tax-Lien History

Liens and tax certificates have a specific history of predatory use against racial minority homeowners in the United States. The most documented modern case is the Washington DC tax-sale scandal, where homeowners who owed as little as $134 in back taxes lost homes worth hundreds of thousands of dollars. The District sold tax liens to private investors, who added legal fees and interest on top of the original debt, then foreclosed when the homeowner could not pay the inflated bill. In 2023, the Supreme Court ruled 9-0 in *Tyler v. Hennepin County* that keeping the surplus from a tax-foreclosure sale violates the Takings Clause.

The $500,000 primary-residence deferral introduced earlier in this chapter is the system's answer. No private investor buys the lien. No foreclosure is initiated. No homeowner is forced from their residence because they cannot write a check in April. Chapter 15 develops it through Jennifer the Retiree, with comparisons to reverse mortgages and other predatory products; Appendix C works the math.

The wealth tax uses those tools. It does not use them to take homes.

6.8 International Control Chains

When the chain of control crosses borders, the same principle applies: the system has jurisdiction over US-located assets, not over persons. A Cayman Islands LLC owns US real estate through a British Virgin Islands trust, controlled by a Swiss family office, directed by a German billionaire in Monaco. Who pays? The German billionaire. The entity chain is metadata. The human is the controller. Enforcement proceeds against the US asset itself: the building can be liened and auctioned. The foreign controller does not need to be present; the asset is present.

Whether the non-compliant party is a sanctioned oligarch, an anonymous owner behind a secrecy jurisdiction, or a sovereign wealth fund claiming immunity, the answer is the same. If no one registers, anyone who does holds the authoritative claim.

Diplomatic immunity and its limits. Embassy properties are exempt under the Vienna Convention. Commercial real estate held by a foreign government for investment is taxable. The line is functional, not formal: diplomatic use is exempt; commercial holdings are not.

Chapter 12 develops the full case that US-located wealth cannot escape US jurisdiction regardless of where the controller lives. Appendix F details the cross-border architecture: bilateral treaties, the Common Reporting Standard, the FATCA precedent, the standing arbitration panel for sovereign-immunity and controller-classification disputes, and the graduated enforcement ladder for non-cooperative jurisdictions.

6.9 Why This Eliminates Shell Games

Every evasion strategy in the current system relies on obscuring control. Create enough layers, and no one can tell who's responsible. The Duty of Control makes layers irrelevant.

Offshore shell company. Incorporated in the Caymans with a nominee director. Who can direct its investments, receive its distributions, dissolve it? Trace the control, find the human, assign the duty.

Irrevocable trust. The trust document says it cannot be revoked. But who appointed the trustee and can replace them? Who can modify the terms? "Irrevocable" is often a legal fiction. There are almost always humans who retain practical control.

Corporate layers. Company A owns Company B owns Company C owns the asset. Three layers of abstraction. But Company A has a board, and the board has members. Those humans control the chain. They bear the duty.

Every structure, no matter how complex, is ultimately controlled by humans. Find the humans with the power to seize, revoke, or override, and you find the duty-bearers.

6.10 Summary

The Duty of Control establishes a simple principle: whoever controls wealth bears the duty to pay.

Four indicators serve as evidence of control:

- **Use:** Power to manage or employ
- **Benefit:** Power to receive income or value
- **Exclusion:** Power to prevent others' access
- **Transfer:** Power to sell, gift, or assign

But indicators alone do not determine duty. The definitive test is the power to seize: who can reclaim the asset, terminate access, and ultimately dispose of it? Indicators identify candidates for control. Seizure power identifies the controller.

Where seizure requires compensating the other party's stake, control is proportional. Where the seizing party can take everything, control is total. The terms of every deal (every loan, every lease, every partnership) determine how duty is assigned.

Follow the chain of seizure power upward until you find a human who cannot be overridden. That human pays.

Only natural persons (and government bodies for public assets) appear as controllers on the ledger. No corporation, trust, LLC, or other legal entity signs. The human behind it signs. Somebody has to put their name on the line. Without a named human, there is no one to hold legally accountable, no one to prosecute for fraud, and no one answerable for the power that wealth confers.

Follow the chain of power upward. At the top, you always find a person. That person pays. No trust, no shell company, no layer of abstraction changes that fact. It only obscures it. The Duty of Control strips away the obscurity.

CHAPTER 7

THE PUBLIC LEDGER, HOW IT WOULD WORK

How would you actually enforce a wealth tax? How would you know what wealth exists, who controls it, and whether they have paid?

The answer is a public ledger: a comprehensive, transparent, tamper-evident record of all wealth in the nation. This chapter explains how such a ledger would work, why the technology already exists, and why it would make tax evasion structurally difficult rather than merely illegal.

7.1 Why a Ledger Is Necessary

The current tax system relies on trust. Taxpayers report their own income, claim their own deductions, and calculate their own liability. The IRS checks a small percentage of returns and hopes the rest are honest.

This works tolerably well for wage earners. Employers report wages directly to the IRS. The government knows what you earned before you file your return. Cheating is difficult because the information is independently verified.

It works terribly for the wealthy. Complex structures obscure ownership. Assets are held through layers of entities. Income is deferred, shifted, and redefined. The IRS doesn't know what the wealthy own because no one is required to tell them and the wealthy can afford the expertise to keep it that way.

A wealth tax without a ledger would face the same problem, magnified. At least income eventually surfaces somewhere in bank deposits, in spending, in lifestyle. Wealth can sit quietly, appreciating, invisible to authorities. Without knowing what wealth exists, you cannot tax it.

A public ledger would solve this problem the same way county land records solve it for real estate. You cannot hide a house. It sits on a specific piece of land, recorded in county records, visible to anyone who looks. The ledger extends this principle to all forms of wealth. Registration is the ultimate assertion of control: tamper-evident, timestamped, cryptographically verified, and instantly recognizable by any court. If you want the strongest possible claim to your assets, you register them on the ledger and bear the duty.

For meaningful wealth (your home, your investments, your business), the ledger is the authoritative record. A registered claim supersedes any competing paper trail. For everyday personal effects below a de minimis threshold set by Congress, traditional proof of ownership still works. But the ledger is always the stronger path.

7.2 Reclaiming the Technology From the Speculators

What Distributed Ledgers Actually Do Strip the marketing away and distributed ledger technology does one thing. It lets independent parties keep synchronized copies of a shared record without trusting each other or a central operator.

Three properties make this work. Entries are append-only. Each entry is cryptographically linked to the one before it, so rewriting history breaks the chain and tampering becomes visible. And the record lives in many independent copies, so no single party can secretly change what it says.

That is the innovation. It is not speed. Every node in the network has to agree on every entry before it is final, which makes distributed ledgers slower than centralized payment networks by design. It is not efficiency. The same data lives in dozens of places on purpose. What you get in exchange is a record many parties can verify and no one can silently rewrite.

One limit has to be named up front. The ledger guarantees the integrity of the record, not the truth of what goes into it. A lie written to a distributed ledger is still a lie, now permanently visible. Chapter 11 and Appendix D elaborate.

What Happened to It The technology is neutral. The people who made it infamous were not.

A distributed ledger is cheap to create and easy to attach a tradeable token to. That turned out to be a convenient way to sell synthetic assets to the public. Cryptocurrencies. NFTs. Meme coins. DeFi protocols. A decade of speculation built on the same underlying plumbing, much of it dishonest, some of it outright fraud.

None of that is a problem with the record-keeping. It is a problem with the people who ran the scams and the regulators who let them. The infrastructure worked exactly as advertised the whole time. What failed was the assumption that every problem benefits from a token attached to it.

What the Technology Is Actually Good At What distributed ledgers do well is exactly what a wealth tax needs. The wealth tax does not need tokens. It does not need a cryptocurrency. It does not need smart contracts, decentralized finance, or any of the speculative infrastructure that made the technology infamous. It needs the one boring piece underneath: a record that many independent parties can verify, that nobody can silently edit, and that stays trustworthy even when individual operators are not.

That is the piece worth reclaiming. Not the speculation, not the ideology, not the libertarian origin story. Just the record-keeping primitive that was buried under a decade of marketing, and that turns out to solve a problem governments have had for a very long time: how to keep an honest, public, comprehensive record of wealth at national scale without requiring citizens to trust the government that maintains it.

7.3 The Architecture

The public wealth ledger would have two components: a canonical record maintained by the government, and distributed mirrors maintained by independent parties. Together, they would create a system that is both authoritative and tamper-resistant.

The Canonical Ledger

The government maintains the official record. This is the ledger with legal force, the one that determines ownership, liability, and enforcement. Think of it as county land records, but for everything.

Authorized officers can append entries: declarations of new assets, transfers of control, updates to valuations. Each entry is timestamped, signed, and linked cryptographically to previous entries. The chain of entries creates a tamper-evident history. You can add to it, but you cannot change what came before without breaking the cryptographic links.

The canonical ledger is the source of truth. Courts recognize its entries as proof of ownership. Tax liability is calculated from its records. Legal protection flows from registration.

Distributed Mirrors

Here is what would prevent government manipulation: the canonical ledger is mirrored by independent parties. Universities, news organizations, watchdog groups, and international institutions maintain synchronized copies. These mirrors receive every update in real-time and verify each entry cryptographically.

If the government tries to delete an entry, the mirrors still have it. If the government tries to modify an entry, the cryptographic hash changes, and the mirrors show the original. If the government tries to add a false entry, the mirrors don't have it, and the discrepancy is visible.

To successfully tamper with the ledger, you would need to compromise not just the government's systems but every independent mirror simultaneously. Universities in different states. News organizations with different political leanings. International institutions beyond US jurisdiction. The more mirrors, the harder tampering becomes.

This is the key property: distributed verification makes manipulation detectable.

Who Can Register

Only natural persons and government bodies can register as controllers (Chapter 6 established this principle and explains why no exceptions are permitted). Entities appear in asset descriptions but never in the controller field.

How Wealth Gets Onto the Ledger

How does wealth get onto the ledger? Almost always through paperwork you are already doing for other reasons. Here is what that looks like in the ordinary cases.

You buy a house. You sign the closing documents the same way you do today. The county recorder files the deed, same as today. What changes is that the deed filing also creates a ledger entry: your name as controller, the purchase price as the declared value. Household contents below the de minimis threshold can ride on the same registration as a single bundled value, the way a homeowner's policy covers dwelling and personal property in one number. You do nothing extra. The ledger populates itself from the paperwork that already exists. Chapter 13 explains which pieces of that entry show publicly and which stay in government-only records.

You open a brokerage account. You fill out the same forms your custodian already uses and answer the same know-your-customer questions your broker is already required to ask. The custodian sends periodic position feeds to the ledger the same way it already sends tax forms to the IRS. Your holdings appear on the ledger at the values the custodian reports. You never touch the ledger directly. Chapter 11 covers how valuation works for the contents of the account.

You start a business. When you register an LLC or corporation with your state, the state registration feeds the ledger automatically. You are listed as the controller of your ownership stake. You pick a valuation method (revenue multiple, book value, rolling average, and so on) and declare an initial value. Until something triggers a reassessment (a sale, a pledge, a capital raise, etc.), your reported value stands. Chapter 11 walks through what happens in a down year.

You inherit a painting. Probate already values your decedent's estate for tax purposes. That valuation moves to the ledger when the estate closes, with you as the new controller. You can accept the estate's appraisal, or you can commission a new one if you disagree. Disputes flow through the process described in Chapter 11. If you buy the painting at auction instead, the auction house reports the transaction and the sale price becomes the ledger value.

You own a patent. Intellectual property is the hardest case because it has no value until something happens to it. A patent you hold without using it sits on the ledger at its registration cost. If you license it, the license revenue establishes a value. If you pledge it as loan collateral, the lender's appraisal becomes the ledger value. If you sell it, the sale price controls. Until one of those events, the patent stays at its prior value. Appendix D walks through the menu of events that trigger reassessment.

7.4 What the Ledger Cannot Do

The architecture above secures the record against tampering. It does not secure the record against lies. A controller who declares a painting at $50,000 when it is really worth $500,000 has not broken the ledger. The ledger recorded exactly what it was told.

Some assets enter the ledger through self-declaration by the controller. Others enter through compelled reporting by third parties who re-assessed the value. For example, banks report pledged collateral, custodians report brokerage positions, and insurers report covered assets. Transactions can trigger reassessment of true market values. Contested values flow through the arbitration process described in Chapter 11.

Where exactly the boundary between self-declaration and compelled reporting falls is a live design question. The easy cases are already covered by existing law.

The hard cases are operating businesses, private art, and intellectual property, assets where nobody but the owner knows what they are worth. This book does not pretend this boundary is already drawn. Appendix D walks through the options and the tradeoffs.

Enforcement does not depend on perfect input. A controller who lies on the ledger and is caught faces tax evasion liability on the same footing as a controller who lies on a 1040 today. What changes is that the lie is now a permanent, timestamped, publicly inspectable entry, and that every third-party assessment is potential evidence for a competing claim or valuation challenge. When a bank appraises collateral at $2 million and the controller registered it at $500,000, that discrepancy is not just an escape assessment trigger. It is ammunition for anyone, a certified appraiser, a competitor, an ex-spouse, who might challenge the registration or file a competing claim. Challenges no longer require an IRS audit. They can come from counterparties, journalists, insurers, or anyone else with reason to notice the gap between the declared value and observed realities.

7.5 A Self-Funding Administrative System

The ledger needs to be maintained. Servers must run. Data must be stored. Mirrors must be synchronized. Who pays for this?

The answer: the users, through modest filing fees. This would make the ledger self-sustaining without requiring taxpayer funding, similar to a county recorder's office but more efficient.

How It Works

Writing to the ledger costs a small filing fee. Declaring a new asset, updating a valuation, transferring control, and other transactions each require a fee, just like recording a deed or filing a business registration.

Maintaining the ledger earns audit stipends. Universities, watchdog organizations, and other institutions that run mirrors and verify records receive compensation for their services. This creates an incentive for independent parties to participate in oversight.

Fees are paid in dollars (or dollar equivalents). No special currency is required. You pay your filing fee the same way you'd pay any government fee.

Hypothetical Fee Structure

The fees are modest, enough to fund operations, not enough to burden ordinary users:

Transaction Type	Filing Fee
Initial asset registration	\$5-\$50
Annual valuation update	\$1-\$10
Control transfer (title change)	\$10-\$100
Dispute filing	\$50-\$500

How these figures were derived. The fee ranges are based on three reference points:

1. **Existing government filing fees.** Recording a deed currently costs \$10-\$100 in most counties. Registering a vehicle costs \$15-\$50. Filing a UCC (Uniform Commercial Code) financing statement costs \$20-\$50. Business registration fees range from \$50-\$500. The ledger fees are calibrated to these existing benchmarks: familiar, accepted, and proven sustainable.

2. **Distributed ledger transaction costs.** At scale, distributed ledger transactions cost fractions of a cent to process. The fees proposed here are orders of magnitude higher than the technical cost, providing ample margin for system maintenance, mirror compensation, and administrative overhead. Even at the low end, the system would be self-sustaining.

3. **Burden analysis.** A typical household with a home, two vehicles, retirement accounts, and bank accounts might have 5-10 registrable assets. Personal effects below the de minimis threshold do not require individual registration and incur no filing fees. At \$5-\$10 per initial registration and \$1-\$5 per annual update, the total annual burden would be \$20-\$100, comparable to current vehicle registration fees. This is trivial relative to the assets' value and the legal protections received.

The ranges allow Congress to adjust fees based on asset complexity. A simple bank account registration might cost \$5; a complex trust structure with multiple beneficiaries might cost \$50. The principle is cost recovery, not revenue generation.

A household with a home, a car, and some investments might pay \$20-\$50 per year in filing fees. A corporation with thousands of assets would pay more, but still a trivial fraction of the assets' value.

Why This Works

Guaranteed demand. You must use the ledger to have legally recognized ownership. This isn't optional; it's like needing a deed to own land or a title to own a car.

Stable and predictable. Fees are set by regulation, not by market speculation. They cover costs, nothing more.

Self-sustaining. The system pays for itself through user fees. No taxpayer subsidy required. The more assets registered, the more revenue for maintenance.

Government record-keeping has always worked this way. The county recorder's office doesn't run on taxpayer funds; it runs on filing fees. The wealth ledger extends this proven model to all assets.

7.6 The Ledger as Ultimate Control

This is where the system's enforcement power comes from: for meaningful wealth, the ledger is the authoritative record of who controls what, and registration is the strongest claim the legal system recognizes.

The Principle

Registration on the ledger is not a burden. It is the ultimate assertion of control. A registered claim is tamper-evident, timestamped, and instantly verifiable by any court. No paper receipt, no handshake deal, no shoebox of documents can match it. If you control wealth and you register it, your claim supersedes all others.

The power runs in the other direction too. If you do not register wealth of meaningful value, anyone else who can demonstrate a claim to it can register it instead, bear the duty, and hold the authoritative position. The ledger recognizes whoever steps up, and due process resolves competing claims. This inverts the current incentive structure entirely. Today, hiding wealth is advantageous: you avoid taxes while still enjoying legal protection. Under this system, hiding wealth means leaving your claim vulnerable to anyone willing to register and pay.

How It Works

If your painting is not on the ledger and someone else registers it, their claim is the one courts recognize. If your loan collateral is not on the ledger, your security interest is weaker than a competing registered claim. Chapter 9 develops these examples in detail.

The ledger becomes the foundation of property rights. Registration is the act that makes ownership definitive. If you want the strongest possible claim, you participate in the system that provides it by registering your assets and bearing the duty that funds it.

Why Registration Is Worth It

Some will ask: why would anyone voluntarily register and pay taxes on their wealth?

Because registration gives you something no other system in history has offered: a claim to your property that is cryptographically verified, publicly recorded, and recognized as authoritative by every court in the country. No one can forge it. No one can silently alter it. No one can assert a competing claim without going through due process to challenge yours. That is worth more than any tax savings from hiding.

The protection runs against the state, not just against private claimants. A registered, duty-paying stake falls squarely within the 5th Amendment's Takings Clause: the government cannot take it for public use without equitable compensation through due process. Chapter 10 develops the constitutional grounding.

When Claims Compete

If anyone can register wealth, what stops someone from registering your car while you are on vacation?

Due process resolves competing claims. When two people register the same asset, the dispute goes to the Judgment Layer described in Chapter 11. Each party presents evidence. The panel determines who actually controls the wealth, and the ledger updates to reflect the determination. During the dispute, the prior registration stands. No one loses their position without a hearing.

The prior registration stands unless its basis fails. When two filings collide, the earlier one holds while the dispute is heard. To displace it, the challenger has to show that the original filing was made in bad faith, or by someone who did not have control at the time. The panel looks at what stood behind the registration: the chain of acquisition, third-party records from custodians, insurers, and lenders, and the duty payments made under it. A registration grounded in that record will outlast a later filing that has nothing but the filing itself. The burden falls on the challenger, and the ledger is what the burden runs against.

Bad-faith registration is a crime. Filing a registration on wealth you know you do not control is the ledger equivalent of filing a fraudulent lien, which is already a criminal offense in every state. The bad-faith filer faces criminal liability, pays all arbitration costs, and has their registration removed. This is not a new legal concept. Courts have handled fraudulent property filings for as long as property records have existed.

The parallel is exact. County recording offices have managed competing claims to real property for centuries. UCC Article 9 has managed competing claims to secured collateral for decades. Two people file deeds on the same parcel; evidence of actual ownership resolves it. Two creditors claim the same collateral; priority rules resolve it. The ledger extends these proven mechanisms to all asset classes. The question of "who really controls this?" is the same question the Duty of Control already answers.

De Minimis: What Must Be Registered vs. What Can Be

Anyone can register any asset on the ledger at any time, regardless of value. A $500 guitar, a $3,000 bicycle, a family heirloom worth $200: if you want the ultimate claim, you register it. Registration is always available and always provides the strongest proof of ownership the system offers.

What changes at the de minimis threshold is the *obligation*. Congress sets a per-item value (for illustration, $10,000) above which registration is required. Failure to register assets above this threshold is tax evasion, because the controller has a duty to declare and is choosing not to. Below the threshold, registration is voluntary. Traditional proof of ownership (purchase receipts, insurance riders, photographs, appraisals, bills of sale) remains legally sufficient for everyday personal effects. Courts have accepted this evidence for centuries. The ledger does not replace it for items you choose not to register.

But the ledger always offers *superior* proof. A ledger entry is tamper-evident, timestamped, and cryptographically verified. It is instantly accessible to courts, insurers, and law enforcement. If your $8,000 watch is stolen, a ledger entry resolves the ownership dispute faster and more decisively than a faded receipt in a filing cabinet. The incentive to register even sub-threshold items is built into the system: the ledger claim is simply better.

The de minimis threshold is not a loophole. It applies per item, but the aggregate of sub-threshold holdings must still be reported as a category total, and the duty runs against that aggregate. Buying a thousand watches at $9,999 each shows up as one line of "Other Assets: $9,999,000" on the ledger. Under-reporting that aggregate is tax evasion, anchored by the records that dealers, insurers, and lenders generate as a matter of course. Structuring purchases to evade aggregate reporting is its own offense, on the model of Bank Secrecy Act structuring.

Congress adjusts the threshold as needed. The principle is administrative efficiency: do not spend more to track an asset than the tax revenue it generates. The ledger is a tool for accountability over meaningful wealth, not an inventory of household goods.

7.7 Privacy and Transparency

A public ledger raises legitimate privacy questions. Chapter 13 addresses them in depth, but here is the essential framework.

The Three-Tier Model

The ledger uses a three-tier information architecture. The public record (Tier 1) shows total wealth, tax burden, and asset categories, searchable by name for the top 10% of wealth holders and public officials, accessible by Ledger ID for everyone else. The government maintains confidential itemized records (Tier 2). Individual assets are disclosed only by consent or court order (Tier 3). Lookup notifications ensure that searching is itself transparent.

Chapter 13 details this architecture and addresses privacy concerns, including the Nordic precedent, the asset aggregation system that protects actionable intelligence, and the current asymmetry where workers have no financial privacy while the ultra-wealthy enjoy near-total opacity.

7.8 Why Trust This Government With This Ledger?

The government that cannot complete a Pentagon audit, that launched healthcare.gov into a smoking crater, that ran Iraq reconstruction, would now be maintaining a tamper-evident record of everyone's wealth. Why would anyone trust that?

The question is fair. Here is how the architecture addresses it, in four parts that work together.

You do not have to trust. You can verify. The architecture above was built around this point. The canonical ledger lives inside the government. The mirrors live outside it. Universities, news organizations, and international institutions hold synchronized copies that update continuously. If the government tries to delete, modify, or fabricate an entry, the mirrors show the discrepancy within minutes. Trust is not the mechanism. Independent verification is.

The government goes first. Before any citizen is asked to put their assets on a ledger, the government puts federal spending on a ledger of the same type. Chapter 14 details this sequence. If the Treasury can run a tamper-evident ledger of its own outlays, the capacity to run a wealth ledger has been demonstrated rather than claimed. The burden of proof is on the state, and the test comes first.

The code is open. The software that runs the canonical ledger and the mirror network is published, auditable, and modifiable by anyone. No hidden back doors. No proprietary secret sauce. Security researchers, cryptographers, and hostile critics can examine every line. When the system claims tamper-evidence, the claim is verifiable by inspection rather than by government assurance.

The Pentagon audit failure is an argument for the ledger, not against it. The Department of Defense cannot pass an audit because it runs 208 separate financial systems that cannot agree on where a single dollar went. That is the exact problem a shared ledger solves. The audit fails because there is no shared record for the auditors to check against. Put the spending on a tamper-evident ledger that Treasury and Congressional oversight see simultaneously, and the audit writes itself.

None of these make the state trustworthy. They make trust unnecessary.

7.9 Existing Precedents

This isn't science fiction. Governments already maintain ledgers of this type.

County land records have tracked real estate ownership for centuries. Every deed, every mortgage, every lien is recorded and publicly searchable. You cannot hide a house.

Vehicle registrations track car ownership nationwide. The DMV knows who owns every registered vehicle. You cannot hide a car (legally).

Securities registration through the SEC tracks stock ownership for public companies. Major shareholders must disclose their holdings. You cannot hide a large stake in a public company.

Estonia uses a blockchain-style integrity layer to protect critical government records, including health and judicial files, against tampering.[1] Citizens can see who accessed their data and when.

These precedents track assets. But can a distributed ledger track government finances at scale? The answer is yes, and three separate pilots have demonstrated it.

The Treasury pilot. The Treasury Department's Bureau of Fiscal Service tested blockchain technology for tracking federal grant payments. They built a permissioned Ethereum network and tokenized grant disbursements, linking award data from the National Science Foundation to actual payment flows. A standard federal financial report (the SF-425) that normally takes eight employees five hours to compile was generated by the blockchain system in seconds. The data was already there, already linked, already verified. Not through automation of the old process, but by making the old process unnecessary. When every transaction is recorded on a shared ledger, the report writes itself.

The DOD supply chain pilot. The Navy and Defense Logistics Agency used SIMBA Chain to track high-value parts through the supply chain, and a separate pilot demonstrated blockchain tracking 600 tons of military equipment more efficiently than the legacy systems it replaced. The Pentagon proved the technology works for defense logistics. Then it went back to the 208 legacy systems that keep failing (Chapter 4 explains why).

The Philippines national ledger. In January 2026, the Philippines launched the "Digital Bayanihan Chain," putting its entire national budget on a blockchain-based ledger. Three government oversight agencies see every entry simultaneously. Citizens can query spending data in natural language using an AI interface. The system was funded by a \$5 to \$10 million grant from Polygon. A developing nation put its entire federal budget on a transparent ledger for a tiny fraction of what the Pentagon spends each year on its failed audit process. The technology is not experimental. It is operational, at national scale.

The public wealth ledger would extend these proven concepts to all forms of wealth. The technology exists. The precedents exist, from county land records to national-scale blockchain ledgers. The question is political will, not technical feasibility.

7.10 Summary

The public ledger is the enforcement mechanism that would make the wealth tax work.

Why it's necessary: You can't tax what you can't see. A ledger makes all wealth visible.

How it would work: A canonical government record, mirrored by independent institutions, creates a tamper-evident system that no single party can manipulate.

How it's funded: Filing fees make the system self-sustaining, like a county recorder's office.

Why it's enforceable: The ledger is the authoritative record of control. Registration is the strongest claim to ownership the system offers. Anyone who controls wealth of meaningful value and does not register it risks a competing claim from anyone who does. Below the de minimis threshold, traditional proof of ownership remains valid, but ledger registration is always the stronger path. The incentive to hide disappears when hiding means leaving your claim vulnerable.

Privacy: The ledger equalizes transparency. Everyone plays by the same rules, not maximum privacy for the powerful and minimum privacy for everyone else.

Legitimacy: Before asking citizens to participate, the government goes first. The same ledger technology applies to federal spending, starting with the Department of Defense. Chapter 14 details the phased rollout. The government must submit to the transparency it asks of citizens.

Counties have recorded land ownership on public ledgers for centuries. What is described here is the same principle, extended to all wealth. The tools are modern. The idea is as old as the republic.

7.11 Notes

1. e-Estonia, "KSI Blockchain," https://e-estonia.com/solutions/cyber-security/ksi-blockchain/.

CHAPTER 8

THE PROPORTIONAL TAX, THE FORMULA

This is the chapter where you can do the math yourself.

The previous chapters established what counts as wealth, who bears the duty to pay, and how the ledger makes enforcement possible. Now comes the formula: exactly how much would you owe?

The answer is simple enough to fit on a napkin. Your tax equals your share of the nation's wealth multiplied by federal spending. That's it. No deductions, no exemptions, no 70,000 pages of code. One formula.

8.1 The Formula

Here is the complete federal tax calculation:

```
YOUR TAX = (Your Wealth ÷ Total US Wealth) × Federal Spending × (Days of Control
    ÷ 365)
```

With current numbers:

```
YOUR TAX = (Your Wealth ÷ $175 Trillion) × $7 Trillion × (Days of Control ÷ 365)
```

For a full year of control, this simplifies to:

```
YOUR TAX = Your Wealth × 4%
```

That's the entire federal tax system. One formula. One rate. One calculation.

Important: This is your *calculated liability*. For homeowners, the **primary residence deferral** allows you to defer taxes on up to **$500,000 of primary residence equity** as a lien at Treasury rate + 1%, paid when the home is sold or transferred. See Chapter 15 for details on this protection.

An interactive calculator at thelasttax.com lets you plug in your own numbers and compare your wealth tax liability against your current federal burden.

Why This Is Better

Simple. This formula fits on a napkin. You don't need an accountant to understand it. You don't need a lawyer to find the loopholes because there aren't any.

Transparent. Everyone can calculate their own liability. Everyone can verify everyone else's. The math is public. The inputs are public. The results are public.

Proportional. The rate is the same for everyone. Four percent of a million dollars is forty thousand. Four percent of a billion dollars is forty million. The wealthy pay more because they have more, not because they face a higher rate.

Automatic. The ledger knows what you control. The formula calculates what you owe. There's nothing to optimize, nothing to defer, nothing to restructure. Your liability follows your wealth.

Won't People Change Their Behavior?

A reasonable objection: if you tax wealth at 4%, won't people rearrange their finances to reduce what they owe? Academic studies of wealth taxes in Switzerland and Denmark found exactly that. When rates went up, reported taxable wealth went down.

But those studies tell you more about the systems than about the people. In Switzerland, the wealthy moved to lower-tax regions. In Denmark, they shifted assets into exempt categories like pensions and housing. Both responses exploited specific design flaws: jurisdiction shopping and exemptions. Under this system, the tax follows the wealth regardless of the owner's address, and the Wealth Test has no exempt categories. The two largest channels of avoidance in the academic literature do not exist here.

Some behavioral response remains real. People may consume more and save less. Business owners may challenge valuations aggressively. These responses are modest compared to jurisdiction shopping and exemption shifting, but they are not zero. The formula handles this automatically: if total wealth on the ledger shrinks, the rate rises to meet spending. Revenue is matched by definition. What changes is the rate, not the revenue. The three-year rolling average circuit breaker (described below) prevents that adjustment from spiraling.

Even an implausibly large behavioral response stays manageable. If 15% of wealth somehow exited the ledger, far beyond what the empirical literature suggests for a system without exemptions or jurisdiction shopping, the effective rate would rise only to about 4.7%, still within the range of long-term equity returns and below the combined federal burden most workers pay today. Appendix C tabulates the rate across the full range of scenarios, from full capture at about 2.9% to a 15% exit at 4.7%.

8.2 The Total Ledger Estimate

The formula requires knowing total US wealth. This is the denominator that makes everything calculable.

The Number

Conservative estimate: $175 trillion. This figure represents US household wealth only, as measured by the Federal Reserve. As the analysis below shows, the total wealth that would appear on the ledger (including foreign-controlled US assets) reaches **$225-250 trillion.**

A note on precision: the Federal Reserve's Z.1 Financial Accounts for Q4 2025 reports household net worth at approximately $184.1 trillion. This book uses $175 trillion as a round, conservative figure that sits deliberately below the latest measured total. Because actual household wealth is higher, the $175 trillion denominator slightly overstates the rate rather than understating it: at the full $184.1 trillion, the effective rate is closer to 3.8%. Erring toward the lower, rounder denominator keeps every worked example on the conservative side. The difference does not change the argument in any material way, and the formula self-corrects: as the real number shifts, the rate adjusts automatically.

This estimate draws from Federal Reserve data on household wealth, but assessing total national wealth is genuinely difficult under the current system. Here's why:

What we can measure (Federal Reserve data):

Category	Approximate Value
Real estate	~$48 trillion[1]
Corporate equities (stocks)	~$56 trillion[1]
Pension entitlements	~$40 trillion[1]
Private business equity	~$18 trillion[1]
Consumer durables	~$8 trillion[1]
Other financial assets	~$17 trillion[1]

What current estimates struggle to capture:

- **Tradeable debt held by creditors:** Banks, loan servicers, and bondholders control approximately $20 trillion in household debt and $22 trillion in business debt as assets. Some of this is reflected in financial sector valuations, but the accounting is murky.
- **Private institutional wealth:** Corporations, nonprofits, and trusts hold assets that aren't fully reflected in household wealth figures.
- **Intellectual property and patents:** Valuable IP often escapes traditional wealth estimates entirely. A pharmaceutical patent worth billions may not appear on any balance sheet at its true market value.
- **Undervalued private businesses:** Closely-held companies are notoriously difficult to value and often underreported.

Foreign-Controlled Wealth: The Missing $70 Trillion

The biggest gap in the $175 trillion estimate is not hidden wealth or undervalued assets. It is foreign-controlled wealth sitting in plain sight.

The Federal Reserve's household net worth figure measures only US-resident households. It explicitly excludes assets owned by foreign individuals, corporations, sovereign wealth funds, and governments. When a Japanese pension fund buys US stocks or a Saudi investor purchases Manhattan real estate, those assets are subtracted from the household sector in the Fed's accounting.

How much wealth are we talking about? According to the Bureau of Economic Analysis, foreign entities controlled approximately **$70.5 trillion** in US assets at the end of 2025.[2] That breaks down roughly as follows:

Category	Value
Foreign direct investment (factories, businesses, subsidiaries)	~$18 trillion (market value)
Foreign portfolio investment (US stocks and corporate bonds)	~$33 trillion
US Treasury securities held by foreign governments and investors	~$9 trillion
Other financial assets (bank deposits, loans, derivatives)	~$10 trillion

To put this in perspective: foreign entities control wealth inside the United States roughly equal to 40% of what American households themselves control. Japan alone holds over $1.2 trillion in US Treasury securities. Foreign investors collectively own a substantial share of the US stock market and US corporate bond market.

This wealth is not in the $175 trillion denominator. Under the current system, that's an accounting curiosity. Under the system described in this book, it matters enormously.

Recall from Chapter 6 that the Duty of Control follows the wealth, not the passport. Foreign controllers of US assets would need to declare on the ledger if they want US legal protection for their holdings (just as foreign owners of US real estate already pay US property taxes). Chapter 12 reinforces this: the tax is on control of US wealth, not on US citizenship.

The actual ledger total would include both US household wealth *and* foreign-controlled US wealth. The combined figure ranges from **$225 to $250 trillion**, determined by how much foreign-controlled wealth registers on the ledger.

What does that do to the formula?

Scenario	Denominator	Effective Rate
US household wealth only (current book estimate)	$175 trillion	4.0%
Including foreign-controlled assets (conservative)	$225 trillion	3.1%
Including foreign-controlled assets (full capture)	$245 trillion	2.9%

This book's headline rate of 4% is conservative. When the ledger captures foreign-controlled US wealth, as the system requires, the effective rate would likely fall to approximately 3%, not rise. Every dollar of foreign-controlled wealth that registers on the ledger lowers the rate for everyone.

This also means the system creates a powerful incentive for the United States to *welcome* foreign investment rather than restrict it. More foreign wealth on the ledger means a lower tax rate for American households. The ledger turns foreign investment into a direct benefit for every American taxpayer.

One important note: the $70.5 trillion figure includes US government debt held by foreigners (~$9 trillion in Treasury securities). Whether government debt instruments belong on the wealth ledger is a policy choice. If they do, the foreign holders pay tax on them, and the denominator grows accordingly. If they don't, the additive figure is closer to $60 trillion. Either way, the effect is substantial.

Why a Clean Ledger Changes Everything

The uncertainty in these estimates reveals a fundamental problem: **no one actually knows how much wealth exists in America or who controls it.**

Under the current system, wealth hides in corporate structures, offshore accounts, complex trusts, and undervalued assets. The Federal Reserve does its best to estimate, but gaps remain.

A public ledger would change this. When the ledger is the authoritative record, and anyone who does not register wealth of meaningful value risks a competing claim from someone who will, the true total emerges. Sub-threshold personal effects are captured as aggregate category totals, not individual entries, so even modest wealth is visible. The ledger doesn't estimate wealth; it *records* it.

This book uses **$175 trillion** as a conservative working figure, yielding an effective rate of **4%**. But as shown above, the true ledger total reaches $225 trillion or more once foreign-controlled US wealth is captured. At $200 trillion, the rate drops to **3.5%**. At $225 trillion, it falls to **3.1%**. At $250 trillion, it drops below **3%**.

The actual rate would be whatever is necessary to fund federal spending. The ledger would reveal the true denominator.

Market Fluctuations

The total fluctuates with market conditions. When stock prices rise, total wealth rises, and the effective rate falls slightly (since the denominator grows). When markets fall, the opposite occurs.

The Three-Year Average Circuit Breaker

A sharp market decline could create a dangerous feedback loop: falling asset values increase the effective tax rate, which forces asset sales, which drives prices down further, which increases the rate again. This is the "death spiral" critics warn about.

The solution: use a three-year rolling average for the total ledger value.

Instead of using the current year's total wealth as the denominator, the formula uses the average of the past three years:

```
EFFECTIVE RATE = Federal Spending ÷ (3-Year Average of Total Wealth)
```

How this prevents panic spirals:

Scenario	Current-Year Method	3-Year Average Method
Year 1: $175T total wealth	4.00% rate	4.00% rate
Year 2: Market crash, $140T	5.00% rate (panic!)	4.29% rate (stable)
Year 3: Partial recovery, $155T	4.52% rate	4.47% rate

With the three-year average, a 20% market crash raises the effective rate by only ~0.3 percentage points instead of ~1.0 percentage point. This prevents the forced selling that would deepen the crash.

Why three years?

- Long enough to smooth out volatility
- Short enough to eventually reflect real changes in wealth
- Matches the business cycle: most recessions last 1-2 years
- Provides predictability for tax planning

Automatic stabilization: During booms, the lagging average keeps rates slightly higher than they would be (cooling speculation). During busts, the lagging average keeps rates lower than they would be (preventing panic). The system naturally dampens extremes.

Now You Can Calculate

With this number, you can calculate your own federal tax liability right now:

1. Add up the value of wealth you control (your equity in your house, car, savings, investments, business)
2. Divide by $175 trillion
3. Multiply by $7 trillion

That's your annual federal tax. No accountant required.

How Debt Works

As Chapter 6 explains through the duty of control, debt is not a "deduction" from your wealth. Instead, debt represents a division of ownership.

If you have a $500,000 house with a $200,000 mortgage, there's one asset with two ownership stakes:

- **Your equity:** $300,000 (you pay tax on this)
- **Bank's lien:** $200,000 (the bank pays tax on this)

The total wealth taxed is still $500,000; it's just split between you and your lender. Tradeable debt (mortgages, student loans, bonds) passes the wealth test, so the holder of that debt pays tax on it.

This means:

- You don't "subtract" your debts to calculate your tax
- You pay tax on the equity you actually control
- Your lender pays tax on the debt they hold as an asset
- The total tax collected reflects the total wealth in the system

The same principle applies to entities of every kind. A corporation's total value is captured through its equity (shareholders bear the duty) and its debt (creditors bear the duty). A family farm's value is split between the owner's equity and the bank's lien. A non-profit's assets trace to the board members who control them. The entity is a pass-through; the humans who control each stake are the taxpayers. See Chapter 6 for the full framework on entity control.

Note: Remember the duty of control. The terms of the deal determine whether control is proportional or total. If the bank must sell at fair market value and return your surplus equity upon default, both parties bear proportional duty on their respective stakes, exactly as described above. But if the loan terms let the bank seize and sell without regard to your equity, keeping the proceeds, the bank may have full seizure power and thus full responsibility for the wealth taxes. The proportional split above assumes responsible lending terms that protect borrower equity. See Chapter 6 for the full framework.

8.3 The Effective Rate

At current spending levels, the effective rate is approximately **4% annually** on wealth you control, based on the conservative $175 trillion denominator. As discussed above, once foreign-controlled US wealth is captured on the ledger, the true rate would likely be lower.

The Calculation

- Current federal spending: approximately $7 trillion per year (FY2025)[3]
- Total US wealth (conservative, US households only): approximately $175 trillion[4]
- Total ledger wealth (including foreign-controlled US assets): approximately $225-250 trillion[2]
- Effective rate (conservative): $7T ÷ $175T = **4%**
- Effective rate (with foreign-controlled wealth): $7T ÷ $225T = **~3.1%**

This book uses the conservative 4% figure throughout its worked examples. The actual rate, once the ledger captures all wealth including foreign-controlled assets, would likely be lower. Every example in this chapter and Chapter 15 overstates the tax owed. That is by design: it means the real-world system would be more favorable to taxpayers than what you see here.

Why 4% Is Sustainable

Critics will argue that a 3-4% annual wealth tax is confiscatory, that it will erode and eventually destroy wealth. This objection only holds if you believe capital is static. If you believe in capitalism, it isn't.

The S&P 500 has averaged approximately 7-10% nominal annual returns over the past century. Real estate, private businesses, and diversified portfolios have historically exceeded the 3-4% threshold as well. Well-deployed capital grows faster than the tax takes. The wealth tax does not ask capital to shrink. It asks capital to share a portion of its returns with the society that enables those returns: the legal system that enforces contracts, the infrastructure that moves goods, the educated workforce that creates value.

Capital that is idle, unproductive, or purely speculative may indeed be taxed down over time. That is a feature: it creates pressure toward productive deployment. Capital put to good use in a functioning capitalist economy generates returns that comfortably exceed 3-4%.

Not every asset class clears that bar every year. A working ranch, a small manufacturer with heavy equipment, a family farm in a down cycle: these operations may generate 2-3% returns on the capital tied up in land and machinery. The system accounts for this. Use-value assessment (Chapter 11) ensures that working farmland is valued at what it produces, not what a developer would pay for the dirt. The primary residence deferral (Chapter 15) provides cash-flow relief. And the actual rate, once foreign-controlled wealth enters the ledger, is likely closer to 3% than 4%, which changes the math for asset-heavy operations significantly.

> True belief in capitalism means believing that the wealth it creates will outpace the contribution it owes.

What This Replaces

This single 4% wealth tax replaces:

Current Tax	Gone
Federal income tax	✓
Payroll taxes (Social Security/Medicare)	✓
Corporate income tax	✓
Capital gains tax	✓
Estate tax	✓
Gift tax	✓
Alternative minimum tax	✓
Net investment income tax	✓

All of these replaced by one formula.

The Rate Varies with Spending

The 4% rate is a function of two variables: federal spending and total ledger wealth.

Using the conservative $175T denominator:

- If Congress spends $8 trillion, the rate rises to ~4.6%
- If Congress spends $6 trillion, the rate falls to ~3.5%

Using a $225T denominator (including foreign-controlled US wealth):

- If Congress spends $7 trillion, the rate is ~3.1%
- If Congress spends $8 trillion, the rate rises to ~3.6%
- If Congress spends $6 trillion, the rate falls to ~2.7%

The formula creates a direct feedback loop. Every dollar of federal spending translates to a calculable increase in everyone's tax rate. Fiscal discipline becomes everyone's business.

The Rising Tide

The formula has a profound implication that is easy to miss: **when total wealth grows and spending stays constant, everyone's tax rate falls.**

Under the current income tax, someone else's success does not lower your taxes. Your neighbor starting a successful business, an immigrant building a company, a new industry emerging. None of it reduces what you owe the IRS. Taxation under the income system is zero-sum: the government sets a rate, and you pay it regardless of what happens around you.

Under the proportional wealth tax, it is the opposite. Every dollar of new wealth created anywhere in the system increases the denominator. If total wealth grows from $175 trillion to $200 trillion while federal spending holds at $7 trillion, the effective rate drops from 4.0% to 3.5%. Everyone's bill falls, not because government spent less, but because the nation grew wealthier.

This is the Henry Ford insight applied at the civic level. Ford understood that paying workers enough to buy his cars expanded the market for everyone. Here, anyone growing wealth expands the denominator for everyone. Your neighbor's prosperity is not your burden. It is your tax cut.

A Floor, Not a Ceiling

The four percent is the floor. It is the constitutional duty every controller of wealth owes the Republic for the privilege of holding it. Once that floor is in place, the body politic is free to build on top of it by statute, for special purposes, for limited periods.

This is not a brackets system in disguise. A surtax of this kind is transparent: named, dated, scoped to a specific project, and visible on the same public ledger as the base rate. It expires on the day the project is funded. There are no perpetual brackets to game because there are no perpetual brackets.

The Civil War income tax was raised to fight a war and phased out when the war was paid for. The lesson is not that special-purpose taxes are dangerous; it is that they must die when their purpose dies. Sunset clauses are the ledger's job, and the ledger does not forget. When the survival of the Republic is the question, those who control the most wealth have the most to lose in a collapse. A wartime surtax is the wealthy paying to preserve the system that makes their fortunes possible. There is no neutral ground for capital when the Republic falls.

Time-limited surtaxes for a railroad, a power grid, a port, a generation of schools, or a war that cannot be avoided are compatible with this system because they ride on a sound base. Permanent progressive brackets are not, because they reintroduce every avoidance incentive Chapters 2 through 4 catalogued. The Henry Ford insight from earlier governs either way: an infrastructure surtax that grows the denominator pays itself back in the rate everyone owes upon completion.

One tax is the floor. One rate is the floor. The ledger holds whatever the body politic chooses to build above it, in plain sight, with an expiration date.

8.4 Two Quick Examples

Set the optional surtaxes aside; the base formula is what almost every taxpayer will ever deal with. To see it in action, here are two examples at opposite ends of the wealth spectrum. Chapter 15 provides detailed profiles for twelve personas at every wealth level, with full asset tables and current-vs-proposed comparisons.

Maria the Teacher

Maria earns $58,000 and controls $117,000 in wealth (modest savings, a retirement account, a paid-off car). Under the current system, she pays approximately $13,700 in federal taxes (income tax, payroll taxes, and the employer payroll share that reduces her compensation). Under the wealth tax: $117,000 x 4% = **$4,680.** Maria saves roughly **$9,020 per year**, a 66% reduction. Her student loan debt is an asset held by the loan servicer, who pays tax on it. Maria pays only on wealth she controls.

Alexander the Billionaire

Alexander is a tech founder controlling $8.3 billion (mostly company stock, plus investments and real estate). Under the current system, he pays approximately $25 million in federal taxes, an effective rate of 0.3% on his wealth. Under the wealth tax: $8.3 billion x 4% = **$332 million**. Alexander pays roughly **$307 million more per year**. His wealth grows by billions annually; even after the tax, he remains extraordinarily wealthy. He simply contributes proportionally to the society that makes his wealth possible.

Same Formula, Different Impact

The formula treats everyone identically: 4% of what you control. But the impact varies enormously depending on whether the current system already taxes you heavily (workers) or barely at all (the ultra-wealthy). Chapter 15 walks through twelve detailed profiles, from a working family to a billionaire, showing exactly who wins, who pays more, and by how much.

8.5 Duration of Control

You pay for the time you control wealth, not just a snapshot on a particular date.

Proportional to Time

If you control an asset for half the year, you pay half the annual duty. If you control it for one day, you pay 1/365 of the annual duty. The ledger tracks control continuously, and liability follows.

No Gaming the Timing

Under the current system, sophisticated taxpayers time their transactions to minimize taxes. Sell losers in December to harvest losses. Defer gains until next year. Transfer assets before the estate tax snapshot.

Under the wealth tax, timing games don't work. If you sell stock in June, you pay for January through June. The buyer pays for July through December. The total tax on the asset is the same regardless of when it changes hands.

Automatic Updates

When control transfers, the ledger records the timestamp. Liability shifts at that moment. There's no year-end calculation, no estimated payments, no quarterly adjustments. The system tracks continuously, and you pay for exactly the time you controlled each asset.

Mid-Year Spending Changes

The formula treats federal spending as a single annual number for simplicity, but Congress routinely passes mid-year supplemental appropriations: disaster relief, emergency military funding, unexpected operational costs. The daily-accrual mechanism handles these the same way it handles control transfers. Each day's duty is calculated against the spending authorized as of that day. If Congress authorizes $500 billion in additional spending on day 200, every controller's daily rate increases from that day forward; the additional revenue is collected without retroactive adjustment to the first 199 days. A taxpayer who watched their representatives vote a supplemental can see their own bill move in proportion the next day.

8.6 The Anti-Bubble Mechanic

Here is an unexpected benefit of the wealth tax: it naturally discourages asset bubbles.

The Mechanism

Under the current system, there's no cost to holding overvalued assets. If your stock is trading at 100 times earnings, you pay nothing extra. Under the wealth tax, higher valuations mean higher taxes. If your stock doubles in price, your tax on that stock doubles. If your house is assessed for more than what the market would bear, you pay a premium.

Incentive Alignment

The mechanism creates pressure for realistic valuations:

- **Overvalue your assets?** You pay more taxes every year.
- **Undervalue your assets?** Escape assessments catch you when you transact (banks, insurers, and auditors report values), and valuation challenges catch you otherwise. You'll owe back taxes plus penalties.

The optimal strategy is honest valuation. Neither gaming high nor gaming low makes sense.

Market-Wide Effects

When speculation drives prices above fundamental value, the wealth tax makes that speculation expensive. Holding overvalued assets costs real money every year. This creates gradual pressure toward realistic pricing. Corrections happen slowly and continuously rather than in sudden crashes.

The wealth tax doesn't prevent all bubbles, but it raises the cost of participating in them.

8.7 Payment in Kind: The Economic Downturn Safety Valve

What happens during a severe economic crisis when taxpayers genuinely cannot pay in cash? During declared economic emergencies (hypothetical criteria: GDP decline exceeding 5%, unemployment exceeding 10%), the government can accept assets or fractional shares of assets in lieu of cash payment. Assets are transferred at their current ledger value and held in a sovereign wealth fund with a mandate to liquidate over 5-10 years. This is a voluntary option for asset holders in lieu of auctioning away tax lien certificates against their holdings.

This prevents the wealth tax from becoming pro-cyclical, making recessions worse by forcing asset sales at the worst possible time. The government eventually gets its revenue. Taxpayers avoid forced liquidation at fire-sale prices. The economy avoids a cascade of forced selling.

Payment in kind is available only during declared emergencies; in normal times, cash payment is required. The government selects which assets to accept (prioritizing liquid, easily valued assets), and retirement accounts are protected from this provision. Appendix B provides additional detail on eligible asset types and safeguards.

8.8 The Feedback Loop

The wealth tax creates accountability in both directions.

Higher Spending Means Higher Rates

If Congress spends more, everyone's tax rate rises. There's no hiding the cost in complex budget projections or future debt. The rate is simple: federal spending divided by total wealth.

Every citizen can calculate exactly how much a new program costs them personally. A $100 billion spending increase raises the rate by about 0.06 percentage points. For someone with $1 million in wealth, that's $600 per year. For someone with $100 million, it's $60,000.

Everyone Has Skin in the Game

Under the current system, many people believe "someone else" pays for government. The wealthy think the middle class pays. The middle class thinks the wealthy pay. Everyone thinks they're overtaxed and others are undertaxed.

Under the wealth tax, everyone pays proportionally. Everyone sees the rate. Everyone knows exactly what government costs them. Fiscal debates become concrete rather than abstract.

The End of Structural Deficits

Under the current system, Congress spends money it does not have. The FY2025 deficit exceeds $1.8 trillion. Interest on the national debt now exceeds $1 trillion a year, growing 8% annually.[5] The country is borrowing money to pay interest on money it already borrowed.

The proportional tax eliminates the mechanism for this. Revenue is not a separate question from spending. It *is* spending. The formula guarantees it: if Congress authorizes $7 trillion in spending, the rate adjusts to collect $7 trillion. There is no gap to fill with borrowed money.

The path to reducing the national debt is not mysterious. Step one: stop borrowing. There is no step two. Under this system, that happens automatically: revenue matches spending by definition. From there, existing debt service (already included in federal spending) gradually pays down the principal. As the debt shrinks, interest expense shrinks, total spending falls, and the rate drops. It is a virtuous cycle: fiscal discipline rewarded with lower taxes for everyone.

Some minimal borrowing still occurs for timing and operational reasons. Short-term cash management is standard in any treasury operation. But the structural $1.8 trillion annual deficit, the hole currently being dug deeper every year, ceases to exist.

This doesn't guarantee wise spending, but it makes every dollar of spending visible. You can't hide costs in complexity when the formula is public and the rate is everyone's business.

8.9 Summary

The proportional wealth tax replaces the entire federal tax system with one formula:

> YOUR TAX = (Your Wealth ÷ Total Ledger Wealth) × Federal Spending

Using the conservative $175 trillion denominator (US household wealth only), this works out to approximately **4% annually**. Once foreign-controlled US wealth (~$70 trillion) is captured on the ledger, the effective rate would fall to approximately **3%**. All worked examples in this book use the conservative 4% figure.

The crossover point is roughly $1.5-2 million in wealth. Below that, most people pay less. Above that, most people pay more. Workers and middle-class families win decisively. The ultra-wealthy, who have escaped taxation through sophisticated planning, finally pay their proportional share.

One formula. No deductions. No exceptions. For the first time, the tax burden falls where the wealth sits.

8.10 Notes

1. Board of Governors of the Federal Reserve System, *Financial Accounts of the United States* (Z.1), Q4 2025 release (March 19, 2026), https://www.federalreserve.gov/releases/z1/.

2. U.S. Bureau of Economic Analysis, *U.S. International Investment Position*, year-end 2025 release, https://www.bea.gov/data/intl-trade-investment/international-investment-position.

3. Congressional Budget Office, "Monthly Budget Review: Summary for Fiscal Year 2025," 2025, https://www.cbo.gov/publication/61307.

4. Board of Governors of the Federal Reserve System, *Financial Accounts of the United States* (Z.1), Q4 2025 release (March 19, 2026), integrated with the Distributional Financial Accounts, https://www.federalreserve.gov/releases/z1/.

5. Committee for a Responsible Federal Budget, "CBO Estimates 2025 Deficit Totaled $1.8 Trillion," October 2025, https://www.crfb.org/blogs/cbo-estimates-2025-deficit-totaled-18-trillion.

CHAPTER 9

ENFORCEMENT, HOW ENFORCEMENT WOULD WORK

How would you actually enforce a wealth tax? The question deserves a serious answer, because enforcement is where most wealth tax proposals fall apart. If the system depends on finding hidden wealth the way the IRS tries to find hidden income, the wealthy will win that game every time. They have better lawyers, more complex structures, and more resources to spend on concealment than any tax authority can spend on investigation.

The system described in this book takes a different approach. It does not rely on finding hidden wealth. It makes hiding wealth self-defeating. The enforcement mechanism is structural, not investigative. Evasion doesn't just risk penalties. It means leaving your claim to wealth vulnerable to anyone willing to register it and bear the duty.

Here is how that would work.

9.1 The Ledger as Enforcement

The public ledger is the enforcement mechanism itself.

The Core Principle

The ledger is the authoritative record of control. For wealth above de minimis thresholds set by Congress, registering your stake and bearing the duty places it under legal protection: a registered claim is the strongest the legal system offers, displaceable only through due process. The lien-and-auction track described later in this chapter operates only against stakes that are unregistered or delinquent. If you control an asset of meaningful value, you register it and bear the duty; if you do not, anyone else who can demonstrate a claim may register it instead and hold the authoritative position.

As Chapter 7 established, this inverts the current incentive structure entirely. The cost of concealment exceeds the cost of compliance.

How It Works

Imagine you own a valuable painting worth $2 million. Under the current system, you might "forget" to report it, hoping the IRS never notices. The painting hangs on your wall, appreciating in value, generating no tax liability.

Under the ledger system, that strategy fails. Your ex-spouse knows about the painting. Your insurance agent knows about it. The dealer who sold it to you knows about it. Any of them can register it on the ledger and start paying the duty. Now you have to challenge their registration through due process, and you are the one who was hiding it. Even if no one else claims it, the painting sits outside the authoritative record: courts have no registered entry to enforce, insurers have no ledger value to cover, and if someone steals it, you are fighting with a paper receipt against anyone who registers it first.

Or imagine you lend $500,000 to a business partner, secured by equipment that isn't on the ledger. The partner defaults. You try to seize the collateral. But the ledger shows no registered claim on that equipment. A competitor who registered it holds the authoritative position. Your security interest loses to their registered claim.

The ledger becomes the foundation of property rights. You want the strongest possible claim to your wealth? Register it. You want courts to recognize your control instantly and unambiguously? Register it. You want no one else to be able to assert a competing claim? Register it and bear the duty.

For meaningful wealth above the de minimis threshold described in Chapter 7, registration is the definitive assertion of control. Everyday personal effects remain yours through traditional proof of ownership.

9.2 The Graduated Enforcement Ladder

When taxes go unpaid, the system doesn't immediately act against assets. Instead, it escalates through a series of graduated steps, each giving the taxpayer opportunity to comply before more serious consequences apply.

The following is a hypothetical system inspired by existing tax enforcement practices around the United States.

Step 1: Notice and Payment Plan

If you miss a payment, you receive notice. You have 60 days to pay or arrange a payment plan. Interest accrues, but no penalties yet.

Most delinquencies resolve here. Life happens, people forget, have temporary cash flow issues, make mistakes. The system accommodates this.

Step 2: Tax Lien Certificate Sale

If you don't pay or arrange a plan within 60 days, the government sells a **tax lien certificate** to private investors (see the Florida model described below). The investor pays your back taxes; you owe the investor the amount plus capped interest; you have 2-3 years to repay. You keep your asset throughout this entire process.

Step 3: Asset Auction (Last Resort)

Only after the lien redemption period expires, and only if you've made no effort to pay, can the asset be sold. Even then:

- The asset is sold at **public auction**, not purchased by the government
- You receive any proceeds above the tax debt and enforcement costs
- This is rare, reserved for persistent non-payment over years

Step 4: State as Buyer of Last Resort

What happens when no private investor wants the lien? Some assets, like obscure art, niche collectibles, or minority stakes in illiquid businesses, may not attract private buyers.

The state steps in as buyer of last resort:

- The government pays out any existing lien holders at face value
- The asset transfers to government ownership
- The asset is held for eventual disposition (sale, donation to museums, etc.)

This is genuinely rare. Most assets have *some* market. But for truly illiquid assets, the state ensures the system doesn't break down.

Fringe Market Bundling

To minimize state purchases, illiquid liens are bundled with liquid ones.

How it works:

- Tax lien certificates are grouped into diversified bundles
- Each bundle contains a mix of liquid assets (real estate, securities) and illiquid ones (art, collectibles, minority stakes)

- Private investors bid on bundles, not individual liens
- The liquid assets make the bundle attractive; the illiquid ones come along for the ride

Example bundle:

Asset Type	Lien Value	Liquidity
Residential real estate	$50,000	High
Public securities	$30,000	High
Commercial property	$40,000	Medium
Art collection	$15,000	Low
Private company stake	$25,000	Low
Bundle Total	**$160,000**	Mixed

An investor might not buy a $15,000 lien on a painting that may never sell. But they'll happily buy a $160,000 bundle where 75% is liquid real estate and securities. The illiquid assets are carried along.

The bundle investor's economics. The bundle is priced for zero recovery on the illiquid pieces. An investor does not pay $160,000 for the example bundle; they bid something like $115,000, assuming the art and the private stake never redeem. At that price the $120,000 of liquid liens alone produce an attractive return as taxpayers redeem with back-taxes plus capped interest, and unredeemed liens convert to the underlying asset at the end of the redemption period. Anything recovered from the illiquid pieces is upside. Distressed-debt funds and bulk lien buyers already operate this way.

Why this works:

- Investors get diversification and overall attractive returns
- The government rarely needs to act as buyer of last resort
- Even obscure assets eventually find their way to market
- The system handles edge cases without breaking

This mirrors how property taxes already work. It's familiar, fair, and defensible.

Enforcement Costs (Poundage)

Poundage is the total of fees, interest, and enforcement costs assessed on delinquent accounts. Each step adds costs that the delinquent taxpayer bears:

- Interest on unpaid amounts

- Administrative fees for lien processing
- Auction costs if it reaches Step 3

This ensures evasion never becomes a competitive advantage. The evader pays for the cost of their own enforcement. Pay voluntarily and pay less. Resist and pay more.

9.3 State Property Tax Enforcement as Precedent

Critics sometimes suggest that wealth tax enforcement is unprecedented. It isn't. States have enforced wealth taxes on real estate for centuries. The mechanisms are well-established and can scale to other asset classes.

Florida Tax Certificates

Florida's property tax system demonstrates how enforcement can work without government seizure.

When property taxes go unpaid, the county doesn't immediately seize the property. Instead, it sells a tax certificate to private investors. The investor pays the back taxes to the county, and in return receives a certificate bearing interest, up to 18% annually in Florida.

The property owner has two years to redeem the certificate by paying the back taxes plus accumulated interest. Most do. The investor earns a return; the county gets its revenue; the owner keeps their property.

If the owner doesn't redeem within two years, the certificate holder can apply for a tax deed. After additional notice and due process, the property transfers to the investor. The original owner loses the property, not to the government, but to a private party who was willing to pay the taxes.

The mechanism anchors to the asset. Either the current owner pays, or someone who will takes over. Owners come and go, and the tax base keeps collecting.

California Escape Assessments

California's Proposition 13 limits annual property tax increases, but "escape assessments" prevent indefinite undervaluation.

When property changes hands, it's reassessed at current market value. When property is improved, supplemental assessments capture the added value. Over time, assessed values track reality, even if individual properties are temporarily undervalued.

Gaming valuations has limits. You can undervalue for a while, but transactions and improvements trigger reassessment, and assessed values drift back toward reality.

Deed Auctions

For long-delinquent properties, most states conduct deed auctions. The property is sold to the highest bidder, who takes clear title and assumes tax obligations going forward.

This clears the backlog. Properties that weren't generating revenue start generating revenue again. New owners, who presumably can afford the taxes, replace old owners who couldn't or wouldn't pay.

The auction keeps the asset paying. Ownership transfers to someone who can and will pay, and the county's revenue continues uninterrupted.

Scaling to All Assets

These mechanisms can extend beyond real estate:

Real Estate Mechanism	Scaled Version
Tax certificate sale	Lien on any registered asset
Deed auction	Asset auction (stocks, vehicles, etc.)
Escape assessment	Valuation updates on transfer or change

The principles are the same. Unpaid taxes create liens. Liens can be sold to investors. Persistent non-payment leads to asset transfer. The wealth stays in the system; only the controller changes.

9.4 Citizen Enforcement Incentives

The public ledger enables something the current system cannot: citizen oversight with financial incentives.

Poundage Funds Evasion Bounties

A portion of the poundage collected from evaders goes to whistleblowers. Anyone who exposes concealed wealth (assets hidden from the ledger entirely, held through undisclosed structures, or declared at values so disconnected from observable reality that they constitute deliberate fraud) earns a share of the recovery.

The result is an army of citizen auditors. Journalists investigating the wealthy. Competitors scrutinizing rivals. Disgruntled employees exposing their bosses. Ex-spouses revealing hidden assets. The incentive to expose evasion is financial and substantial.

Evasion bounties address concealment and fraud. If an asset appears on the ledger but the controller and an appraiser disagree about its value, that is a valuation challenge, a separate process described in Chapter 11. The line between the two is clear: honest disagreement about value is a civil dispute. Hiding assets or filing declarations that no reasonable person would consider genuine is evasion.

How Evasion Bounties Work

The evasion bounty operates through formal filing. Here's the process:

1. **Evidence gathering.** Because the ledger's public Tier 1 records show every citizen's name, total declared wealth, and asset categories, anyone can see whether a neighbor's mansion, luxury cars, and lifestyle are consistent with their declared wealth. A whistleblower who spots a discrepancy, whether they're a neighbor, an ex-spouse, a competitor, or a disgruntled employee, gathers evidence: documents, photographs, testimony, or any other material that suggests declared values are wrong or assets are missing from the ledger entirely.

2. **Formal filing.** The whistleblower files an evasion bounty claim with the tax authority, providing their evidence. This is similar to the IRS whistleblower program that already exists.

3. **Government investigation.** The tax authority, which has full access to Tier 2 records (individual asset details, transaction history, and valuations), investigates the claim. They compare the whistleblower's evidence against the itemized records and determine if evasion occurred.

4. **Targeted Tier 2 access.** If the claim has merit and the whistleblower's assistance would aid the investigation, a court can authorize limited, supervised

access to specific Tier 2 records relevant to the claim. This follows the same due process framework that governs all individual asset disclosure: judicial authorization, limited scope, documented access.

5. **Bounty payment.** If evasion is confirmed and taxes recovered, the whistleblower receives a percentage of the recovery (typically 15-30%, similar to existing IRS whistleblower awards).

What this means: The public Tier 1 data, names, totals, and asset categories, gives every citizen enough information to notice when something doesn't add up. The evasion bounty then provides a formal channel for turning that observation into an investigation. The whistleblower doesn't need special access to see that someone is wealthy. They provide evidence that the declared values are wrong.

Public Data Enables Pattern Analysis

Both individual public records and aggregate data are available for analysis. Watchdog organizations can analyze patterns: compliance rates by industry, wealth concentration by region, average declared values for asset classes.

Investigative journalists can work at both levels. At the systemic level, a reporter can discover that "compliance rates in the art market are 30% lower than other asset classes." At the individual level, a reporter can compare a public figure's declared wealth against observable indicators. This dual-level transparency creates pressure for both systemic reform and individual accountability.

Why This Prevents Corruption

Under the current system, enforcement is discretionary. The IRS decides who to audit. Political pressure can protect friends and target enemies. Selective enforcement is possible because the process is opaque.

Under the ledger system, aggregate compliance data is public. If compliance rates suddenly improve for politically connected industries while others remain flat, journalists will notice. If evasion bounty claims against certain individuals are consistently rejected without investigation, patterns emerge. The aggregate transparency makes selective enforcement visible and therefore politically costly.

9.5 Why Banks Would Benefit

Here is an unexpected constituency for the wealth tax: banks.

The Trump Case

In 2024, a New York court found Donald Trump liable for civil fraud, entering a judgment of approximately $464 million in disgorgement and interest.[1] The core allegation: he systematically inflated asset values when seeking loans from banks, while deflating the same values when reporting to tax authorities.

His triplex apartment was valued at $327 million to banks, more than any New York City apartment has ever sold for.[2] The same property was valued far lower for tax purposes. His golf courses, his buildings, his brand: all had two values, one for lenders and one for the IRS.

In August 2025, a New York appeals court vacated the penalty as an unconstitutionally excessive fine. The underlying fraud findings were not fully reversed, but the headline consequence disappeared.

This outcome illustrates the problem. Even when a court finds that someone systematically maintained dual valuations for the same assets, enforcement of consequences remains contested and reversible. The current system makes it possible to operate with two sets of books for years, and even after being caught, the penalties may not stick. Banks relied on these inflated valuations when extending credit. They thought they had adequate collateral. They didn't.

The Problem for Banks

This isn't unique to Trump. Borrowers have systematic incentives to inflate asset values when seeking loans. Banks conduct due diligence, but verification is expensive and imperfect. Sophisticated borrowers can present misleading valuations that pass initial scrutiny.

The result: banks extend credit based on inflated collateral values. When borrowers default, the collateral is worth less than expected. Losses accumulate.

How the Ledger Solves This

Under the ledger system, every asset has one declared value, the value on which taxes are paid. You cannot tell banks your property is worth $100 million while telling the IRS it's worth $30 million. The ledger shows one number.

Banks can verify collateral values instantly by checking the ledger. If a borrower claims their portfolio is worth $50 million, the bank can confirm it in seconds. No expensive appraisals. No reliance on borrower representations. Just check the public record.

Why Banks Might Support This

Banks would pay wealth tax on their own assets, their buildings, their reserves, their investments. But they would also:

- **Eliminate valuation fraud:** No more borrowers gaming collateral values
- **Reduce due diligence costs:** Ledger verification replaces expensive appraisals
- **Improve lending efficiency:** Faster, more reliable credit decisions
- **Reduce losses:** Collateral values are verified, not claimed

The trade-off might favor banks. They pay more in taxes but lose less to fraud. The net effect could be positive.

9.6 Why Evasion Becomes Structurally Difficult

Every evasion strategy that works under the current system fails under this one.

Hiding Wealth Means Losing Control

You can hide assets from the ledger. But hidden assets sit outside the authoritative record. You cannot pledge them as collateral through any compliant institution. You cannot insure them against the ledger's verified values. And anyone who knows about them can register them, bear the duty, and hold the superior claim.

The cost of hiding exceeds the cost of paying. A 4% annual tax is expensive. But leaving your wealth vulnerable to competing claims is more expensive.

The Ledger Is Public

Under the current system, your tax return is confidential. Only the IRS sees it. If you underreport, discovery depends on IRS investigation, and the IRS is underfunded and overwhelmed.

Under the ledger system, your declarations are public. Journalists can investigate. Competitors can verify. Watchdogs can scrutinize. If your lifestyle doesn't match your declared wealth, someone will notice.

Citizen Enforcement Creates Constant Vigilance

Whistleblowers have financial incentives to expose evasion. Your disgruntled employee knows what assets the company really has. Your ex-spouse knows what you're hiding. Your competitor knows your business is worth more than you declared.

Millions of potential auditors, each with financial incentive to expose fraud. No safe harbor for concealment.

The Hardest Case: Wealth Nobody Else Sees

The system works best when third parties generate valuations as a normal part of doing business: banks appraise collateral, insurers underwrite coverage, brokerages report positions. But some wealth never passes through a third party. Gold bars in a safe. An uninsured wine cellar. Cryptocurrency on a hardware wallet. Art in a private warehouse. If the owner never pledges it, never insures it, and never sells through a regulated channel, no institution reports it and the ledger only knows what the owner declares.

This is a real limitation. The system does not pretend otherwise. Three things constrain it. First, unregistered wealth of meaningful value sits outside the authoritative record: it cannot be used as collateral through compliant institutions, any competing registrant holds the superior claim, and it cannot be converted through any compliant channel without triggering ledger reporting. Second, deliberate concealment is tax evasion, subject to the same criminal penalties that apply to a false income tax return today. Third, the evasion bounty means that the neighbor who saw the delivery truck, the ex-spouse who knows about the storage unit, and the contractor who built the vault all have a financial incentive to report what they know. Perfect concealment requires perfect secrecy from every person who has ever seen the asset.

The residual risk is real but bounded. It is the same risk every property tax system tolerates: some wealth escapes. The question is whether the amount that escapes is large enough to matter. For the vast majority of wealth holders who want to actually use what they own, the cost of hiding exceeds the cost of declaring.

9.7 Criminal Penalties

The enforcement mechanisms described above are primarily civil: liens, auctions, poundage fees, and competing claims against unregistered wealth. But what about deliberate fraud?

Tax fraud remains a crime. Just as willful tax evasion is a federal crime today (carrying penalties of up to 5 years in prison and $250,000 in fines under 26 U.S.C. § 7201), deliberate concealment or fraudulent undervaluation under the wealth tax would carry criminal consequences.

Congress would establish specific penalties through implementing legislation, but the principle is clear: the civil enforcement mechanisms handle mistakes, disputes, and ordinary non-compliance. Criminal penalties address willful fraud, meaning deliberate schemes to deceive the system.

What constitutes criminal fraud:

- Deliberately concealing assets from the ledger while continuing to use them
- Creating false documentation to support fraudulent valuations
- Conspiring with others to hide wealth or manipulate records
- Systematic patterns of undervaluation that cannot be explained as good-faith errors

What does not constitute criminal fraud:

- Good-faith valuation disputes (handled through the challenge process)
- Mistakes or omissions corrected during amnesty periods
- Disagreements about valuation methodology
- Late payments or temporary non-compliance

The distinction matters. The system is designed to make compliance easy and evasion structurally difficult. Most people would comply because it's rational to do so. Criminal penalties exist for the small minority who deliberately attempt to defraud the system, and they would face consequences similar to those for tax fraud today.

9.8 Summary

Enforcement under the wealth tax is structural, not investigative.

The ledger as enforcement: The ledger is the authoritative record of control. Above de minimis thresholds, registration is the definitive assertion of ownership, and anyone who does not register wealth of meaningful value risks a competing claim from anyone who does. Below the threshold, traditional proof of ownership remains valid.

Lien plus poundage: Unpaid taxes trigger liens on equivalent assets, with auction if unresolved, plus a fee covering enforcement costs. Evasion becomes more expensive than compliance.

Proven mechanisms: State property tax enforcement (tax certificates, escape assessments, deed auctions) provides precedent that scales to all asset classes.

Citizen enforcement: Public ledger plus evasion bounties and valuation challenges creates millions of potential auditors with financial incentives to expose fraud and correct undervaluation.

Bank benefits: A single source of truth eliminates valuation fraud, potentially making banks net beneficiaries despite paying wealth tax themselves.

The result: evasion becomes structurally difficult rather than merely illegal. The rational choice is to declare honestly and pay proportionally.

9.9 What Comes Next

Part II has presented the solution: a wealth tax built on three pillars. The **Wealth Test** defines what counts as taxable wealth. The **Duty of Control** determines who pays. The **Public Ledger** and proportional formula make the system enforceable.

But a proposal this ambitious faces serious objections. Critics will argue it's unconstitutional, that valuation is impossible, that the wealthy will flee, and that privacy will be destroyed. These objections deserve honest responses.

Part III takes each objection in turn, stating each challenge fairly in its strongest form before responding. If the objections cannot be answered, the proposal fails. If they can be answered, the path forward becomes clearer.

The most fundamental challenge comes first: the claim that a federal wealth tax is simply unconstitutional. Under current law, that claim is correct. Chapter 10 explains what to do about it.

End of Part II: The Solution

9.10 Notes

1. Civil fraud judgment entered February 2024: $354.9 million disgorgement plus $98.6 million prejudgment interest, totaling approximately $464 million. Vacated on Eighth Amendment excessive fines grounds by the Appellate Division First Department on August 21, 2025. See https://www.nbcnews.com/politics/donald-trump/judgment-trump-civil-fraud-case-officially-entered-464-million-rcna140256 and https://www.dandodiary.com/2025/08/articles/director-and-officer-liability/n-y-court-affirms-trump-civil-fraud-ruling-vacates-massive-damages/.

2. New York Attorney General filings in *People of the State of New York v. Donald J. Trump et al.*, 2022, https://ag.ny.gov/sites/default/files/tto_release_properties_addendum_-_final.pdf. The highest-priced NYC residential sale on record is Ken Griffin's $238 million purchase at 220 Central Park South in January 2019.

CHAPTER 10

"IT'S UNCONSTITUTIONAL"

10.1 The Objection Stated Fairly

The Constitution contains two provisions requiring that "direct taxes" be apportioned among the states according to population:

Article I, Section 2: "Representatives and direct Taxes shall be apportioned among the several States... according to their respective Numbers."

Article I, Section 9: "No Capitation, or other direct Tax shall be laid, unless in Proportion to the Census."

If the federal government levies a "direct tax," it must collect the same amount per capita from each state. If California has 12% of the population, it must pay 12% of the tax, regardless of how much wealth Californians actually have. In 1895, the Supreme Court decided *Pollock v. Farmers' Loan & Trust Co.* and struck down a federal income tax, ruling that taxes on income from property are direct taxes requiring apportionment. Apportionment is unworkable for any tax that scales with wealth, so the decision effectively prohibited federal income taxation.

A wealth tax is even more clearly a tax on property than an income tax was. Under current Supreme Court precedent, a federal wealth tax is unconstitutional. This is a serious legal argument. This book does not dismiss it. It addresses what comes next.

10.2 The Amendment Path

The constitutional objection describes current law. It does not describe a permanent barrier. Article V exists precisely so future generations can adapt the fundamental law, and every major reform in American history that ran into a constitutional barrier overcame it the same way. Slavery was constitutionally protected until the 13th Amendment. State exclusion of women voters was constitutionally permitted until the 19th. Federal income taxation was constitutionally prohibited until the 16th Amendment overturned Pollock.

The 16th is the directly relevant precedent. Chapter 2 traces the full history: fourteen years of failed workarounds after Pollock, then ratification in under four years once Congress finally proposed the amendment. The Court said "you can't do this under the Constitution as written." The response was to rewrite the Constitution, and once it was rewritten, the Court upheld the new income tax in *Brushaber v. Union Pacific Railroad* (1916).

The wealth tax amendment asks for less than the 16th did. In 1909, the lift was genuinely novel: could the federal government tax citizens directly at all, on any basis other than apportionment? That question reached the foundations of federal power, and it took fourteen years to win. A wealth tax amendment asks something smaller. Direct federal taxation is already established. Every working American has paid one for over a century. The question is no longer whether the federal government can reach citizens directly, but whether the same power, already conceded for income, also reaches wealth. That is an extension, not an invention.

Constitutional change can also move quickly. The 26th Amendment (voting age to 18) was ratified in 100 days. The 12th took six months. The slow part of constitutional change is building political will. Once that political will exists, the process itself moves fast.

Appendix A provides a section-by-section analysis of the proposed amendment text, including the two-thirds congressional supermajority and three-fourths state ratification requirements.

10.3 The Amendment Process

The Constitution provides two paths for amendment. Both are difficult but achievable.

How Amendments Happen

Proposal requires either:

- Two-thirds of both houses of Congress, OR
- A convention called by two-thirds of state legislatures (34 states)

Ratification requires:

- Three-fourths of state legislatures (38 states), OR
- Conventions in three-fourths of states

No presidential signature is required. The president can support or oppose an amendment, but cannot veto it.

Historical Success Rate

Twenty-seven amendments have been ratified. The most recent, the 27th Amendment (concerning congressional pay), was ratified in 1992, though it was originally proposed in 1789.

Major reforms have succeeded through this process:

- Abolition of slavery (13th)
- Equal protection and due process (14th)
- Voting rights regardless of race (15th)
- Women's suffrage (19th)
- Direct election of senators (17th)
- Presidential term limits (22nd)

The process is deliberately difficult. It requires broad consensus across regions and political perspectives. But when that consensus exists, amendments happen.

What It Takes

Successful amendments require:

Broad public support. The issue must resonate beyond partisan lines. The income tax amendment succeeded because farmers in Kansas and workers in New York both felt the injustice of a system that taxed their labor while exempting accumulated wealth.

Sustained advocacy. Fourteen years of organizing preceded the congressional vote on the 16th Amendment. Movements must outlast individual election cycles.

A political moment. Eventually, the pressure builds until it becomes irresistible. Politicians who once opposed reform find it easier to support than resist. The 16th Amendment passed the Senate 77-0 because by 1909, opposition had become politically untenable.

A wealth tax amendment would require the same: broad support, sustained advocacy, and a political moment. This book is part of building that support.

An Honest Assessment of the Difficulty

The 26th Amendment analogy is instructive but imperfect. Lowering the voting age had no organized economic opposition. A wealth tax amendment would face the most expensive lobbying campaign in American history.

The scale and identity of that opposition is itself worth examining honestly. The 16th Amendment took eighteen years from Pollock to ratification, against modest opposition. A wealth tax amendment would face far more. A realistic timeline: ten to fifteen years from the moment serious organizing begins. Chapter 14 acknowledges this honestly.

The question is whether the prize justifies the effort. A republic where wealth answers to society. A tax system that fits on a napkin. An end to the buy-borrow-die aristocracy. The case made throughout this book is that it does.

10.4 Model Amendment Language

What would a wealth tax amendment actually say? Here is one possible formulation. Note that this is illustrative, and the actual language would be refined through the legislative process:

Amendment: The Wealth Tax Amendment

Section 1. The Sixteenth Amendment is hereby repealed. All federal taxes on income, including but not limited to taxes on wages, salaries, dividends, interest, capital gains, and corporate profits, are hereby abolished in such manner and time as Congress shall prescribe, not to exceed six years after ratification of this Amendment.

Section 2. The total taxes levied upon wealth shall be proportionate to the annual expenditures of the federal government as authorized by Congress. Each person shall be liable for a share of such taxes equal to the proportion and duration of wealth under that person's control as recorded in the public ledger established pursuant to this Amendment.

Section 3. Congress shall establish and maintain a public ledger recording all wealth within the jurisdiction of the United States, the persons controlling such wealth, and the declared value thereof. The public ledger shall be the authoritative record of control over wealth within the jurisdiction of the United States, subject to challenge and amendment only through due process of law.

Section 4. Where control of wealth is subject to revocation, override, or nullification by another, tax liability shall rest upon the person possessing superior authority over such wealth.

Section 5. As used in this Amendment, "person" means a natural person. No entity created by law (corporation, trust, partnership, limited liability company, or otherwise) shall be recorded as a controller of wealth on the public ledger. Government bodies may be recorded as controllers of public assets, but shall bear no tax liability on such assets.

What This Does

Authorizes proportional wealth taxation without the apportionment requirement that makes it unworkable. The amendment explicitly removes the constitutional barrier.

Establishes the public ledger as the authoritative record of wealth and control. The ledger is not just a policy choice. It is constitutionally mandated, and registration is the definitive assertion of control.

Establishes the duty of control as the basis for liability. The amendment enshrines the principle that control, not nominal ownership, determines who pays.

Restricts ledger controllers to natural persons and government bodies. No corporation, trust, or other legal entity may be recorded as a controller; the human who controls the entity registers under their own name, and government bodies bear no tax on the public assets they hold.

Phases out existing taxes over up to six years, providing transition time for the new system to be built and validated.

Why It's Structured This Way

Clear authority. No ambiguity about whether Congress can levy a wealth tax. The amendment explicitly grants the power.

Proportional by definition. The formula is in the Constitution itself: your share of taxes equals your share of wealth times federal spending.

Enforceable. The ledger requirement is constitutional, not just statutory. Future Congresses cannot undermine enforcement by defunding the ledger.

Democratic oversight. Congress still controls spending. The amendment does not set tax rates. It ties rates to spending decisions made through the normal legislative process.

10.5 The Constitutional Shield

The amendment authorizes the wealth tax. It also establishes something the current tax code does not: a constitutional shield around every duty-paying stake.

The principle. The duty pays for the infrastructure that recognizes property. Courts, registries, enforcement: the institutions that make ownership meaningful exist because the public maintains them. A controller who pays the duty has done what is asked in exchange for that recognition. The same institutions that recognize the stake cannot then extinguish it without due process and equitable compensation. The shield is the natural complement of the duty, not an extra grant on top of it.

Against private claimants. A registered, duty-paying stake stands on the ledger until displaced through the Judgment Layer. Chapter 11 walks through how that resolution works in practice. The point for the constitutional argument is narrower: a competing claimant cannot wipe out a registered stake by registering on top of it. The earlier filing holds while the dispute is heard, and the burden falls on the challenger to show the original filing was made in bad faith or without genuine control. Due process, applied uniformly, decides every contested claim.

Against government taking. When the government acts to take a registered stake for public use, the 5th Amendment's Takings Clause requires equitable compensation. This is not a new doctrine. It is the same protection that applies today when a state condemns a parcel to widen a road or run a transmission line. What the amendment changes is the universe to which that doctrine applies. Today, the Takings Clause protects only the property forms the legal system already recognizes: real estate, certain financial instruments, registered intellectual property. Under the amendment, every form of registered, duty-paying wealth is property of the kind the clause was written to protect. The clause does not need to be expanded. The ledger is what brings the rest of the wealth inside it.

What the shield does not cover. The protection is grounded in the duty. A controller who chooses not to pay steps outside the protection by that act. The lien-and-auction track that follows is not a taking. It is the same machinery that resolves an unpaid property tax today, applied uniformly across asset classes, and it operates against a stake whose holder has already failed the obligation that grounds the protection. No registered duty-payer is exposed to the lien track. Only the unregistered and the delinquent are.

The constitutional case for the wealth tax is not only that the amendment removes the apportionment barrier. It is also that the system, properly designed, creates a stronger and more uniform property right than the current arrangement. The duty is what builds the right. The amendment is what makes it durable.

10.6 The Real Question

The constitutional objection asks the wrong question. The question is not "is it constitutional?" The question is "should it be?"

Reframe the Debate

Critics treat current law as immutable. It is not. The Constitution is a legal document created by humans, amended by humans, and subject to further amendment by humans. The Founders made amendment difficult but possible. They expected future generations to adapt.

Article V exists for a reason. Amending the Constitution is not betrayal of the Founders' vision. It is fulfillment of it. They gave us the tools. Using them honors their legacy.

The Choice

The country faces a choice:

Option 1: Accept that wealth can never be taxed at the federal level. Accept that the Constitution, as currently interpreted, permanently exempts accumulated wealth from proportional contribution. Accept that the direct tax clause, originally a compromise to protect slaveholders, will forever protect billionaires.

Option 2: Amend the Constitution to enable accountability. Use the process the Founders provided. Change the law to match our values.

This is how democracy works. We identify problems. We debate solutions. We change the rules when the old rules no longer serve us. The constitutional objection is not a reason to abandon the wealth tax. It is a reason to pursue an amendment.

10.7 Summary

The constitutional objection to a federal wealth tax is legally serious and correct under current precedent. A wealth tax is a "direct tax" requiring apportionment, and apportionment is unworkable.

But this objection confuses current law with permanent law. The Constitution can be amended. It has been amended twenty-seven times. The 16th Amendment specifically overcame a Supreme Court decision (Pollock) that blocked income taxation.

The path is clear:

1. Build public support for wealth taxation
2. Sustain advocacy across election cycles
3. Reach the political moment when opposition becomes untenable
4. Propose and ratify an amendment

Constitutional barriers have been overcome before. The 16th Amendment proved it. The question is not whether the Constitution permits a wealth tax today. The hard part has never been the legal procedure. The hard part is convincing enough people that the current arrangement is intolerable.

10.8 What If the Amendment Stalls?

The amendment is the goal. But political timelines are unpredictable, and the work does not have to wait.

The federal spending ledger described in Chapter 14 requires no amendment. Congress can authorize it tomorrow. Putting the Pentagon's budget on a tamper-evident ledger, proving the technology works, and establishing the principle that government submits to the same transparency it asks of citizens: all of this is statutory. It builds capacity, demonstrates feasibility, and creates political momentum.

Several states already levy annual wealth taxes on real estate. Nothing prevents a state from extending that principle to other asset classes within its borders, testing valuation methods, enforcement mechanisms, and the ledger infrastructure at a smaller scale. State-level experimentation is how the income tax built support before the 16th Amendment, and it is how this system could build support too.

These are not substitutes for the amendment. A patchwork of state wealth taxes inherits the structural failures Chapter 4 described, inconsistent enforcement and political vulnerability, and adds the jurisdiction shopping Chapter 12 examines: wealth migrating to whichever state taxes it least. The amendment is what makes the system national, uniform, and durable. But the road to the amendment runs through proving that the pieces work, and proving the pieces work does not require waiting for ratification.

CHAPTER 11

"YOU CAN'T VALUE EVERYTHING"

The second major objection to a wealth tax is practical: how do you value assets that don't have clear market prices? Public stocks are easy, check the exchange. But what about private businesses? Art collections? Intellectual property? Complex financial instruments?

Valuation challenges are real. But most of what critics call impossible is already handled by existing property tax law, and the rest is resolved by a functioning dispute resolution process. This chapter shows both.

11.1 The Objection Stated Fairly

Critics argue that a wealth tax is unworkable because many assets cannot be reliably valued:

Private businesses don't trade on exchanges. There's no ticker symbol, no daily price quote. How do you value a family restaurant? A tech startup? A law firm partnership?

Art and collectibles are unique. Each painting, each vintage car, each rare wine collection is one of a kind. Comparable sales may not exist. Valuations are subjective.

Intellectual property is intangible. What's a patent worth? A trademark? A copyright? The value depends on future revenue that may or may not materialize.

Illiquid assets can't be easily sold. Real estate in a declining market. Minority stakes in private companies. Restricted stock that can't be traded for years.

The argument concludes: if you can't value assets reliably, you can't tax them fairly. A wealth tax would be arbitrary, contentious, and ultimately unenforceable.

This is a legitimate concern. Here is how existing law already addresses most of it.

11.2 Valuation Law Already Exists

The objection assumes the system has to invent a valuation framework from scratch. It does not. Property tax law has handled most of what critics call impossible for a century, and the wealth tax extends mechanisms that are already proven at scale. The work here is not to design new rules but to show how the existing rules already do the job.

California's supplemental assessments. When a property in California changes hands, undergoes construction, or suffers damage, the county assessor issues a supplemental assessment that updates the taxable value effective on the event date. The owner does not wait for the next annual cycle, and the county does not re-value every property on a schedule. Events trigger updates, and between events the prior value stands. The wealth ledger operates on the same principle, extended from real property to all asset classes. The event list is different (sales, pledges, capital raises, insurance underwriting, declared impairments) but the logic is identical.

Agricultural use-value assessment. Working farmland is assessed at its value as agricultural land, not at its development potential. A 200-acre farm in a county where developers would pay $20,000 an acre for the dirt is taxed on its crop-yield value, not the speculative land value. This is a standard statutory mechanism in state property-tax codes across the country. The wealth ledger uses the same principle for farmland, for working commercial real estate, and for operating businesses. The value on the ledger reflects the economic use of the asset, not a theoretical maximum a buyer might pay in a speculative market.

Assessor-initiated reassessment on transaction triggers. County assessors do not run comprehensive re-valuations of every property every year. They reassess when a transaction trigger fires: a sale, a pledge, a substantial improvement, a recorded damage claim. Between triggers, the prior year's assessed value stands. This keeps administrative costs bounded and limits the surface area for opportunistic re-valuation. The wealth ledger uses the same approach. A private business whose ownership has not changed, whose equity has not been pledged, whose insurance has not been updated, and whose controller has not declared an impairment simply retains its prior declared value. Nothing new to value means nothing new to report.

"If you can pledge it, you can value it." Banks, insurers, and the controllers themselves already generate valuations as a normal part of doing business. Those valuations are what the ledger collects. A mortgage lender appraises the house. An art insurer appraises the collection. A commercial bank values the inventory and equipment backing a business loan. The wealth tax does not ask these institutions to do new work; it asks them to report the work they already do. This is one mechanism among several, and it sits inside the broader organizing principle: the system uses existing valuation infrastructure rather than inventing new infrastructure.

11.3 Valuation Methods by Asset Class

Different assets require different valuation approaches. None of these methods are new; they are used constantly in commerce, lending, and insurance. Across all asset classes, values update on triggering events and between events the prior value stands. The worked examples below show how each class picks up that principle.

Straightforward Assets

Several major asset classes present no meaningful valuation challenge. **Public securities** (stocks, bonds, funds) have prices quoted every trading day; the ledger pulls them automatically. **Bank accounts and retirement accounts** (401(k)s, IRAs) have stated balances reported by custodians. **Cryptocurrency** has exchange prices multiplied by holdings. **Real estate** uses comparable sales, professional appraisal, or assessed values, methods counties have used for property tax purposes for centuries. These categories collectively represent the majority of American household wealth, and none require inventing new methods.

Depreciating assets (vehicles, boats, aircraft, equipment with industry-standard schedules) have published depreciation guides (KBB, NADA, Aircraft Bluebook) that the ledger pulls from annually. Owners do not file updates. Triggering events still override the schedule when they happen: a sale, a total loss, a new appraisal for insurance, or a pledge as collateral all establish a new value that supersedes the schedule. This is the same pattern as public securities, where prices update from market data without owner action.

Private Businesses

Method: Controller-elected at registration. Common methods include revenue multiples, EBITDA multiples, book value, and rolling averages of prior-year valuations. The controller picks the method that best fits the business type at initial ledger registration. The choice is tied to the asset's ledger classification, and switching methods later requires a re-registration event that is disclosed on the ledger. A controller cannot cherry-pick boom-year methods and bust-year methods.

Difficulty: Medium, bounded by process.

Private business valuation is more complex than public securities but well-established in commercial practice. Business owners already use these methods when seeking loans, selling stakes, or planning estates. The wealth tax applies the same methods to the same assets.

- **Revenue multiples:** Value equals revenue times an industry-standard multiple (e.g., 2x revenue for a service business)
- **EBITDA multiples:** Value equals earnings before interest, taxes, depreciation, and amortization times a multiple (e.g., 5x EBITDA)
- **Book value:** Value equals assets minus liabilities as shown on the balance sheet
- **Rolling average:** Value equals the average of declared values over a trailing window (e.g., three years), which smooths cyclical volatility

Pre-revenue startups. A company that has raised $50 million in venture funding but has no revenue and no earnings produces zero under revenue multiples and EBITDA multiples. The answer is straightforward: if the company has completed a priced funding round, that round establishes the ledger value. Investors valued the company when they wrote the check, and that valuation is the best available evidence. If no priced round has occurred, book value applies: cash on hand plus intellectual property at development cost. In either case, the value updates at the next triggering event (a new round, a sale, or a declared impairment).

Between-trigger behavior. Once a private business is on the ledger at its initial declared value, the value does not update on a schedule. Updates occur when a triggering event fires: a sale, a pledge, a capital raise, insurance coverage, or a declared impairment by the controller. Between events, the prior value stands. This is the California supplemental principle applied to operating businesses. If nothing has happened to the business that generates new valuation data, there is no new valuation to report. Appendix D enumerates the full event list.

Honest down years. A controller who needs to devalue an asset (revenue drop, customer loss, equipment damage) creates a triggering event by filing a declared impairment on the ledger with supporting evidence: updated financials, a third-party assessment, or other independent confirmation. If accepted, the declaration becomes the new ledger value. A false impairment is tax evasion on the same footing as a false income tax return, and disputes flow through the Judgment

Layer below. Every impairment is a public ledger entry visible to lenders, insurers, customers, and investors. A controller who claims impairment year after year is publishing the case against their own creditworthiness.

Art, Collectibles, and Intellectual Property

Art valuation is subjective but not arbitrary. If you can insure it, you can value it: insurance appraisals, auction records of comparable works, and certified expert assessments provide anchors. The same applies to wine collections, vintage cars, rare books, and other collectibles. Intellectual property follows a similar principle: if a patent generates licensing revenue, that revenue establishes a value. If it has attracted acquisition offers, those offers establish a value. IP that generates no revenue and has no acquisition interest has minimal value, and minimal tax liability. Appendix B provides the detailed valuation methods for each of these asset classes.

11.4 Self-Reporting with Market Verification

The previous section established the organizing principle: existing law already handles most valuation. This section describes how that principle operates at the level of the individual controller.

Controllers declare the value of their assets. They pay taxes based on their declared values. The government does not need to independently appraise millions of assets. But it also does not need to trust the declarations blindly, because **you cannot hide value from everyone**. Every time you interact with the financial system (a loan, an insurance policy, a sale, an appraisal), you reveal what your assets are really worth. The ledger collects those revelations and compares them to the declaration.

Escape Assessments

Certain transactions automatically trigger revaluation, extending the California supplemental framework from real estate to all asset classes.

Transactions that trigger escape assessment:

Transaction	What It Reveals
Sale or transfer	Actual market price
Collateral pledge	Bank's assessed value
Insurance coverage	Insured value
Refinancing	Appraised value
Estate transfer	Probate valuation
IPO (initial public offering) or capital raise	Market capitalization

How it works: If you declare your house is worth $300,000 but pledge it as collateral for a $500,000 loan, the bank's valuation becomes the new ledger value. If you insure your art collection for $5 million but declare it at $1 million, the insurance value triggers reassessment.

Back taxes apply: When an escape assessment reveals undervaluation, you owe back taxes on the difference, plus modest interest. No penalties for honest mistakes caught through normal transactions.

Third-Party Valuation Reporting

Financial institutions already assess asset values constantly. The ledger simply collects these assessments.

Who reports:

Institution	What They Report
Banks	Collateral values for loans
Insurance companies	Coverage amounts and appraisals
Brokerages	Securities holdings and values
Auditing firms	Fair market values in financial statements
Appraisal companies	Professional valuations (when commissioned)

How it works: When you apply for a loan, the bank assesses your collateral. That assessment is reported to the ledger. When you insure valuable property, the insurer's appraisal is reported. When your company is audited, the auditor's fair value assessments are reported.

These reports create a **market consensus** around asset values. If your declared value diverges significantly from third-party reports, the discrepancy is flagged for review. Under the ledger's authoritative-record principle, every third-party valuation also serves as potential evidence for a competing claim or valuation challenge. A bank that appraises your collateral at three times your declared value has not just triggered an escape assessment. It has created a public record that any certified appraiser can use to file a valuation challenge, and that any person with a competing claim to the asset can use to support a registration filing.

Privacy note: Third parties report values, not personal details. The ledger sees "Asset ID 7X9K2M valued at $2.3M by First National Bank" not your name, address, or loan terms.

When escape assessments and third-party reporting produce a value that conflicts with the controller's declaration, the dispute goes to the Judgment Layer described below.

11.5 The Judgment Layer

The mechanisms above (trigger-based updates, third-party reporting, self-declaration with honest adjustment) work because a functioning dispute resolution process stands behind them. Controllers trust that their declarations are treated fairly. Challengers trust that legitimate disputes can be filed without prohibitive cost. The system as a whole trusts that contested values are resolved by evidence and process, not by administrative fiat or negotiation under pressure.

This is the Judgment Layer, and it is a structural component of the wealth tax. It is not an exception-handling afterthought. Every assertion in this chapter about self-declaration, trigger-based updates, and between-trigger stability assumes the Judgment Layer exists and works.

Who Can File a Challenge

Three parties can file a valuation challenge:

1. **The tax authority** (the federal agency administering the wealth tax) can audit a declared value and file a challenge if the evidence supports it.
2. **A certified appraiser** can file a challenge against a third party's declaration when the appraiser has professional grounds to believe the value is understated. Successful challenges earn a bounty scaled to the recovered tax. Frivolous challenges expose the challenger to cost-shifting, described below.
3. **Another controller** can file a challenge against a related asset's declaration if the declaration affects the challenger's own tax liability (for example, a business partner disputing a co-owner's impairment declaration).

How Arbitration Works

A challenge goes to an independent arbitration panel modeled on existing tax courts and commercial arbitration bodies. The panel receives both sides' evidence (appraisal reports, transaction comparables, market analysis, the controller's response), holds a hearing if either side requests one, and issues a binding valuation decision within a defined window. A working target of 90 days covers straightforward cases; complex disputes can run longer with documented justification.

Panel members are drawn from a roster of certified appraisers, valuation specialists, and tax court judges with expertise in the asset class at issue. A panel hearing a private-business dispute includes members who understand private-business valuation. A panel hearing an art dispute includes members who understand art-market valuation. Expertise is tied to the dispute, not assigned generically.

The early years will be the hardest as controllers test the system with a wave of challenges. The first years of the wealth tax would see a surge of filings as asset holders probe how the Judgment Layer handles their particular situation. This is expected, not a crisis. The transition timeline in Chapter 14 runs four years of parallel operation (Years 3 through 6) before the old system is repealed, and that parallel period is when the surge hits, while the old system is still collecting revenue and the stakes of any individual dispute are bounded by the "pay the lower of" rule. By the time the wealth tax stands alone, the caseload has settled into steady state and the panel roster has scaled to meet it.

Costs and Defaults

Filing costs are scaled to the asset class and the amount in dispute, modeled on existing court filing fees. Ordinary challenges are affordable enough that legitimate disputes get heard. Frivolous challenges face a cost-shifting rule: if the panel finds the challenge lacked a reasonable basis, the challenger pays the full cost of arbitration and the controller's reasonable defense expenses.

During a pending dispute, the prior year's declared value stands. The controller pays tax based on that prior value, and any additional tax owed if the challenge succeeds accrues at the Treasury rate plus one percent, which is the same deferral mechanism that applies to primary-residence wealth tax under Chapter 15. A challenge does not force a controller into a sudden cash call.

Outcomes

If the challenge succeeds, the ledger value updates to the panel's determination, effective retroactively to the tax year in dispute. Back taxes are assessed at the new value with interest at Treasury plus one percent. A separate penalty (typically 15% of the underpayment) applies only if the panel finds the original declaration was made in bad faith. Honest disagreements over valuation methodology do not trigger penalties.

If the challenge fails, the controller's declared value stands and the challenger pays the arbitration costs. A pattern of failed challenges by the same party triggers additional review and, at the panel's discretion, a bar on future filings without pre-screening.

No Forced Purchase

The government never buys the asset in dispute. A controller who owes back taxes pays them through the standard wealth tax mechanism: direct payment, primary-residence deferral at Treasury plus one percent, or the enforcement liens described in Chapter 9. Nothing in this system authorizes the state to take the asset itself.

11.6 Eleanor's Bad Year: A Worked Example

Eleanor is 58. She founded a specialty manufacturing business in her 30s, ran it successfully through three economic cycles, and now owns 90% of it. The business accounts for roughly 90% of her net worth. In a normal year, revenue is $40 million and EBITDA is $6 million. Her ledger value for the business, set at registration using a 5x EBITDA method, is $30 million. Her wealth tax liability on the business is substantial but manageable.

Then a bad year hits. Her main customer segment contracts sharply. Revenue drops to $22 million. EBITDA drops to $1.8 million. Her industry has seen cyclical downturns like this before, and she expects to return to normal within two to three years. Until then the numbers are ugly.

Under the current income tax, Eleanor pays little on the business this year because her income-based liability already reflects the drop. Under the wealth tax as commonly imagined, Eleanor would be taxed at the boom-year value during a bust-year reality. This is precisely the scenario critics invoke when they say the tax is unworkable for founders.

Here is how the wealth tax actually handles Eleanor's year.

Step 1: Eleanor reports the impairment. She logs into the ledger and files a declared impairment for the business. Her reported EBITDA drops from $6 million to $1.8 million. Her elected valuation method (5x EBITDA, locked at registration) produces a new ledger value of $9 million, down from $30 million. The new value takes effect for the current tax year, and her wealth tax liability drops proportionally.

Step 2: Nothing further happens if nobody challenges. If the tax authority reviews her return and finds the impairment plausible, her filing stands. Her tax for the year reflects the $9 million value. No appraisal, no arbitration, no dispute.

Step 3: If someone challenges, the Judgment Layer processes it. If the tax authority has evidence the revenue drop is overstated, or if a certified appraiser files a challenge alleging the impairment is cosmetic, the dispute goes to an arbitration panel. Eleanor provides her financials: audited statements, customer contracts, industry context. The panel reviews the evidence and issues a determination within the defined window.

Step 4: The prior value stands during the dispute. While the challenge is pending, Eleanor's tax liability is calculated at the prior year's value ($30 million), not at the contested new value ($9 million). Any additional tax she may owe if the challenge succeeds accrues at the Treasury rate plus one percent. If she prevails, the additional accrual is waived and the $9 million value takes effect for the disputed year. If she loses, the additional tax is owed with interest, but at a deferral rate that is modest and predictable.

Step 5: The result is process, not a magic number. Eleanor's case is answered by the Judgment Layer, not by a rule that specifies what a manufacturing business in a cyclical downturn is worth. The wealth tax does not need to know the exact correct value of her business during a bad year. It needs a mechanism that turns her declaration into an accepted filing or a contested one, and that resolves the contest fairly.

Two things this worked example shows. The wealth tax does not force Eleanor to sell her business to pay the tax. And the tax does not punish her for a cyclical downturn. The system adjusts because she adjusts it, and the enforcement mechanism is the Judgment Layer rather than a rigid schedule.

11.7 Edge Cases

The California supplemental framework and the Judgment Layer between them cover most of what looks like edge cases. Two categories still deserve specific treatment.

Illiquid Assets

Some assets cannot be easily sold. A minority stake in a private company with no buyers. Real estate in a depressed market. Restricted stock that cannot be traded for years. Uniquely specialized equipment with no working market.

Illiquidity affects value. A minority stake worth $10 million if freely tradeable might be worth $7 million given restrictions. The controller's elected valuation method should reflect this discount at registration, and the tax liability adjusts accordingly. For genuinely unique assets with no comparables, conservative estimates are defensible and the Judgment Layer is the backstop when the tax authority disagrees.

De Minimis Threshold

The de minimis threshold (Chapter 7) ensures everyday personal effects are not individually tracked. Congress sets a per-item value below which traditional proof of ownership suffices, with possible variation by asset category. Aggregate values are still reported as category totals, preventing the threshold from becoming a loophole.

11.8 Approximate Justice Beats Precise Injustice

Critics demand perfect valuation before accepting any wealth tax. But perfection isn't the standard for any tax system. Income taxes estimate deductions. Property taxes lag market changes. Estate tax valuations are negotiated. Every system functions despite imperfection.

The relevant comparison is the status quo. Under the current system, a billionaire whose wealth grows by $10 billion pays nothing on that growth. Under a wealth tax with imperfect valuation, they pay approximately 4% of approximately $10 billion. Even with significant valuation error, the result is more equitable than zero.

Most wealth is easy to value: public securities, real estate, and bank and retirement accounts. The hard cases (private businesses, art, IP) represent a minority of total wealth, and even these have workable methods used daily in commerce. Approximate justice is better than precise injustice.

11.9 Summary

The valuation objection treats an existing problem as if it were a new one. Property tax law has handled most of what critics call impossible for a century, and the wealth tax extends those mechanisms rather than inventing new ones.

Existing law, not new mechanism. California's supplemental assessments handle event-triggered reassessment. Agricultural use-value assessment handles land whose economic use differs from its speculative potential. Assessor-initiated reassessment on transaction triggers handles operating businesses and real estate. These are all existing statutory mechanisms used at scale by state and county tax authorities every day.

Trigger-based updates, not annual re-valuation. A private business on the ledger does not get re-valued on a schedule. Its value changes when a triggering event fires: a sale, a pledge, a capital raise, insurance coverage, a declared impairment. Between events, the prior value stands. This keeps administrative cost bounded and prevents opportunistic re-valuation.

Controller-elected methods, locked at registration. At the moment an asset is registered, the controller picks a valuation method from a fixed menu (revenue multiples, EBITDA multiples, book value, rolling averages, use-value for working farmland, and so on). The method is tied to the asset's classification, and switching methods requires a disclosed re-registration event. A controller cannot cherry-pick boom-year methods and bust-year methods.

Trust the declaration, enforce the breaks. Controllers self-declare. The system accepts the declaration at face value. If someone challenges, the dispute goes to the Judgment Layer. A false declaration exposes the controller to tax evasion liability on the same footing as a false income tax return. The valuation trusts the controller until the trust is broken, and the enforcement mechanism is the breaking.

The Judgment Layer is structural, not optional. A functioning dispute resolution process stands behind every other mechanism in this chapter. Independent arbitration panels with asset-class expertise. Scaled filing costs that admit legitimate disputes and deter frivolous ones. Prior value stands during disputes, with any additional tax deferring at Treasury plus one percent. No forced purchases, ever.

Process, not magic numbers. Eleanor's bad year is answered by process. The wealth tax does not need to know the exact correct value of her business during a cyclical downturn. It needs a mechanism that turns her declaration into an accepted filing or a contested one, and that resolves the contest fairly. That mechanism is the Judgment Layer, and it is how the chapter's promise is kept.

Approximate justice is better than precise injustice.

CHAPTER 12

"THE RICH WILL JUST LEAVE"

The third major objection is capital flight. If we tax wealth, the wealthy will simply relocate, taking their money, their businesses, and their jobs with them. The country ends up with less revenue, not more.

This objection sounds plausible. But the mechanics tell a different story. The wealthy can leave. Their wealth, for the most part, cannot. And the mechanisms to handle departure already exist.

12.1 The Objection Stated Fairly

The capital flight argument has several components:

The wealthy are mobile. Unlike workers tied to jobs and communities, the ultra-wealthy can live anywhere. If taxes become too burdensome, they will move to lower-tax jurisdictions.

They will take their assets offshore. Wealth can be transferred to foreign accounts, foreign corporations, and foreign trusts. The US will lose visibility and control.

Investment will flee. If the US becomes a high-tax jurisdiction, capital will flow elsewhere. Businesses will relocate. Jobs will follow.

The country ends up worse off. The revenue gained from taxing the wealthy will be less than the revenue lost from their departure. The middle class will bear more of the burden, not less.

This is a common argument against any tax increase on the wealthy. It deserves a serious look at the evidence.

12.2 The Wealth Stays Even If the Owner Leaves

This system taxes wealth, not people. That is what defeats the capital flight argument. Every wealth tax that failed in the past century taxed residents on their holdings, so changing residency escaped the tax. This one taxes wealth on its location, regardless of where the controller lives. Most US wealth is tied to US jurisdiction or land and definitionally cannot leave.

Real Estate Does Not Move

You cannot move 50 acres in Montana to Ireland. You cannot relocate a Manhattan apartment to Singapore. You cannot transfer a California vineyard to the Cayman Islands.

Real estate is, by definition, immovable. It stays where it is regardless of who owns it. If the owner leaves the country, the land remains, and remains subject to US jurisdiction.

Real estate represents approximately $48 trillion of US wealth. None of it can flee.

US Businesses Have US Operations

A business headquartered in the US, with US employees, US customers, and US operations, cannot simply relocate. The legal entity might reincorporate abroad, but the actual business (the factories, offices, stores, and workers) stays put.

Take a retail chain with 1,000 US stores. The owner can move to Monaco. The corporation can reincorporate in Ireland. But the stores remain in the US, serving US customers, employing US workers. The wealth represented by those operations is US wealth, regardless of where the owner sleeps. And the Irish corporation does not sign the ledger. The human owner does, from Monaco, from Dublin, from anywhere. The ledger requires a natural person as the controller. Reincorporation changes the legal wrapper. It does not change who puts their name on the line.

US Intellectual Property Requires US Courts

Patents, trademarks, and copyrights derive their value from legal enforcement. A US patent is valuable because US courts will enjoin infringers and award damages. A US trademark is valuable because US law prevents counterfeiting.

If you want US courts to protect your intellectual property, you need US jurisdiction. You can move to Switzerland, but your US patents still depend on US enforcement. The wealth represented by that IP is tied to the US legal system.

The Wealth That Can Move

Some wealth is genuinely mobile:

- Cash in foreign bank accounts
- Securities in foreign brokerages
- Ownership of foreign businesses
- Cryptocurrency (theoretically)

But this represents a minority of total wealth. And even mobile wealth often depends on US connections: US customers, US markets, US legal protections.

The vast majority of US wealth is tied to US jurisdiction. The owner can leave; the wealth cannot.

12.3 Citizenship Is Irrelevant

The wealth tax proposed in this book is not based on citizenship. It is based on control of wealth within US jurisdiction.

The Principle

If you control wealth in the United States (real estate, businesses, intellectual property, securities), you pay US taxes on that wealth. It does not matter if you are American, French, Saudi, or Singaporean. Control US wealth, pay US taxes.

This is how property taxes already work. Foreign nationals who own US real estate pay US property taxes. They do not get an exemption because they are not citizens.

The Implication

Renouncing US citizenship does not exempt you from the wealth tax. If you remain a French citizen living in Paris but own a Manhattan apartment, you pay wealth tax on that apartment. If you are a Singaporean national but control a US business, you pay wealth tax on that business.

The question is not "where do you live?" or "what's your passport?" The question is "what US wealth do you control?"

The Enforcement Mechanism

If a foreign controller does not pay, the same enforcement mechanisms apply. Liens can be placed. The wealth can be auctioned to someone who will pay. And if a controller stops paying altogether, their registration lapses and their claim is no longer the authoritative one. Anyone else who steps up to register the asset and bear the duty holds the superior position.

The wealth does not escape, only the owner does. And if the owner wants to maintain control of US assets, they pay US taxes.

Exit Tax as a Backstop

The existing HEART Act already treats expatriation as a deemed sale of unrealized gains. Congress can strengthen the clawback period or add a final wealth-tax settlement if flight ever becomes material. It has not needed to. The primary enforcement is simpler: the ledger is the authoritative record of control over US wealth, and anyone who wants to hold the strongest claim registers and bears the duty.

12.4 Where Would They Go?

The capital flight argument assumes attractive alternatives exist. The reality is more complicated. No single jurisdiction replicates what the wealthy actually use the US for: the deepest capital markets, the most reliable contract enforcement, 330 million consumers, and courts that will still be standing in thirty years. Switzerland, Singapore, Monaco, and Dubai each trade one of these for tax savings. None offer the combination. The wealthy know this, which is why most of them stay, and why the ones who leave keep their businesses here.

Historical Evidence: What Actually Happens

Capital flight threats have been made for over a century, since the first income tax debates. The historical record is instructive.

France: The Paper Exodus

When France maintained its wealth tax, the Impôt de Solidarité sur la Fortune (ISF), from 1989 to 2017, critics claimed it caused massive capital flight. Roughly

10,000 wealthy households are estimated to have left over the ISF's three decades.[1] That sounds alarming until you remember France has nearly 30 million households. The departures represented a tiny fraction of the population.

More importantly, most "departures" were paper relocations. Wealthy French established residency in Belgium or Switzerland while keeping their Paris apartments, their Riviera villas, their French businesses. They just filed a change of address.

Why did this work? France made one of the two mistakes Chapter 4 named: taxing the person instead of the wealth. The ISF exempted non-residents' financial assets from the tax. A wealthy Frenchman could move to Belgium, keep every share in every French company, and owe zero wealth tax on any of it. The wealth never moved. Only the address changed. And the tax, designed to follow the person rather than the wealth, simply evaporated.

France's economy continued functioning throughout the ISF era. Paris remained a global financial center. French businesses thrived. The apocalyptic predictions never materialized. When Macron repealed the ISF in 2017, replacing it with a tax on real estate only, he was conceding the obvious: a residence-based wealth tax on financial assets does not work.

The system proposed in this book does not have France's design flaw. The tax follows the wealth, not the person's address. French shares in French companies would still be taxable under a system like this one, regardless of whether the owner lives in Paris or Brussels. Filing a change of address would accomplish nothing.

Sweden: Kamprad's Misdirection

IKEA founder Ingvar Kamprad is the poster child for wealth tax flight. He left Sweden in 1973, citing tax burden, first moving to Denmark before relocating to Switzerland in 1976. He became the example cited in every capital flight argument.

But the full story is more revealing than the headline.

First, Kamprad returned to Sweden in March 2014 at age 87, seven years after Sweden had already repealed its wealth tax. He had spent 41 years outside Sweden but chose to come home. His stated reason was his wife Margareta's death in 2011. Sweden was home. His family was there. His roots were there. The tax savings were not worth permanent exile.

Second, IKEA's Swedish operations never left. The stores stayed. The factories stayed. The product design center in Älmhult stayed. Thousands of Swedish workers kept their jobs for the four decades Kamprad lived abroad. The productive wealth represented by IKEA's Swedish operations remained in Sweden the entire time.

Third, and most revealing: the far larger tax avoidance had nothing to do with Kamprad's personal departure. In 1982, he transferred ownership of the IKEA group to the Stichting INGKA Foundation, a Dutch-registered entity. The IKEA brand and trademarks were placed under Inter IKEA Systems B.V., also in the Netherlands. Every IKEA store worldwide now pays a 3% franchise royalty to the Dutch entity, draining taxable income from every country IKEA operates in. A 2016 European Parliament report estimated this structure avoided approximately €1 billion in European taxes between 2009 and 2014 alone.

This was a transfer pricing story, not a capital flight story. The corporate restructuring would have worked regardless of where Kamprad slept. Sweden's residence-based wealth tax could not follow ownership that had been restructured under a foreign entity, even though the factories, the employees, and the customers were all still in Sweden.

The system proposed here handles both problems. The Duty of Control (Chapter 6) traces through corporate structures, foundations, and holding companies to the ultimate human controller. And the tax follows US-located wealth regardless of the owner's address. Kamprad could have moved to Switzerland AND restructured through Dutch foundations, and his IKEA stores operating on American soil would still be taxable. The stores do not move. The tax does not move. Only the owner moves, and the owner's address is irrelevant.

Norway: The Proof It Works

In 2022, Norwegian billionaire Kjell Inge Røkke announced he was moving to Switzerland, citing Norway's wealth tax (which had recently been increased). By 2024, approximately 300 multimillionaires and billionaires had followed. Capital flight advocates declared victory.

Then the numbers came in.

Every one of Røkke's businesses remained in Norway. The Aker group (Aker BP, Aker Solutions, Aker Horizons, Aker BioMarine, and others) continues to operate from Norway with approximately 18,000 Norwegian employees. Røkke himself stated: "My capital will continue working in Norway." Corporate taxes, payroll taxes, and all other business-related taxes continued flowing to the Norwegian government.

What Norway lost was Røkke's personal wealth tax on his shares, estimated at 175 million kroner annually. Under Norwegian law, non-residents are not subject to wealth tax on shares in Norwegian companies. His shares in TRG (which owns 68% of Aker ASA) fell off the wealth tax rolls the moment he changed his address, even though those shares represent ownership of Norwegian operations, Norwegian employees, Norwegian infrastructure. The tax followed the address, not the asset.

And here is the result that matters: despite 300 wealthy Norwegians leaving, Norway's wealth tax revenue actually *increased*, from 27 billion kroner in 2022 to an estimated 34 billion kroner in 2025. The broad tax base kept growing. The ultra-wealthy departures were a small fraction of total revenue.

Norway demonstrates that even a flawed wealth tax survives the departure of its richest citizens. Under the system proposed in this book, Røkke's departure would change nothing at all. His shares represent ownership of operations on Norwegian (or American) soil. The tax follows the asset. If he wants the authoritative claim to those shares, he registers and pays. If he does not, anyone else who registers them holds the superior position. His mailing address in Lugano is irrelevant.

California: Still Full of Billionaires

California has the highest top marginal rate in the nation at 14.4% on wage income above $1 million (12.3% income tax plus 1% mental health surtax plus uncapped State Disability Insurance since SB 951 took effect in 2024),[2] and remains home to more billionaires than any other state. Silicon Valley, Hollywood, and the venture capital industry stayed. Amenities, networks, and opportunities outweigh tax savings for most wealthy individuals.

New Jersey: The Millionaire's Tax

When New Jersey enacted a millionaire's tax in 2004, Princeton researchers found that only 0.1% of affected taxpayers left. Revenue from the tax far exceeded revenue lost from departures.

Eduardo Saverin: The Exception That Proves the Rule

Facebook co-founder Eduardo Saverin is the most famous recent example of tax-motivated expatriation. In September 2011, months before Facebook's 2012 IPO, Saverin renounced his US citizenship; he had already moved to Singapore in 2009. His Facebook stake was valued at roughly $1.7-2.4 billion at the time of renunciation based on pre-IPO secondary-market valuations, and rose to approximately $4-5 billion at the May 2012 IPO. By expatriating before the IPO, he avoided hundreds of millions in capital gains taxes.

Capital flight advocates cite Saverin as proof that the wealthy will flee. But the details complicate the narrative:

First, Saverin is the exception, not the rule. Despite decades of high taxes on the wealthy, he is one of the very few billionaires to actually renounce citizenship. Most stay.

Second, Saverin paid an exit tax. Under the HEART Act, his expatriation triggered a deemed sale of his assets. He paid taxes on his unrealized gains at the time of departure, estimated at $365-500 million depending on the source. He did not escape tax-free.

Third, Saverin's case is precisely the scenario the wealth tax addresses. Under the current system, Saverin could accumulate billions in unrealized gains, then expatriate and pay a one-time exit tax. Under a wealth tax, he would have paid 4% annually on his Facebook shares from the moment he controlled them. By the time he considered leaving, he would have already contributed his proportional share for years.

Fourth, Saverin gave up something real. He can never live in the United States again without a visa. He cannot vote. He cannot hold US office. He is permanently excluded from the country where he built his fortune. For most wealthy Americans, this is not an acceptable trade-off.

The lesson: Even the most famous case of tax expatriation involved paying substantial exit taxes, and it is rare precisely because the costs of leaving are high. A wealth tax makes the calculation even less favorable: you pay your share while you are here, not just when you leave.

Lessons From History

The historical evidence points in a consistent direction. Capital flight threats are common; actual departures of productive wealth are rare. And under the system proposed in this book, the dynamic shifts further, because every country that "lost" revenue to capital flight lost it because the tax followed the person's address, not the wealth. This system follows the wealth. The person's address is irrelevant. If they leave and their wealth stays, the wealth is taxed. If they leave and abandon their registration, anyone else can step up and claim it. Either way, the system works.

12.5 What About the Next Stripe?

Consider capital formation instead of departure. What if the next Stripe never incorporates here? The choice gets made once, before there is any wealth to tax.

The answer turns on what the tax tracks. The ledger does not care where a company is incorporated. It cares where the wealth lives. A payments company incorporated in Dublin that serves US customers, processes US transactions, employs US engineers, and relies on US courts is a US operation in an Irish wrapper. Duty of Control (Chapter 6) looks through the wrapper. The US portion appears on the ledger regardless of where the holding company files its articles.

Stripe itself is the example. Patrick and John Collison grew up in Dromineer, County Tipperary, went to MIT and Harvard, and could have returned home to an island with a 12.5% corporate rate and an EU market at the door. They chose

San Francisco. Not because the US was cheaper (it was not) but because the talent, the capital, the customers, and the courts were worth more than any tax savings. That is the revealed preference of the exact founders the objection worries about.

12.6 Let Them Try. They Can't Take Montana with Them.

That is the single sentence this chapter keeps returning to. The wealth that matters, the land, the businesses, the infrastructure, the legal protections, is rooted in US jurisdiction. Owners who want those benefits pay for them. Owners who leave can be wished well, but the assets remain, and remain taxable, under the control of whoever steps up to the ledger next.

12.7 International Coordination Exists Already

The US does not need to build a new enforcement architecture from scratch. The diplomatic template is already in place: FATCA compels over 100 countries to report on US persons under threat of withholding, and the OECD's Common Reporting Standard has made automatic cross-border financial disclosure the global default. Extending these frameworks to cover controller reporting for US-situs wealth is an amendment to existing treaties, not a new institution. Appendix F walks through the full picture: FATCA precedent, CRS reciprocity, bilateral Wealth Transparency Agreements, a standing arbitration panel for controller-classification disputes, and graduated enforcement offramps for non-cooperative jurisdictions.

But the coordination layer is a multiplier, not the foundation. The core enforcement works unilaterally, because the wealth this chapter cares about is the wealth that cannot leave.

12.8 Summary

The capital flight objection sounds serious but does not withstand scrutiny when examined against the evidence.

Most wealth cannot move. Real estate, US businesses, and US intellectual property are tied to US jurisdiction regardless of where the owner lives.

Citizenship is irrelevant. The tax is on control of US wealth, not on US citizenship. Foreign owners of US assets pay US taxes, and foreign corporations do not register as controllers: the natural persons who control them do.

The design is different. Every country that lost revenue to capital flight taxed the person's address, not the wealth. This system taxes the wealth. Changing your address changes nothing.

The historical record is clear. The wealthy have threatened to leave for a century. Mostly, they do not. And when they do, the wealth stays. The existing coordination infrastructure (FATCA, CRS, MLATs, the tax treaty network) is detailed in Appendix F; none of it does the heavy lifting for the core argument.

The simple response: let them try. They cannot take Montana with them.

12.9 Notes

1. Eric Pichet, "The Consequences of the French Wealth Tax: An Empirical Analysis," summarized in Tyler Cowen, "The Economic Consequences of the French Wealth Tax," Marginal Revolution, September 2024, https://marginalrevolution.com/marginalrevolution/2024/09/the-economic-consequences-of-the-french-wealth-tax.html.

2. California Senate Bill 951 (signed September 2022) eliminated the wage cap on State Disability Insurance contributions effective January 1, 2024. The SDI rate was 1.1% in 2024 and rose to 1.2% in 2025, applying without limit on top of the 12.3% top income tax bracket and the 1% Mental Health Services Tax. California Employment Development Department, "Contribution Rates, Withholding Schedules, and Meals and Lodging Values," https://edd.ca.gov/en/payroll_taxes/rates_and_withholding/.

CHAPTER 13

"WHAT ABOUT PRIVACY?"

The fourth major objection concerns privacy. A public ledger of all wealth sounds like a surveillance state. Everyone's finances exposed. Criminals targeting the wealthy. Stalkers finding their victims' assets. The cure worse than the disease.

This objection deserves an honest response. It also has a concrete answer: the system is designed with a specific privacy architecture that addresses each of these concerns structurally.

13.1 The Objection Stated Fairly

The privacy concerns critics raise are these:

Exposure of personal finances. A public ledger would reveal everyone's wealth. Your neighbors could see what you are worth. Your employer could see your assets. Your ex-spouse could track your finances.

Criminal targeting. Visible wealth creates targets. Criminals could identify wealthy individuals for robbery, kidnapping, or extortion. The ledger becomes a shopping list for bad actors.

Harassment and stalking. Activists could target wealthy individuals. Stalkers could find their victims' assets. Public shaming could follow unpopular investments or business dealings.

Chilling effects. People might avoid accumulating visible wealth. Entrepreneurs might not start businesses. Investors might not take risks. The economy could suffer.

Government overreach. A comprehensive wealth database gives the government unprecedented power. Future administrations could misuse the information. The potential for abuse is real.

These concerns come from reasonable intuition. But they are overwhelmingly contradicted by evidence. Countries that have adopted wealth transparency have not experienced the catastrophes that critics predict. The fears are theoretical. The evidence is real.

13.2 What's Public vs. What's Private: The Three-Tier Model

The ledger uses a three-tier information architecture that balances public accountability with practical security. The tiers dissolve most of the concerns above.

Tier 1: Public Record

Every controller has a Tier 1 record containing the same information: real name, total declared wealth, tax burden, compliance status, and asset categories with totals. The difference is how that record can be found.

Name-searchable records. Controllers in the top 10% of declared wealth and all elected or appointed public officials have records that anyone can find by searching their name. This is where the accountability argument has force. The asymmetry that exists today (maximum privacy for those with maximum resources) is concentrated at the top of the wealth distribution. Public scrutiny belongs where concentrated economic power and public authority reside, not at the household level.

Ledger ID records. Everyone else has a record that is accessible only through their Ledger ID, a long alphanumeric identifier (similar to a case number or IBAN) assigned at registration. You can look yourself up anytime. You can share your Ledger ID voluntarily: with a bank when applying for a loan, with an insurer, with anyone you choose. But no one can browse or search the records of ordinary citizens by name.

The threshold is percentile-based, not dollar-based. It adjusts automatically as wealth distribution changes. At current levels, the top 10% begins at approximately $1.9 million in net wealth.[1] This captures the vast majority of wealth concentration (the top 10% controls roughly 67% of all household wealth) while keeping the family with a house and a 401(k) out of the public spotlight.

Why the top 10%? The case for public transparency is strongest where the stakes are highest. Controllers above this threshold hold enough wealth to exert meaningful economic influence: large employers, major property holders, significant shareholders. Below it, the accountability benefit of name-searchability diminishes while the privacy cost remains constant. A nurse with $400,000 in retirement savings does not need her financial life searchable by coworkers and neighbors. A controller of $50 million in assets does need that accountability, because $50 million buys the kind of influence that affects other people's lives.

Public officials are name-searchable regardless of wealth. The public has a right to know whether the people who write tax law are complying with it.

Here is what a Tier 1 record looks like (identical for both name-searchable and Ledger ID records):

Field	Value
Name	Jane Rodriguez
Total Declared Wealth	$5,550,000
Annual Tax Burden	$55,500
Compliance Status	Current

Asset Category	Category Total
Real Property	$1,200,000
Financial Securities	$3,400,000
Business Interests	$800,000
Other Assets	$150,000

That is what the public sees. Not which stocks. Not which properties. Not which business. Categories and totals.

Tier 2: Government Record (Confidential, Full Itemization)

The tax authority maintains a complete, itemized record for each citizen:

- Individual asset identities, types, locations, and values
- Transaction history (acquisitions, dispositions, transfers)
- Valuation methodology for each asset
- Full audit trail

This is equivalent to what the IRS already knows about wage earners today: every dollar, every source, every deduction. The ledger simply extends this level of government knowledge to all forms of wealth, not just wages.

Tier 2 records are confidential. They are protected by the same statutory framework that currently protects tax returns (Internal Revenue Code, or IRC, section 6103), with criminal penalties for unauthorized disclosure.

Tier 3: Individual Asset Disclosure (By Due Process or Consent)

Specific assets can be individually disclosed from their category under two circumstances:

Voluntary disclosure. You choose to reveal a specific asset. This happens when you use an asset as loan collateral, when you insure it, or when you voluntarily disclose for any other reason. The disclosure is limited to the specific asset and the specific party.

Judicial order. A court orders disclosure of specific assets through existing legal mechanisms: subpoenas, discovery orders, or warrants. The same court rules that already govern bank records in lawsuits cover ledger assets too.

The key principle: **you cannot simultaneously assert control over a specific asset and hide it within a category.** If you want courts to enforce your ownership, insurers to cover your losses, or banks to lend against your holdings, the specific asset must be individually identified. Otherwise, it stays aggregated.

Lookup Notifications

Borrowing from Norway's 2014 refinement: when someone searches your record, you receive a notification identifying who looked. This accountability mechanism reportedly reduced frivolous searches in Norway by approximately 90% while keeping the system fully transparent.

The information remains public. Anyone can look. But looking is itself a transparent act. Your nosy neighbor can check your wealth, but you will know they checked. This creates social accountability for the act of searching, not a barrier to it.

13.3 What Actually Happens When Wealth Is Public

The privacy objection assumes that making wealth visible would be unprecedented and dangerous. It is not unprecedented. Norway has published every citizen's tax return since 1863, a practice rooted in the same tradition of fiscal openness that runs through Norwegian public life. Sweden and Finland do the same. These are among the wealthiest, safest, most stable democracies on Earth.

Norway's Two-Century Experiment

In Norway, you can look up anyone's taxable income, total wealth, and taxes paid. This information has been public for over a century and a half. In 2001, Norway put the data online, making it searchable from any computer. The predicted catastrophes never materialized.

What did happen:

Tax compliance improved. Research shows that firms subject to audits increased wage reporting by 18% and reported employee numbers by 22% relative to control groups. When people know their neighbors can see whether they are paying, they pay. Third-party information reporting combined with withholding reduces personal income tax non-compliance to roughly 1%.

Corruption remained low. Norway ranks among the five least corrupt countries on Earth, according to Transparency International. Denmark and Finland, which operate similar transparency systems, consistently rank first and second. Transparency correlates with institutional trust, not institutional decay.

No targeting epidemic. After two centuries of public wealth data, Norway has no documented pattern of criminal targeting tied to tax transparency. Norwegian police have investigated this question and concluded that the public tax registry is not a significant source of criminal intelligence.

The Honest Cost

Research by economist Ricardo Perez-Truglia, using Norway's 2001 online transition as a natural experiment, found that income transparency increased the happiness-income correlation by 29%. Put simply: wealthy Norwegians became happier knowing their relative position. Poorer Norwegians became less satisfied after learning theirs.

Transparency has a psychological cost. Visibility of inequality sharpens awareness of inequality, and awareness stings.

But weigh that sting against this: an estimated $492 billion is lost annually to tax havens globally.[2] Between $21 trillion and $32 trillion in private wealth sits hidden in secrecy jurisdictions, untaxed and unaccountable.[3] The cost of secrecy is not measured in feelings. It is measured in schools that do not get built, infrastructure that crumbles, and a tax burden that falls disproportionately on those who can least afford it.

The burden of proof is on those who claim transparency is dangerous. Norway has been running this experiment for over 160 years. The results are in.

13.4 The Current Asymmetry

The three-tier model addresses the design question. But there is also a fairness question worth examining: who has privacy now?

Ordinary Americans Have Limited Financial Privacy

If you earn wages, your employer reports every dollar to the IRS. Taxes are withheld automatically. Your bank reports interest income. Your broker reports dividends and capital gains. If you own a home, it is in public records: anyone can look up your property, its assessed value, and what you paid for it. Your mortgage is recorded. Your property taxes are public.

The Wealthy Enjoy Extensive to Near-Total Opacity

If you are wealthy enough to afford sophisticated planning, your finances are opaque. Assets are held through trusts, LLCs, and offshore entities. Beneficial ownership is hidden behind layers of abstraction. The truly wealthy can achieve almost complete financial opacity through offshore trusts in secrecy jurisdictions, nominee directors and shareholders, shell companies within shell companies. They enjoy the benefits of ownership while bearing none of the accountability.

The current system does not provide privacy. It provides *asymmetric* privacy. Maximum privacy for those with maximum resources to achieve it. Minimum privacy for everyone else.

The ledger eliminates the asymmetry. Not by giving workers more privacy, but by giving the wealthy less.

13.5 The Asset Aggregation Mechanism

Asset aggregation is the system's primary protection against actionable intelligence. The public sees the totals from the Tier 1 record (introduced above), not the specific composition within each category. They cannot tell:

- Whether your real property is one mansion or three rental units
- Whether your securities are concentrated in one company or diversified across hundreds
- Whether your business interest is a controlling stake or a minority position
- What percentage of your wealth is liquid versus tied up in illiquid assets
- The specific identity of any individual asset

The information most useful to a criminal is not "how much do they have" but "how quickly can they access it." A kidnapper gains little from knowing you have $5.5 million if they cannot tell whether it is locked in real estate or sitting in a brokerage account. Aggregation removes the actionable intelligence while preserving the accountability.

This is not a novel technique. Statistical disclosure control methods (suppression, coarsening, aggregation) are well-established practice at the Census Bureau, the IRS Statistics of Income program, and financial regulators worldwide. The mechanism is straightforward: the government's Tier 2 database holds full itemization; the public Tier 1 view runs a simple aggregation query by category.

Cash and equivalents fold into "Other Assets" because a separate cash total would tell anyone with bad intentions exactly how much liquid wealth a controller has on hand. The four categories (Real Property, Financial Securities, Business Interests, Other Assets) are broad enough that individual assets cannot be inferred from the totals, but specific enough that the public can see the general shape of a person's wealth.

13.6 Statutory Grounding and the Durability Problem

The three tiers are grounded in statute, and each sits on top of law that already exists. Section 6103 of the Internal Revenue Code, which makes unauthorized disclosure of tax return data a federal crime, extends to the full Tier 2 record. The same court rules that already govern bank records and subpoenas in lawsuits govern Tier 3 individual asset disclosure. The Tier 1 public record is defined by statute at both the threshold (the top 10% of declared wealth) and the field level (what displays, what stays aggregated).

A future administration cannot collapse the tiers through a software update. Any change requires an act of Congress. And any attempt to make the change quietly runs straight into the mirror network.

Changes Are Structurally Visible

The distributed mirrors do more than catch someone editing a single record. They catch someone editing the rules.

Tier 2 records are mirrored under encryption. Mirror operators can verify structural integrity (record counts, hash chain continuity, access logs) but cannot read the contents; that is the point of the encryption. Verifying that the public Tier 1 aggregates correctly summarize those encrypted records requires zero-knowledge proofs: cryptographic methods that prove a statement is true (here, that a public total is the correct sum of encrypted records) without revealing the underlying data. Chapter 14 uses the same technique for classified spending, and the methods to deploy these proofs at national scale still need development. What the mirrors can read directly is the rules. If a future tax authority tried to drop the name-searchable threshold from the top 10% to the top 50%, every mirror operator (universities, international bodies, news outlets, civil society groups) would see the change the moment it happened. The same goes for any attempt to redraw the aggregation categories or narrow the Tier 3 court-order requirements. Every rule change shows up as a public edit against the prior version.

Every alteration is on the record, and every alteration leaves a trail that a later Congress, a later court, or a later administration can use to walk back malfeasance.

13.7 Due Process for Individual Asset Revelation

Individual assets remain aggregated unless there is a reason to disclose them individually. The reasons fall into two categories: consent and compulsion.

Consent-Based Disclosure

You choose to reveal a specific asset when doing so serves your interests:

Loan collateral. A bank needs to verify that a specific asset exists and has sufficient value to secure a loan. You authorize the bank to see the specific asset within your category. The bank verifies against the government's Tier 2 records. The disclosure is limited to that asset and that institution.

Insurance. An insurer needs to know what they are covering. You authorize disclosure of the specific asset being insured. The insurer sees the asset's identity, value, and relevant details. Nothing else in the category is revealed.

Voluntary public disclosure. You can always choose to make any of your assets public. Nothing prevents a business owner from publicizing their holdings for marketing, credibility, or any other reason.

Compulsion-Based Disclosure

Courts can order individual asset disclosure through existing legal mechanisms:

Court proceedings. If you claim ownership or possession of a specific asset in court, whether in a divorce, a business dispute, or a creditor action, that asset must be individually identified. You cannot hide behind a category total while simultaneously asserting legal rights over a specific item. The act of asserting control is itself an act of disclosure.

Discovery and subpoena. Courts already have broad power to order production of specific financial records in a lawsuit. Bank statements, brokerage accounts, business records, and tax returns can all be compelled by subpoena. The same power applies to ledger assets: a court can order an individual asset disclosed from its category total when it is relevant to a case before it.

Criminal investigation. Law enforcement with proper warrants can access the full Tier 2 record, including individual asset details. This is no different from current subpoena powers over bank accounts and brokerage records.

Separation of powers. Requests for individual asset disclosure from within a category are processed through the judiciary, not the tax authority. This prevents the executive branch from using itemized wealth data for political purposes. A judge must authorize the individual disclosure, creating a check on government power.

This framework leverages decades of established due process law. It does not invent new powers. It applies existing powers to a new record system.

13.8 You're Not a Target Just Because You're Visible

The most emotionally compelling privacy argument is the safety argument: if criminals can see who is wealthy, the wealthy become targets. This argument feels intuitive. The evidence points in the other direction.

The Forbes 400 Test

The Forbes 400 is a public list of the four hundred wealthiest Americans. Their names, photographs, net worth estimates, and sources of wealth are published annually and available to anyone with an internet connection. Bloomberg maintains a daily-updated index of the world's five hundred richest people.

These are the most visible wealthy people on Earth. If visibility created targeting, the Forbes 400 would be under constant siege. They are not. The crime rate against publicly listed billionaires is not meaningfully different from the crime rate against comparably situated individuals who are not on the list. Criminological research confirms that criminals target based on opportunity and visible proxies (a Range Rover in the driveway, a social media post from a luxury vacation), not databases. A ledger entry adds almost nothing to what behavioral observation already reveals.

Existing Transparency Has Not Created Crime Waves

The Forbes 400 is not the only test case. Wealth information is already public across multiple domains:

- **Property records** have been public for centuries. Homeowners are not uniquely victimized as a result.
- **SEC filings** reveal insider ownership of public companies. No crime wave against executives has resulted.
- **Political donations** are public record. This has not made major donors targets.
- **Public officials** disclose their finances. This has not led to widespread targeting.
- **Executive compensation** is disclosed in public filings, down to the dollar.

If making wealth information public were inherently dangerous, these existing disclosures would have created the very problems that critics predict for the ledger. They have not. Norway's century-and-a-half of published tax returns has produced no documented pattern of criminal targeting. The safety argument against transparency is not supported by evidence from any country that has actually tried it.

13.9 Mutual Assured Transparency

When everyone's wealth is visible, nobody has an informational advantage. This creates a form of accountability that secrecy makes impossible.

Politicians Under Scrutiny

A congressman who votes against a wealth tax while holding $50 million in assets faces a different kind of accountability when that $50 million is public knowledge. Voters can evaluate whether their representatives are legislating in the public interest or in their own financial interest. Currently, members of Congress file financial disclosures, but these are limited, often delayed, and frequently incomplete. The ledger makes this accountability automatic.

Citizens Can Verify the System

Under the current system, citizens must trust that the tax code is fair without the ability to verify. They cannot know whether their wealthy neighbor pays a lower effective rate. They cannot see whether corporate executives bear a tax burden proportional to their wealth. They suspect the system is unfair, and polling consistently confirms this suspicion, but they cannot prove it.

The ledger lets them prove it. Or, if the system works as designed, it lets them see that it works. Either outcome is better than suspicion.

Transparency Replaces Suspicion with Knowledge

Financial secrecy does not create trust. It creates suspicion. Polling shows that 60% of Americans believe wealth distribution is unfair. When the public cannot see what the wealthy pay, they assume the worst, and they are often right. Norway's experience demonstrates the alternative: visibility creates compliance pressure. Tax compliance in countries with public tax data consistently exceeds compliance in countries without it. Transparency replaces the quiet certainty that the system is rigged with knowledge, and knowledge is a better foundation for social cohesion.

13.10 Remaining Protections

The transparency-first approach does not mean transparency without exceptions. Certain populations face genuine risks that justify limited accommodations.

Domestic Violence Survivors

The ledger cannot solve domestic violence. This needs to be said first, because the protection described here is a narrow accommodation inside a much larger safety problem. Keeping someone alive who has left a person who wants to hurt them is the work of protective orders, shelters, law enforcement, and courts. A registry does not replace any of that. What it can do is refuse to become one more tool in the wrong hand.

The mechanism borrows from the address confidentiality programs most states already run for survivors of stalking, domestic violence, and trafficking.

Who qualifies. Anyone with a documented domestic violence case, an active protective order, or equivalent court-recognized safety status. The threshold matches the state programs already in place. No new eligibility rules, no new court review. If a state has already recognized the threat, the ledger recognizes it.

How it works. The survivor files with the court that handles protective orders in their jurisdiction. The court forwards the request to the tax authority. The survivor does not need to appear in the tax system at all. The court handles the communication, and the ledger acts on the court's instruction.

What suppression looks like. The Tier 1 public record goes dark. The name is pulled from name-searchable results even if the person is above the percentile threshold, and category totals are hidden from public display. The Ledger ID is reassigned, so anyone who knew the old ID cannot find the new record. Tier 2 records stay intact at the tax authority, because the survivor still owes the tax and still files returns. Tier 3 court-ordered disclosures still work, because suppression is not a shield against a subpoena.

Lookup notifications. Searches against the suppressed record are logged and sent to the court, not to the survivor. If an abuser types her name into the public website, the search lands in the court's monitoring queue along with his identity. The survivor is not the one watching the notification arrive.

How it travels. State address confidentiality programs already coordinate across state lines, and the ledger suppression follows the same pattern. A survivor who relocates does not need to re-petition from scratch. The protection is tied to the person, not to the state where the petition was first filed.

What it does not do. It does not stop a law enforcement officer from pulling the record through a lawful request, though every such request is logged. It does not stop a court-issued subpoena in a custody case. It does not solve the hardest problem: some of the most dangerous people to survivors are people with legal authority to compel disclosure. Those problems exist now. They continue to exist under the ledger. This book does not pretend otherwise.

The fine details of this petition process (how fast suppressions take effect, what paperwork the court requires, how the interstate handoff works, how reviews are scheduled) belong to the agencies that will build it, not to this book. The mechanism is named. The protocol is not. And what this book refuses to claim is that any registry can replace the work of keeping people safe who depend on staying invisible.

Judges, Prosecutors, and Undercover Agents

Security-sensitive government personnel can receive similar accommodations. Federal judges, prosecutors handling organized crime cases, and undercover law enforcement agents face specific, documented threats that justify temporary restrictions on public visibility. The mechanism is the same: judicial order, documented threat, limited duration, government records fully intact.

Data Breaches

The ledger's public-facing data, Tier 1, contains names, wealth totals, and asset categories. It does not contain Social Security numbers, bank account numbers, passwords, brokerage credentials, or home addresses. A breach of Tier 1 reveals nothing beyond what is already publicly accessible by design.

A breach of the government's Tier 2 records would be more serious, exposing individual asset details. But this risk is equivalent to the existing risk of an IRS breach, which society already accepts as the cost of tax administration. The distributed mirror architecture (described in Chapter 7) limits single-point-of-failure risk. And unlike credit card numbers or passwords, wealth data cannot be directly exploited: knowing someone owns $2 million in real estate does not give you access to that real estate.

Government Abuse and Scope Creep

The most serious privacy objection is not a data breach. It is a future administration deciding the ledger is too useful to leave alone. The concern comes in two versions.

The capture scenario. A hostile administration takes over the tax authority and starts using itemized wealth data as a political weapon: donor lists against activists, asset profiles on disfavored groups, audits deployed as punishment. The ledger concentrates more financial information in one place than any federal system in American history, and concentrated information is a target.

The scope-creep scenario. The ledger exists to collect a wealth tax. A future Congress notices the data and adds riders: capital controls, targeted exit taxes, asset freezes against sanctioned groups, social-credit-style penalties tied to what you own. Each rider is defensible on its own terms, and each makes the ledger do something the original amendment did not contemplate.

The answer is structural, not rhetorical.

Individual asset disclosure flows through the courts, not the executive. The tax authority holds the Tier 2 records, but the executive branch cannot pull an individual's itemized holdings without a court order, under the same rules that govern bank records and tax returns today. That constraint is imperfect. Federal courts have been known to rubber-stamp requests. But it is a real constraint with a track record and a reform path.

The mirrors prevent silent manipulation of the rules. As described earlier in this chapter, any executive-ordered change to the tiers, the thresholds, or the suppression rules shows up as a public edit the moment it happens. Universities, international bodies, and news outlets holding mirror copies cannot be quietly coerced without leaving a trail.

The constitutional amendment in Chapter 10 authorizes the ledger for one thing: collecting the tax. It does not authorize the ledger as a general surveillance tool. Any attempt to repurpose it for capital controls, political targeting, or social regulation would require a new amendment, or a court ruling that civil society would have standing to challenge.

The same zero-knowledge proof technique can be applied to Tier 2 access: a cryptographic proof that the government queried only the records it was authorized to query, verifiable by any citizen, without exposing the underlying data. This is a design direction, not a solved problem. The methods for access-control verification at this scale require development beyond what currently exists. But it is the right direction: replacing "trust us" with "verify us" at every layer of the system.

None of this is a guarantee. A determined hostile state can erode any constraint. The mirrors raise the cost of abuse and leave a trail, but they do not make abuse impossible. What they do change is what happens after. A later administration or a later court can use the audit trail to undo the damage.

The current system offers none of this. The IRS already has the capacity to misuse wealth data, and has been used for political targeting within living memory. The mitigation today is institutional norms and the hope of reform. Under the ledger, the mitigation is the same norms plus a permanent record of every attempted change. The second is strictly stronger, even when neither is strong enough.

13.11 The Trade-Off

There is a trade-off. Here it is, stated plainly.

What the System Gains

Revenue. $492 billion is lost to tax havens annually. Between $21 trillion and $32 trillion in private wealth hides in secrecy jurisdictions. A transparent system makes hiding structurally difficult. Even recovering a fraction of this is significant revenue.

Accountability. The wealthy can no longer hide behind opacity. Their contributions, or lack thereof, are visible to the public they share a society with.

Fairness. Everyone plays by the same rules. No special privacy for those who can afford to engineer it. The teacher and the billionaire face the same transparency.

Trust. Citizens can verify that the system works. Suspicion, which currently corrodes public faith in institutions, gives way to knowledge.

Enforcement. Tax evasion becomes structurally difficult when all wealth is recorded, all ownership is attributed, and all tax burdens are public.

What the System Costs

The ability for the wealthy to hide. That is the core loss. Ordinary people's financial lives are already visible, through employer reporting, property records, and bank disclosures. The only people who lose meaningful privacy under this system are those who currently enjoy privacy that others do not.

Some comfort. There is a psychological cost to having your wealth visible, even at the category level. Some people will feel exposed. This discomfort is real. It is also the cost of a system that works.

The Price Is Worth Paying

Polling consistently shows strong cross-partisan support for taxing wealth. A January 2026 Navigator Research survey found that 79% of Americans support raising taxes on the rich, including 94% of Democrats, 78% of independents, and 63% of Republicans.[4] A separate Economist/YouGov poll from January 2026 found that 80% of Americans view wealth inequality as a problem and 78% say taxes on billionaires are too low.[5] These numbers have held steady or increased since earlier polling first documented majority support across all party affiliations. People dramatically underestimate how unequal the current distribution actually is. When they learn the truth, the number who support accountability goes up, not down.

The trade-off is not privacy versus surveillance. It is privacy for the powerful versus accountability to the public. The current system chose privacy for those who can afford it. The ledger makes a different choice: equal transparency, equal rules, equal accountability.

That is a price worth paying for a system that actually works.

13.12 Summary

The privacy objection raises concerns that feel intuitive but collapse under evidence.

The three-tier model balances accountability and security. The public sees names, total wealth, tax burden, compliance status, and asset categories. The government maintains confidential, fully itemized records. Individual assets are revealed only by consent or judicial order. Most citizens are searchable only by Ledger ID, not by name.

The Nordic precedent is clear. Norway has published tax returns for over 160 years. Compliance improved. Corruption remained low. The predicted catastrophes, targeting, harassment, chilling effects, never materialized. The burden of proof is on those claiming transparency is dangerous, and no evidence from any transparent country supports their claim.

The tiers are statutory, and changes are visible. The three tiers sit on existing law (section 6103 and the civil procedure rules that govern subpoenas), and the distributed mirrors make any unilateral change to the rules visible the moment it happens. The architecture is not a guarantee against a hostile administration. But even in the worst case, a real privacy for the middle class plus hard visibility into concentrated wealth beats today's asymmetry, where the wealthy have near-total opacity and everyone else has almost none.

Asset aggregation protects actionable intelligence. The public cannot determine what is liquid, what is illiquid, or what specific assets you hold. They can see your total wealth and whether you have paid your taxes. That is enough for accountability without creating meaningful targeting risk.

Visibility does not equal vulnerability. The Forbes 400, SEC filers, property owners, political donors, and public officials have been visible for decades without experiencing the crime waves that critics predict. Criminals use behavioral signals, not registries.

The trade-off is real but worth it. The cost is discomfort for those accustomed to opacity. The benefit is $492 billion in recovered revenue, accountability for the powerful, and a tax system that actually works.

Privacy, as currently practiced, is a shield for power. The privacy objection asks us to protect the opacity of the few at the expense of accountability for all. Two centuries of Nordic evidence show that transparency strengthens democracy without the catastrophes its opponents predict. The question is not whether a society can function with visible wealth. Societies already do. The question is how long a republic can survive without it.

The objections are real. Constitutional barriers, valuation challenges, capital flight, and privacy concerns are not trivial, and this book has not treated them as trivial. Each has been stated in its strongest form and answered with evidence, precedent, and structural design.

Now that the objections have been addressed, the question that remains is whether it can be built. Part IV turns from defense to construction: how to transition from the current system, how to prove the technology, and what the change means for you personally.

13.13 Notes

1. Federal Reserve, *Survey of Consumer Finances* (2022 data, released October 2023), https://www.federalreserve.gov/econres/scfindex.htm; tabulated at https://dqydj.com/net-worth-percentile-calculator-united-states/.

2. Tax Justice Network, *The State of Tax Justice 2024*, November 2024, https://taxjustice.net/reports/the-state-of-tax-justice-2024/.

3. James S. Henry, *The Price of Offshore Revisited: New Estimates for "Missing" Global Private Wealth, Income, Inequality, and Lost Taxes*, Tax Justice Network, July 2012, https://www.taxjustice.net/cms/upload/pdf/Price_of_Offshore_Revisited_120722.pdf. Updated estimates published in subsequent Tax Justice Network reports suggest the figure may now be higher.

4. Navigator Research, "Four in Five Americans Support Raising Taxes on the Rich and Corporations to Reduce the Deficit," January 2026, https://navigatorresearch.org/four-in-five-americans-support-raising-taxes-on-the-rich-and-corporations-to-reduce-the-deficit/.

5. Economist/YouGov Poll, "Majorities of Americans Say Wealth Inequality Is a Problem and Want Government Intervention," January 2-5, 2026, https://today.yougov.com/politics/articles/53821-majorities-americans-say-wealth-inequality-is-problem-want-government-intervention-january-2-5-2026-economist-yougov-poll.

CHAPTER 14

THE TRANSITION, FROM HERE TO THERE

The transition from the current tax system to a wealth tax is a multi-year process requiring three things: a constitutional amendment, the technology to enforce it, and a phased rollout that proves itself before replacing the old system. What follows is one possible path. The actual timeline and sequence would be determined through the legislative process; walking through a concrete scenario makes the transition tangible.

14.1 The Amendment

The wealth tax requires a constitutional amendment. Two-thirds of both houses of Congress propose; three-fourths of state legislatures ratify. No presidential signature, no judicial review.

The conventional wisdom says amendments take decades. The historical record says otherwise. The 26th Amendment (voting age to 18) took 100 days from proposal to ratification. The 20th took 11 months. The 16th, the income tax amendment that this proposal most directly tracks, took less than four years to ratify once Congress proposed it; the fourteen years before that were spent trying to work around Pollock instead of changing the Constitution. The slow part of constitutional change is building political will. The constitutional process itself moves fast once that will exists.

Building the will is the hard part. The last substantive amendment was ratified in 1971, over fifty years ago. Today's political environment is more polarized than any in living memory. Anyone who promises easy is not being honest. But difficult is not impossible, and several factors make a wealth tax amendment more achievable today than the income tax amendment was in 1909:

- **The frustration is already there.** "Billionaires pay less than teachers" is common knowledge. The public is primed.
- **The solution is ready.** This book provides a complete, defensible proposal.
- **The hard constitutional work is done.** Direct federal taxation is already established. Every working American has paid one for over a century. A

wealth tax amendment asks for an extension of that authority, not an invention of it.

- **Communication is instant.** A viral moment can shift opinion overnight; coordinated advocacy can reach every state simultaneously.

Realistic timeline: anywhere from two years if a political crisis creates the moment to twenty or thirty years against organized opposition. Even the longest path ends with a system worth building. The 16th Amendment took eighteen years from Pollock; women's suffrage took over seventy years of organized advocacy; the abolition of slavery required a civil war. The difficulty of the fight says nothing about whether it is worth fighting. And the intervening years are not empty: the spending ledger pilot, state-level experimentation, and voluntary registration infrastructure described later in this chapter build capacity and political momentum regardless of when the amendment arrives.

14.2 The Six-Year Phased Transition

Cutting the old system before the new one is proven is reckless. The transition runs both in parallel for six years, with the wealth tax capped so no taxpayer pays more than their current burden until the system proves itself. Defined performance thresholds at each phase pause the transition if targets are missed.

Year 1: Foundation. The amendment is ratified. Congress authorizes ledger development through a competitive procurement. A transition agency is created. Asset classification standards, valuation methods, and reporting formats are defined. The old system continues at 100 percent.

Year 2: Voluntary registration. Asset owners can begin registering on the ledger, with early registration incentivized. Pilot programs run on specific asset classes (real estate in selected counties, public securities nationwide). Problems surface and get fixed. No wealth tax revenue is collected yet.

Year 3: Capped collection begins. Registration becomes mandatory for all assets above the de minimis threshold. Wealth tax collection begins, but everyone pays the *lower* of their current burden or their calculated wealth tax liability. An alternative minimum tax of 2 percent applies to wealth above $100 million, ensuring the ultra-wealthy cannot game the "lower of" rule to pay nothing. **Off-ramp:** if registration is below 80 percent or revenue is below 75 percent of projections, Year 4 implementation is delayed.

Year 4: Validation. Full wealth tax liability is calculated for everyone, but collection remains capped for most taxpayers. The system demonstrates equivalent revenue. Courts begin recognizing ledger entries as proof of ownership. The Judgment Layer is tested at scale. **Off-ramp:** systemic problems delay Year 5 phase-over and continue the "pay the lower of" rule.

Year 5: Phase-over. Old taxes drop 25 percent. The wealth tax cap rises proportionally. The AMT threshold drops to $50 million. **Off-ramp:** before repealing old taxes in Year 6, Congress must certify that wealth tax revenue meets or exceeds old-system revenue, registration is substantially complete, enforcement is functioning, and no systemic market disruptions have occurred. A failed certification keeps the old system in place; the wealth tax continues as a supplementary revenue source until issues are resolved.

Year 6: Full transition. Federal income tax, payroll tax, corporate tax, estate tax, and capital gains tax are all repealed. The wealth tax is the sole federal revenue source. Graduated enforcement, evasion bounties, and valuation challenges are all active.

A wealth tax creates one logistical challenge worth naming: if every wealthy taxpayer pays annually on the same date, concentrated selling pressure could destabilize markets. The fix is borrowed from Florida's property tax system: early payment earns discounts (4 percent in November, 3 percent in December, 2 percent in January, 1 percent in February).[1] Most taxpayers pay early, the cash-flow impact spreads across four months, and asset sales spread accordingly. Monthly and quarterly payment options are available for retirees on fixed incomes, business owners with seasonal cash flow, and anyone who prefers smaller increments. Appendix C walks through the schedule.

The transition has reversal paths. If a phase encounters persistent problems in one asset class but works in others, the wealth tax continues where it works and the old system continues where it does not. If the wealth tax fails entirely, it is suspended, but the constitutional amendment remains in place for future implementation. The current system is already failing; it is just failing slowly and invisibly. A system with checkpoints and correction mechanisms is safer than one that drifts toward collapse with no feedback loop.

14.3 Replacing Hidden Transfers

As Chapter 4 documented, the tax code delivers approximately $64 billion annually to 23 million working families through refundable credits. Eliminating income taxes eliminates the delivery mechanism. This proposal replaces it with a statutory commitment, not a promise.

Four pieces become statutory at the amendment and enabling-legislation level:

The commitment. Enabling legislation establishes a direct support program at the same time federal income taxes end, not later.

A funding floor. Set at the aggregate value of the EITC, the refundable Child Tax Credit, and the partially refundable credits the program replaces, indexed so it does not erode. A future Congress that wants to cut below the floor has to legislate explicitly, in public, against a program whose beneficiaries are visible.

Eligibility parity. Defined in the statute using the same factors that determine current EITC and CTC eligibility (household income and family size). A family that qualifies today qualifies on day one of the new program.

Delivery through existing infrastructure. The Social Security Administration handles distribution. It already runs a fixed monthly payment schedule for tens of millions of Americans. No new agency, no new bureaucracy.

The honest caveat: a future Congress can weaken the floor, narrow eligibility, or repeal the program entirely. What changes is how hard that is to do. The current EITC can be narrowed through technical amendments to the Internal Revenue Code that few voters notice. The direct support program is a visible, named, standalone program delivering monthly payments to 23 million families. Cutting it requires an explicit vote against a program those families know by name.

Beyond the floor, Congress retains authority over benefit levels, the calculation formula, cost-of-living adjustments, interactions with state programs, and administrative review. Program design belongs to the people who build anti-poverty programs for a living. This book's job is to guarantee the money, the channel, and the floor.

The ledger makes delivery auditable. Every disbursement, every eligibility determination, every administrative sanction posts to the same tamper-evident record Chapter 7 described for the wealth tax itself. Means-testing creep, contractor skimming, state-level variation, and administrative sanctions all become visible. The ledger does not design the program; it removes the darkness in which program-design failures usually operate.

The transition has zero gaps in coverage. Years 1-4: EITC and CTC continue unchanged while the direct support program is designed and stood up inside the SSA. Year 5: income tax rates drop 25 percent, the direct support program begins parallel operation, and families receive whichever is higher. Year 6: income taxes are repealed. The EITC and CTC end with them, and the direct support program takes their place at the statutory floor or higher.

14.4 Building the Ledger: Government Goes First

The public ledger is the technical foundation of the system. Initial development costs $2 to $5 billion over four years; annual operation runs $500 million to $1 billion, largely self-sustaining through transaction fees. The current IRS budget is approximately $12 billion per year. The architecture follows Chapter 7: a canonical government ledger plus distributed mirrors operated by universities, news organizations, and international institutions. The technology is not experimental. Distributed ledger platforms like Hyperledger Fabric exist at scale; the Philippines built a national-budget ledger for under $10 million. Appendix D provides the full technical specifications, the scale requirements, and the resilience protocols including circuit breakers, federated verification, and air-gapped recovery.

Before asking citizens to put their wealth on a public ledger, the government puts the federal budget on one first. This is moral authority, not just proof of concept. Chapter 4 documented the scale of the problem: the Pentagon has failed its financial audit eight consecutive years, its spending scattered across more than 208 financial systems that cannot be reconciled. Chapter 7 documented that the technology works: the Treasury pilot that reduced five-hour reports to seconds, the Navy supply chain pilot that outperformed legacy systems, the Philippines national ledger that put an entire federal budget on-chain.

The spending ledger rolls out in phases:

Phase 1: Civilian pilot. Start with a mid-sized civilian agency. All contracts, grants, and disbursements go on a permissioned ledger. Every dollar from appropriation to final payment is recorded with a unique identifier, a timestamp, and a cryptographic link to the authorization that approved it.

Phase 2: Agency expansion. Over the next two years, expand to additional civilian agencies. Each deployment tests the system at greater scale.

Phase 3: Defense transition. Transition defense spending onto the ledger, starting with non-classified procurement and logistics, where most audit failures occur.

Phase 4: Full federal budget. Within five to seven years, the entire federal budget operates on the ledger.

Deploying inside DOD infrastructure first provides a benefit beyond accounting: the Department of Defense operates the most attacked network on Earth. By the time the wealth ledger launches for private citizens, the underlying technology will have survived years of adversarial pressure from the most capable threat actors on the planet. No civilian stress test could replicate that. The DOD already runs red-team programs and "Hack the Pentagon," a bug bounty that has paid civilian researchers to identify thousands of vulnerabilities since 2016.

Approximately $100 billion per year flows through classified intelligence programs. The mechanism is tiered transparency:

- **Tier 1: Fully public.** All civilian agency spending, real-time, open access.
- **Tier 2: Verified but delayed.** Sensitive defense and law enforcement spending goes on the ledger with a one-to-five-year disclosure delay. Cleared congressional committees see it immediately.
- **Tier 3: Zero-knowledge proof verified.** The most sensitive classified spending uses zero-knowledge proofs (cryptographic methods that prove a statement is true without revealing the underlying data, introduced in Chapter 13). The system can prove mathematically that classified spending falls within congressionally authorized limits and that funds were disbursed to authorized recipients, without revealing what was purchased.

This crosses every political divide. Fiscal conservatives see waste reduction. Progressives see anti-corruption. Libertarians see taxpayer rights. Military families see resources that actually reach the troops. Once the public sees what transparency reveals (the waste identified, the fraud exposed, the billions recovered) they will not want to go back to opacity.

Onboarding wealth onto the ledger is itself a phased undertaking:

Phase	Timeline	Asset Class	Registration Method
1	Year 2	Public securities, bank accounts, retirement accounts, vehicles	Automatic data feeds from brokerages, banks, custodians, DMVs. Owners verify.
2	Year 2-3	Real estate	County property records feed into the federal ledger. Owners verify valuations.
3	Year 3	Private businesses	State business registrations plus owner-declared valuations using controller-elected methods.
4	Year 3-4	Art, collectibles, IP, cryptocurrency	Self-declaration with supporting documentation (insurance policies, appraisals).

People who register assets that should have been reported previously pay wealth tax going forward but face no penalties for past non-compliance. The goal is getting everything on the ledger, not punishing past behavior. After the amnesty deadline, failure to register assets above the de minimis threshold constitutes tax evasion, and late registration incurs fees. Anyone with a competing claim to unregistered wealth may file to register it themselves.

14.5 The Coalition

Constitutional amendments require political will, and political will is built by naming every constituency that could be a plausible yes. Every previous major amendment was ratified by a coalition whose breadth was itself the argument. The 16th Amendment passed the Senate 77 to 0 because opposition had become politically untenable across every region and nearly every faction. This proposal can assemble a coalition that wide, and the breadth is the argument. Purer pole positions cannot.

Populists, left and right. "Make the billionaires pay their share" polls north of 70 percent across both parties and has for a decade. The duty of control is the principle that wins them: the system asks the same question of every controller regardless of voting pattern. Alexander pays. Victoria pays. Maria does not.

Small business. A level playing field against competitors with armies of tax lawyers. Predictable liability. Jake the plumber saves $10,000 a year. Maya the contractor pays more because she has more, with primary-residence deferral as a cash-management tool in lean years. No entity-level tax, controller-elected valuation methods, trigger-based reassessment so a down year does not require a fight.

Fiscal conservatives. The formula ties the rate to spending. A $100 billion spending increase raises the rate by about 0.06 percentage points. Voters can see it. Legislators cannot hide it. The structural deficit ceases to exist by construction. That is a fiscal discipline mechanism stronger than any balanced-budget amendment ever proposed.

Organized labor. Payroll taxes are the most regressive federal tax, and they land squarely on union members. The wealth tax eliminates them entirely, including the employer's share that suppresses every wage offer in the economy by 7.65 percent. For a union electrician earning $85,000, that is a combined $13,000 in eliminated payroll burden. And constitutional amendments require sustained campaigns across 38 state legislatures; organized labor is the only institution in American life with the infrastructure to do that work.

Farmers. Use-value assessment for working farmland, lifted directly from existing state property-tax law. Trigger-based valuation so the farm sits at its registered value between events. Controller-elected rolling-average methods that smooth cyclical swings. The explicit promise that no family is forced to sell the farm for lack of cash to pay the tax. And no estate tax forcing the next generation to liquidate.

Racial-justice advocates. A tax structure that stops widening the racial wealth gap its predecessor widened. Payroll taxes eliminated, falling hardest on the service sectors where Black and Latino workers are concentrated. The direct support program's statutory floor, replacing hidden transfers with transparent ones. Primary-residence deferral, protecting home equity as the asset class where Black wealth is overwhelmingly concentrated. Stepped-up basis eliminated, closing the mechanism that erases a lifetime of appreciation for people who already had assets to appreciate. None of this closes the gap on its own. All of it stops the current system from widening it.

Others who belong in the room. Tax reformers who want one formula instead of 70,000 pages. Blockchain builders who want the technology's original promise reclaimed for civic purposes. Small congregational faith communities whose concerns are addressed through use-value assessment and distributed control. The professional class spending 6 billion collective hours a year on tax compliance. Each finds their concern answered in the design.

This book deliberately does not answer what the first political move should be. State-level resolutions, federal spending-ledger pilots, constitutional convention pressure, congressional hearings on the Pentagon audit: all are plausible, all depend on conditions this book cannot predict. First-move sequencing belongs to the coalition itself. This book's job is to make the mechanism defensible enough that the coalition can assemble around it without relitigating the design.

Eventually the pressure becomes irresistible. Public frustration reaches a tipping point. Politicians who opposed reform find it easier to support than resist. The amendment passes. That is how the 16th passed. That is how the 19th passed. That is how the 26th passed in 100 days. And the coalition above, wider than any of those, is why it can happen again.

14.6 Summary

The transition from the current system to a wealth tax is achievable, and faster than you might think.

The amendment. History shows constitutional change moves fast once the political will exists; the slow part is building that will, and the work has been underway for decades.

The six-year transition. Year 1: amendment ratified, infrastructure begins. Years 2-4: voluntary registration, capped collection, validation. Year 5: old taxes reduced 25 percent. Year 6: old taxes repealed. No taxpayer pays more than their current burden until the system is proven, and off-ramps at every stage allow pause or reversal.

Direct support is statutory. The 23 million families currently receiving the EITC and refundable Child Tax Credit get a direct support program with a funding floor, eligibility parity, and delivery through the Social Security Administration. No filing requirement. No audit risk. No new bureaucracy.

Government goes first. The federal spending ledger runs in parallel with the wealth tax transition, starting with civilian agencies and expanding to the DOD. By the time the amendment passes, the technology is proven at scale and the state has demonstrated willingness to submit to the same transparency it asks of citizens.

The coalition is the argument. Populists, small business, fiscal conservatives, organized labor, farmers, racial-justice advocates, tax reformers, blockchain builders, faith communities, and the compliance-fatigued professional class each have something specific to gain. The breadth is wider than the 16th Amendment's, and the breadth is the reason no purer pole position can win the fight.

When Americans decided 18-year-olds should vote, it took 100 days. When the country decides billionaires should pay their share, it can happen just as fast.

14.7 Notes

1. Florida Statutes § 197.162, https://www.flsenate.gov/Laws/Statutes/2024/197.162.

CHAPTER 15

WHAT IT MEANS FOR YOU

What would you pay under the wealth tax? How does it compare to what you pay now? Are you a winner or a loser?

This chapter makes it personal. Not abstract policy, but concrete numbers. The answer depends on your situation, and the detailed examples below cover different wealth levels, explain special situations, and give you the tools to calculate your own liability. An interactive calculator at thelasttax.com lets you run your own numbers without working through the worked examples by hand.

But first, the question you're probably already asking: What about retirees? What about people who own their homes but live on fixed incomes? The system has specific protections for them, explained upfront before getting to the numbers.

15.1 Protecting Homeowners and Retirees from Predatory Finance

Before calculating anyone's tax bill, there is a critical protection built into the system worth understanding first. This is a direct response to the predatory financial products that already target asset-rich, cash-poor retirees.

The Problem This Solves

Right now, retirees with home equity but limited income face a gauntlet of predatory options:

Reverse mortgages promise "access to your equity" but charge fees of 2-5% upfront plus ongoing interest rates of 6-8%. A $400,000 home can generate $200,000 in fees and interest over 15 years, leaving heirs with nothing.

Home equity loans require monthly payments that strain fixed incomes. Miss payments and you lose the home.

"Equity sharing" schemes take 20-40% of your home's future appreciation in exchange for cash today. These companies profit enormously from housing appreciation while retirees get a fraction of their equity's value.

Property tax loans in some states charge interest rates of 12-18% on delinquent property taxes, creating debt spirals that end in foreclosure.

The wealth tax deferral system offers something better: **government-backed financing at Treasury rates**, with no predatory fees, no risk of foreclosure, and full transparency.

The Primary Residence Deferral

For your primary residence, you have a choice: pay annually, or defer.

How deferral works:

- Taxes on the first **$500,000 of primary residence equity** can be deferred
- The deferred amount is recorded as a lien on the property
- Interest accrues at **Treasury rate + 1%** (currently ~5%, vs. 8-18% for private alternatives)
- The lien is paid when the home is sold, refinanced, or transferred at death
- You keep your home; the government eventually gets paid
- **No fees, no points, no closing costs**
- Home equity **above** the cap is taxed normally and cannot be deferred

About the $500,000 cap: This threshold is a recommendation, not a constitutional requirement. Congress would set the actual amount through implementing legislation. The suggestion of $500,000 reflects the fact that it covers the vast majority of American homes; the median single-family home price is approximately $400,000. The recommendation also includes indexing the cap to the national median home price, so it automatically adjusts with the housing market.

Why a cap matters: Without a limit, the deferral could be abused. A billionaire could claim a $50 million mansion as their "primary residence" and defer $2 million in annual taxes indefinitely. The cap ensures the deferral protects ordinary homeowners while preventing the wealthy from using it as a tax shelter. If your primary residence is worth $2 million, you can defer taxes on the first $500,000 of equity, but you owe taxes on the remaining $1.5 million just like any other wealth.

Comparison to private alternatives:

Option	Interest Rate	Upfront Fees	Risk of Foreclosure
Reverse mortgage	6-8%	2-5% of home value	Yes (if you leave)
Home equity loan	8-10%	1-3%	Yes (if you miss payments)
Property tax loan	12-18%	Varies	Yes
Wealth tax deferral	**~5%**	**None**	**No**

Why this matters: A 75-year-old widow in a paid-off $400,000 home doesn't need to engage with predatory lenders. The tax accrues against the home's value at a fair rate. When the home eventually sells (whether she moves to assisted living or her heirs inherit), the accumulated taxes are paid from the proceeds.

The wealth is still tracked. The tax is still owed. But no one is forced into predatory financing or from their home for lack of cash flow.

Example: Jennifer the Retiree

Jennifer is a 72-year-old widow with a paid-off home worth $400,000 and modest savings of $50,000. Her total wealth is $450,000. Her annual income is $48,000 (Social Security plus small pension).

Her wealth tax: $450,000 × 4% = $18,000 per year

Her options:

1. **Pay from income:** $18,000 is manageable from $48,000 income, leaving $30,000 for living expenses
2. **Defer on home equity:** Use the primary residence deferral for some or all of the tax on her home

If Jennifer chooses full deferral on her home equity, the tax on her $400,000 home ($16,000/year) accrues as a lien at ~5% interest, while she pays only the $2,000 annual tax on her savings. If she defers for 10 years, the accumulated lien totals approximately $200,000. Her home, appreciating at a modest 3% annually, would be worth about $537,000 by then, leaving roughly $337,000 in equity for her or her heirs after the lien is paid. The government eventually collects at fair rates.

Compare to her current options for accessing home equity:

- A reverse mortgage costs $8,000-$20,000 in upfront fees plus 6-8% interest
- A home equity loan requires monthly payments
- Property tax delinquency in some states triggers 12-18% interest loans

The wealth tax deferral is the **best financing option available to her**: lower rates, no fees, no risk of losing her home.

The result: Jennifer keeps her home. The government eventually collects at fair rates. No predatory lenders profit from her situation.

Why This Is Better Than the Status Quo

The primary residence deferral beats every private alternative a retiree currently faces:

Current System	Wealth Tax System
Property taxes due regardless of circumstances	Deferral available on primary residence
Predatory lenders offer "solutions" at 8-18%	Government deferral at ~5%
Fees and closing costs eat equity	No fees
Risk of foreclosure	No foreclosure for using deferral
Complex, confusing options	Simple, automatic

Why These Protections Are Essential

Without these protections, opponents would have a devastating talking point: "This system evicts grandmothers from their homes." With them, the story changes: this system protects retirees from predatory lenders while ensuring everyone eventually pays their fair share. The wealth is still tracked. The tax is still calculated. It's just collected in a way that's fairer to retirees than the current system.

15.2 How to Calculate Your Liability

The formula is simple:

> `YOUR TAX = (Wealth You Control ÷ Total Ledger Wealth) × Federal Spending`

Using the conservative figures from Chapter 8 ($175 trillion denominator, $7 trillion spending), this simplifies to:

> `YOUR TAX = Wealth You Control × 4%`

Remember: the 4% rate is the high-end estimate. It uses only US household wealth as the denominator, excluding approximately $70 trillion in foreign-controlled US assets that also appear on the ledger (see Chapter 8). The actual rate falls closer to 3% once the full denominator is captured. All examples in this chapter use the 4% figure, meaning the real-world tax would be lower than what you see here.

How Debt Works

Debt is not a deduction from your wealth; it is a division of ownership. You pay tax on your equity, and your lender pays tax on the debt they hold as an asset. A $500,000 house with a $200,000 mortgage means you pay tax on $300,000 and the bank pays tax on $200,000. (For the full explanation and edge cases, see Chapter 8.)

Step by Step

Step 1: Add up the wealth you control.

- Home equity (market value minus mortgage balance)
- Retirement accounts (401k, IRA, pension)
- Investment accounts (brokerage, savings)
- Vehicles (value minus any loan balance)
- Business equity (your ownership stake minus business debt)
- Other assets (art, collectibles, cryptocurrency, etc.)

Step 2: Multiply by 4%.

- Wealth you control × 0.04 = annual wealth tax

Step 3: Compare to current taxes.

- Add up your current federal taxes (income tax + payroll tax)
- Compare to the wealth tax
- The difference is your gain or loss

15.3 Detailed Persona Profiles

Here are twelve detailed examples representing different situations.

Maria the Teacher

Profile:

- Age: 34
- Occupation: Public school teacher

- Annual income: $58,000
- Family: Single, no children

Wealth Maria Controls:

Asset	Value
Savings account	$12,000
Retirement account (403b)	$85,000
Car (Honda Civic, paid off)	$15,000
Personal property	$5,000
Total Wealth	**$117,000**

Note: Maria has $25,000 in student loans. Her loan servicer holds this debt as an asset and pays tax on it. Maria pays tax only on wealth she controls.

Current Federal Taxes:

- Income tax: ~$4,800
- Employee payroll tax: ~$4,400
- Employer payroll tax (reduces her effective compensation): ~$4,400
- **Total federal burden: ~$13,700** (24% of income)

Wealth Tax:

- $117,000 × 4% = **$4,680**

Result: Maria saves ~$9,020 per year.

Maria's wealth is modest, but her income is taxed heavily. Under the wealth tax, she pays based on what she controls, not what she earns. She keeps more of her paycheck. She can save faster. The system rewards her for building wealth rather than punishing her for earning income.

And the $9,000 in direct tax savings is only part of the story. With the employer's payroll obligation eliminated, Maria's school district has $4,400 per teacher in freed budget capacity. The double dividend described in Chapter 2 applies: Maria's next contract negotiation starts from a higher baseline.

DeShawn and Keisha, Working Family

Profile:

- Ages: 28 and 26
- Occupations: Home health aide (DeShawn) and retail associate (Keisha)
- Combined income: $48,000 ($28,000 + $20,000)
- Family: Married, two children (ages 3 and 5)

Wealth DeShawn and Keisha Control:

Asset	Value
Car equity ($8,000 car - $3,000 loan)	$5,000
Savings account	$1,200
Personal property	$3,000
Keisha's retirement account (just started)	$800
Total Wealth	**$10,000**

Current Federal Taxes and Transfers:

Item	Amount
Federal income tax (before credits)	~$1,650
Employee payroll taxes (both workers)	~$3,670
Employer payroll taxes (both workers, suppresses wages)	~$3,670
Earned Income Tax Credit (received)	-$3,500[1]
Child Tax Credit (received)	-$4,000
Net federal position	**-$2,180 (net recipient)**

DeShawn and Keisha currently receive $7,500 in refundable federal tax credits (EITC and CTC), making them net recipients of $2,180 per year from the federal government (Chapter 4 explains this hidden transfer mechanism). **This is the population that any honest reform must address.**

Wealth Tax:

- $10,000 × 4% = **$400**

The Honest Math:

If the wealth tax simply replaces the income tax and nothing else, DeShawn and Keisha lose ground. They save $5,320 in eliminated employee-side taxes (income + payroll) but lose $7,500 in credits. The net change is -$2,180. They are worse off by almost exactly the amount they currently receive in transfers.

This is why the direct transfer program described in Chapter 14 is essential, not optional. Under the full proposal:

Item	Amount
Wealth tax ($10,000 × 4%)	$400
Direct support program (replaces EITC/CTC)	-$7,500
Net position under wealth tax	**-$7,100 (net recipient)**

They pay $400 in wealth tax. They receive $7,500 in direct transfers. Their net position is -$7,100, better than their current net position of -$2,180, and they also benefit from the employer-side payroll savings.

DeShawn's home health agency currently pays $2,142 in employer payroll taxes on his $28,000 salary. Keisha's retailer pays $1,530 on her $20,000. When those obligations disappear, both employers have room to increase wages. In low-margin service sectors with tight labor markets, this is not theoretical. Home health aides and retail workers are in chronic demand. Employers competing for these workers will bid wages up when their cost of employment drops 7.65%.

The full picture for DeShawn and Keisha:

- Wealth tax liability: negligible ($400/year)
- Direct transfers: equivalent to current EITC/CTC ($7,500)
- Wage increase potential: $3,670 in freed employer capacity
- Filing requirement: none (currently they must file taxes to receive EITC, exposing them to IRS audit risk; EITC claimants are audited at rates comparable to millionaires)
- Net result: at minimum equivalent to current, and likely better as wage increases materialize

Under the direct support program, the benefit reaches DeShawn and Keisha without a tax return to file every April, without the audit risk that currently falls disproportionately on EITC claimants, and without the wait until spring for money the household budget needs in January.

Result: DeShawn and Keisha are protected, not harmed.

The system does not pretend the EITC does not exist. It replaces a hidden transfer buried in the tax code with a transparent one delivered directly. No filing. No audit risk. No waiting until tax season for money the family needs in January.

Jake the Plumber

Profile:

- Age: 35
- Occupation: Owner-operator of a plumbing LLC (one helper)
- Annual income: $90,000 (household, joint filing with spouse)
- Family: Married

Jake runs a service business: most value sits in vans, tools, inventory, and receivables, with minimal goodwill above the equipment. Like every controller of a private business, Jake picks a valuation method at ledger registration, and the business appears as a single number on his ledger entry.

For a service business like Jake's, **book value** is the natural choice. It is simple, defensible, and matches how he already thinks about the business for insurance and accounting purposes. (Chapter 11 details the full menu.) His van, tools, inventory, customer receivables, and business cash total about $140,000; his standard commercial debt (van loan and line of credit) totals about $40,000. Book value is $140,000 minus $40,000, or **$100,000**. The lenders bear duty on the $40,000 under the proportional-control rule (Chapter 6); Jake does not.

Wealth Jake Controls:

Asset	Value
Plumbing LLC (book value)	$100,000
Home equity	$100,000
Retirement savings	$60,000
Other savings	$20,000
Total Wealth	**$280,000**

Note: The lenders holding Jake's van loan and line of credit pay tax on those amounts. Jake pays only on what he genuinely controls.

Current Federal Taxes:

- Income tax and self-employment tax (combined): ~$21,000
- **Total federal burden: ~$21,000** (~23% of household income)

Wealth Tax:

- $280,000 × 4% = **$11,200**

Result: Jake's household saves ~$10,000 per year.

Income tax and self-employment tax disappear, and the plumbing LLC itself is not taxed a second time. The business is valued once, using Jake's elected method, and that single number is one factor in his household duty. No separate entity-level tax. No double counting.

The Johnsons, Dual-Income Professional Family

Profile:

- Ages: 42 and 40
- Occupations: Software engineer and marketing manager
- Combined income: $185,000
- Family: Married, two children

Wealth the Johnsons Control:

Asset	Value
Home equity ($450k - $180k mortgage)	$270,000
Retirement accounts (combined)	$320,000
College savings (529 plans)	$45,000
Brokerage account	$40,000
Car equity ($45k - $12k loan)	$33,000
Personal property	$30,000
Total Wealth	**$738,000**

Note: The bank holding the $180,000 mortgage and $12,000 car loan pays tax on that debt. The Johnsons pay tax only on their equity.

Current Federal Taxes:

- Income tax: ~$23,600
- Employee payroll taxes: ~$14,000
- Employer payroll taxes (reduces their effective compensation): ~$14,000
- **Total federal burden: ~$52,000** (28% of income)

Wealth Tax:

- $738,000 × 4% = **$29,520**

Result: The Johnsons save ~$22,500 per year.

The Johnsons' high income subjects them to substantial taxation under the current system. Their accumulated wealth is modest relative to their income. They win.

The Carters, First-Generation Wealth Builders

Profile:

- Ages: 48 and 45
- Occupations: Hospital administrator (Denise) and owner of a commercial cleaning company (Marcus)
- Combined income: $250,000
- Family: Married, one child in college
- Both are first-generation college graduates. Marcus started his business with a $15,000 loan from his mother.

Wealth the Carters Control:

Asset	Value
Home equity ($520k - $180k mortgage)	$340,000
Marcus's business equity (after $80k in commercial debt)	$420,000
Retirement accounts (combined)	$380,000
College savings (529 plan)	$55,000
Denise's brokerage account	$85,000
Vehicles and personal property	$60,000
Total Wealth	**$1,340,000**

Note: The bank holding the $180,000 mortgage and lenders holding the $80,000 in business debt pay tax on those amounts. The Carters pay tax only on their equity.

Current Federal Taxes:

- Income tax: ~$37,000
- Employee payroll taxes: ~$13,000
- Employer payroll taxes (reduces their effective compensation): ~$13,000
- Marcus's self-employment tax: ~$11,300
- **Total federal burden: ~$74,000** (30% of income)

Wealth Tax:

- $1,340,000 × 4% = **$53,600**

Result: The Carters save ~$20,000 per year.

The Carters sit just below the crossover point. They are a family that built $1.3 million through labor, professional credentials, and a small business started with almost nothing. No inheritance. No stepped-up basis to lose. No capital gains strategy to unwind.

Under the current system, the Carters pay 30% of their income in federal taxes. Under the wealth tax, they pay 4% of their wealth. They win, and they win because the current system punishes their income while exempting the kind of inherited, appreciating wealth they were systematically excluded from building.

Two things worth noting. First, the primary residence deferral covers up to $500,000 of home equity. The Carters' $340,000 in home equity is fully deferrable if they ever need the cash-flow relief. Second, Marcus's business is valued using his elected method (book value, in his case), and his commercial debt stays with the lenders. He pays on what he actually controls.

The Carters are not an edge case. They are the system working as designed: rewarding the people the current code punishes most.

Maya the Contractor

Profile:

- Age: 55
- Occupation: Owner of a general contracting LLC (25 years)
- Annual income: $220,000 (household, joint filing with spouse)
- Family: Married

Maya's business has grown into a real operation, and she has a strategic choice to make at registration. The business has equipment depreciated on paper but holding market value, a commercial building that has appreciated above book, and work-in-progress that swings year to year because construction is cyclical. Book value, a rolling-average method, and an EBITDA multiple (a measure of annual profit before accountants adjust it) each give a different number with different tradeoffs. Chapter 11 details the menu and the reasons a controller like Maya might favor one method over another.

For this illustration, Maya elects a **rolling-average method**, which smooths cyclical swings over a trailing window. The method produces a ledger value of

$750,000 for the contracting LLC. Her business debts (equipment loans, building mortgage, and line of credit, totaling about $550,000 under standard commercial terms) are borne by the lenders under the proportional-control rule (Chapter 6); Maya does not pay on them.

Wealth Maya Controls:

Asset	Value
Contracting LLC (rolling average)	$750,000
Home equity	$500,000
Retirement savings	$700,000
Other savings and investments	$550,000
Total Wealth	**$2,500,000**

Note: Lenders holding Maya's equipment loans, building mortgage, and line of credit pay duty on those amounts. Maya pays only on her equity.

Current Federal Taxes:

- Income tax and self-employment tax (combined): ~$56,000
- **Total federal burden: ~$56,000** (~25% of household income)

Wealth Tax:

- $2,500,000 × 4% = **$100,000**

Result: Maya's household pays ~$44,000 more per year.

This is the mechanism working as intended. Maya has built up substantial wealth relative to her income, and she pays more for it. The $44,000 comes out of the investment returns her $2.5 million generates.

In a tight year (a cyclical downturn, a major piece of equipment that needs replacing, a bid that fell through), Maya can elect the primary-residence deferral on up to $500,000 of her home equity to defer roughly $20,000 of tax and preserve the cash for another business investment. The deferred amount accrues as a lien at Treasury plus one percent. She might choose to repay the lien once cash flow recovers, which prevents interest from accruing. The deferral is a cash-management tool for lean years, not a way to permanently reduce her bill.

The Heberts, Cattle Ranchers

Profile:

- Ages: 56 and 53
- Occupation: Third-generation cattle ranch, 1,200 acres in east Texas
- Combined income: $120,000 (cattle sales, hay sales, lease income)
- Family: Married, two adult children, one working the ranch
- Two full-time hired hands

Wealth the Heberts Control:

Asset	Value (Market)	Value (Use-Value)
Ranch land (1,200 acres)	$2,400,000	$960,000
Equipment and livestock	$380,000	$380,000
Home equity (on-ranch house, paid off)	$280,000	$280,000
Retirement savings	$140,000	$140,000
Vehicles and personal property	$60,000	$60,000
Total	**$3,260,000**	**$1,820,000**

Note: The ranch carries a $200,000 equipment loan. The lender bears duty on that amount. The Heberts' total above reflects their equity only. Use-value assessment (Chapter 11) values the land at its agricultural productivity, not at the $2,000/acre a developer might pay. The county already does this for property tax purposes in most agricultural states.

Current Federal Taxes:

- Income tax: ~$14,000
- Self-employment tax: ~$17,000
- Payroll taxes on two hired hands (~$70,000 combined wages): ~$10,700 (both halves of FICA)
- **Total federal burden: ~$41,700** (35% of income)

Wealth Tax (use-value):

- $1,820,000 x 4% = **$72,800**

At a 3% rate (once foreign wealth enters the ledger):

- $1,820,000 x 3% = **$54,600**

Result at 4%: The Heberts pay roughly $31,100 more per year. At 3%, the gap narrows to $12,900 more.

This is the honest hard case. The Heberts' ranch generates a 6.6% return on use-value assets, which clears the 4% rate, but not by much. In a bad year (drought, falling cattle prices), returns could dip below the tax. The primary residence deferral covers up to $500,000 of their home equity, providing cash-flow relief if they need it.

But the full picture includes what disappears. Self-employment tax: gone ($17,000). Payroll taxes on their hired hands: gone ($10,700). That is $27,700 in eliminated taxes before the wealth tax is calculated. And the biggest number is the one that never appears on a tax return: when the Heberts die, the ranch passes to their son with no estate tax. Under current law, a $3.26 million estate could trigger a six-figure estate tax bill that forces a sale. Under the wealth tax, the son goes on the ledger and pays 3-4% annually. The ranch stays in the family.

The Heberts pay more in annual federal taxes than they do today. They also keep their ranch across generations for the first time in the history of the federal tax code.

Bill the TV Star

Profile:

- Age: 42
- Occupation: Lead actor on a hit network drama
- Annual income: $5,000,000 (salary, paid as W-2 by the production company)
- Family: Married, two children

Bill is the wage earner at peak career. No carried interest, no qualified small business stock, no long-term capital gains rate on his pay. Every dollar that lands in his bank account already had close to 40% taken out for federal taxes. His tax accountant is the highest-priced one in town, and the accountant's job is mostly to make sure nothing gets missed, not to find an angle. The angles do not exist for a salaried employee.

Wealth Bill Controls:

Asset	Value
Home equity ($4.5M home - $1.5M mortgage)	$3,000,000
Vacation home equity ($1.5M - $500k mortgage)	$1,000,000
Retirement accounts	$2,000,000
Brokerage and after-tax savings	$8,500,000
Vehicles, art, personal property	$500,000
Total Wealth	**$15,000,000**

Note: The banks holding the $1.5M home mortgage and $500k vacation mortgage pay tax on that debt as their asset. Bill pays tax only on his equity.

Current Federal Taxes:

- Income tax (effective ~35% on $5M of W-2 wages): ~$1,750,000
- Employee payroll taxes (Social Security + 1.45% Medicare on all wages + 0.9% additional Medicare on wages above $250k MFJ): ~$125,000
- Employer payroll taxes (the production company's share, which suppresses gross compensation): ~$83,000
- **Total federal burden: ~$1,958,000** (~40% of income)

Wealth Tax:

- $15,000,000 × 4% = **$600,000**

Result: Bill saves roughly $1,358,000 per year.

Bill is the cleanest case for the labor-vs-capital distortion in the current code. Compare him to David, the entrepreneur in the next profile. Bill and David control roughly the same amount of wealth ($15M and $11.6M), yet Bill pays nearly seven times more in federal tax under the current system. The difference is not what they own. The difference is the form their compensation takes. Bill gets paid in W-2 wages. David gets paid in salary plus pass-through distributions, with the corporate planning that comes with running his own company. The current code treats them as if they live in different countries.

Under the wealth tax, the distinction disappears. Bill pays $600,000 because he controls $15M. David pays $464,000 because he controls $11.6M. The system stops sorting taxpayers by what their lawyers can name their compensation and starts sorting them by how much of the country's productive base they actually hold.

Bill has no buy-borrow-die strategy because he has no asset base to borrow against the way an heir does. He has no stepped-up basis to wait for. His pay hits a W-2 and gets taxed at the top marginal rate the moment payroll runs. This is what "doing everything right" looks like under the current code: a 40% effective rate on income because every rung of the tax-shelter ladder is closed to a salaried worker, no matter how high the salary. Under the wealth tax the ladder is gone. There is one base, one rate, one number. Bill does not have to do anything right anymore. He just has to own what he owns.

David the Entrepreneur

Profile:

- Age: 52
- Occupation: Founder/CEO of a manufacturing company
- Annual income: $350,000 (salary + distributions)
- Family: Married, three children (two in college)

Wealth David Controls:

Asset	Value
Business equity (60% ownership, after $300k debt)	$8,200,000
Home equity ($1.2M - $400k mortgage)	$800,000
Vacation home equity ($600k - $300k mortgage)	$300,000
Retirement accounts	$1,200,000
Investment accounts	$600,000
Vehicles	$150,000
Other assets	$350,000
Total Wealth	**$11,600,000**

Note: The banks holding David's mortgages ($700k total) and the business lender holding the $300k business debt pay tax on those assets. David pays tax only on his equity.

Current Federal Taxes:

- Income tax: ~$95,000
- Self-employment/payroll: ~$25,000
- Corporate taxes (pass-through, his share): ~$180,000
- **Total federal burden: ~$300,000**

Wealth Tax:

- $11,600,000 × 4% = **$464,000**

Result: David pays $164,000 more per year.

David pays more under the wealth tax. His business equity, built over decades, now generates annual tax liability.

But consider what he gains:

- **Simplicity:** No more complex corporate tax planning
- **Stability:** Predictable annual liability, no surprises
- **Level playing field:** Competitors with better tax lawyers no longer have an advantage
- **No exit trap:** He can sell the business without a massive capital gains hit

For many entrepreneurs, the simplicity and predictability are worth the higher cost.

The Hendersons, Affluent Retirees

Profile:

- Ages: 72 and 70
- Occupations: Retired (former physician and attorney)
- Annual income: ~$300,000 (~$120,000 in Social Security and withdrawals they spend; the rest in dividends and realized capital gains from their investment portfolio)
- Family: Married, adult children

Wealth the Hendersons Control:

Asset	Value
Home (paid off)	$850,000
Investment portfolio	$1,800,000
Retirement accounts	$1,200,000
Vacation property equity ($400k - $150k mortgage)	$250,000
Vehicles	$80,000
Other assets	$170,000
Total Wealth	**$4,350,000**

Note: The bank holding the $150,000 vacation property mortgage pays tax on that debt. The Hendersons pay tax only on their equity.

Current Federal Taxes:

- Income tax on withdrawals/dividends: ~$35,000
- Social Security taxation: ~$8,000
- **Total federal burden: ~$43,000**

Wealth Tax:

- $4,350,000 × 4% = **$174,000**
- With primary residence deferral (up to $500,000 of home equity): **$154,000** cash annually

Result: The Hendersons pay $111,000 more per year (using the deferral).

The Hendersons are wealthy. They have $4.35 million in assets. Under the current system, they pay minimal taxes because they've structured their withdrawals carefully and most of their wealth sits in appreciated assets they don't sell.

Under the wealth tax, they pay 4% on what they control. This is a significant increase, but they have significant wealth.

Can they afford it? Their $3 million in liquid investments (portfolio + retirement accounts) generates roughly $120,000-$180,000 in returns annually. The $154,000 annual cash payment is well within their investment returns. The primary residence deferral covers up to $500,000 of their $850,000 home equity, reducing their cash obligation by $20,000 per year. The deferred amount accrues as a lien at Treasury rate + 1%, payable when the home is sold or transferred.

The Hendersons are not the sympathetic case. They're millionaires who've been paying almost nothing relative to their wealth. The system is working as designed.

Victoria the Investor

Profile:

- Age: 58
- Occupation: Investor (inherited wealth)
- Annual income: ~$800,000 (dividends, interest)
- Family: Divorced, adult children

Assets:

Asset	Value
Stock portfolio equity ($45M - $5M margin loan)	$40,000,000
Real estate holdings	$18,000,000
Art collection	$8,000,000
Other investments	$4,000,000
Total Wealth	**$70,000,000**

Note: The bank holding Victoria's $5 million margin loan pays tax on that debt as their asset. Victoria pays tax only on her equity.

Current Federal Taxes (using buy-borrow-die):

- Income tax on dividends: ~$160,000
- Borrows against assets for living expenses (not taxable)
- Unrealized gains: $40,000,000+ (never taxed under current system)
- **Total federal burden: ~$160,000**
- **Effective rate on wealth: 0.23%**

Wealth Tax:

- $70,000,000 × 4% = **$2,800,000**

Result: Victoria pays $2,640,000 more per year.

Victoria's effective rate of 0.23% on $70 million in wealth illustrates the buy-borrow-die strategy described in Chapter 2. Under the wealth tax, the loophole closes. She pays 4% on what she controls, the same rate that applies to every other controller of wealth, and the buy-borrow-die gap between her and Maria stops being a feature of the system.

Alexander the Billionaire

Profile:

- Age: 45
- Occupation: Tech founder/CEO
- Annual income: ~$1,000,000 (salary; wealth grows by billions)
- Family: Married, young children

Wealth Alexander Controls:

Asset	Value
Company stock equity ($7.5B - $200M margin loans)	$7,300,000,000
Other investments	$800,000,000
Real estate	$150,000,000
Art, vehicles, other	$50,000,000
Total Wealth	**$8,300,000,000**

Note: The banks holding Alexander's $200 million in margin loans pay tax on that debt as their asset. Alexander pays tax only on his equity.

Current Federal Taxes:

- Income tax on salary: ~$400,000
- Minimal stock sales (avoids capital gains)
- Wealth grew by $2+ billion last year (untaxed)
- **Total federal burden: ~$25,000,000** (including some strategic sales)
- **Effective rate on wealth: 0.3%**

Wealth Tax:

- $8,300,000,000 × 4% = **$332,000,000**

Result: Alexander pays $307,000,000 more per year.

Alexander currently pays 0.3% on his wealth. Under the wealth tax, he pays 4%, a $307 million annual increase on wealth that grows by billions each year. He can afford it. The harder question is what it means.

What It Means to Let Alexander Keep $8.3 Billion

Someone will stop at Alexander's number and ask the hardest question in this book. If the diagnosis is neo-feudalism, why does the remedy leave Alexander with $8.3 billion? Isn't a 4% skim just a modern version of feudal dues? The lord pays his tithe and keeps the manor, and the serfs are still the serfs, just with a better receipt.

The honest answer is that this book is taxing the aristocracy, not ending it. Those are different things, and the difference matters.

A proposal designed to actually decompose concentrated wealth would look different from this one. It would impose ceilings, forced divestitures, or hard wealth caps. It would tell citizens how much they are allowed to have. That is a legitimate political position, and people who hold it are welcome to organize around it. It is not the position this book takes, for two reasons. First, a coalition that spans populists, small business, fiscal conservatives, and the tax-compliance-fatigued professional class does not assemble around ceilings. Second, a wealth tax that cannot survive the next administration is not a wealth tax, and a decomposition program has never survived a single democratic transition anywhere it has been attempted.

What this book offers instead is the middle position, and the middle position is principled, not a hedge. The left wants more heat on billionaires. The right wants less interference with them. The middle position says both framings are the wrong frame. What we need is an incentive structure that makes wealth accountable to productive use. That structure is one neither pole can assemble, because it forces both of them to stop fighting about the billionaire and start arguing about the budget. Neither pole is willing to leave that fight alone.

Here is the incentive this proposal installs. Wealth deployed into operations, products, IP, or startups generates returns that exceed the tax. Wealth left idle does not. Today, the dominant strategy is to hold appreciated assets until death resets the basis, borrowing against the hoard to live. Under this proposal, keeping $8.3 billion requires deploying $8.3 billion, or watching it erode at the tax rate every year against whatever it would otherwise have yielded. The easiest way for Alexander to reduce his tax bill is to divest what he cannot deploy. Release patents to the public domain or sell them to startups. Sell minority stakes to operators who will run them. Donate idle real estate to communities that will use it. The current system rewards hoarding. This one rewards letting go.

And one more thing worth remembering, because it is easy to forget when the number at the top of the section is $8.3 billion: billionaires do not set the federal budget. Congress does. Citizens do, through the representatives they elect. Alexander's $332 million is not a ransom he negotiates with Congress. It is a share he owes of a bill Congress has already written. The wealth tax does not ask him to justify his fortune. It asks him to stop treating the society that makes his fortune possible as optional, and it asks him to put his wealth to work where it can be seen.

Alexander remains extraordinarily rich. He simply pays. A republic where wealth answers to society is a republic that taxes the wealth and requires the wealth to earn its keep. Wealth that is not earning is burning, and every citizen whose taxes would otherwise be higher has a direct stake in every dollar Alexander chooses to deploy.

15.4 Winners and Losers

Who wins and who loses under the wealth tax?

Winners

Group	Why They Win
Workers with modest savings	Currently pay 20-30% on income; would pay 4% on modest wealth
Middle-class homeowners	Home equity taxed at 4%, but income taxes eliminated
Young professionals	High income, low wealth = big savings
Small savers	Every dollar saved is taxed less than every dollar earned

Pay More (With Protections)

Group	Situation
Affluent retirees	Higher total liability; primary residence deferral available
Successful entrepreneurs	Business equity creates liability; pay from business income or distributions
Wealthy investors	Buy-borrow-die no longer works; pay 4% annually
Billionaires	Finally pay proportionally; ample liquidity to pay

The Crossover Point

The crossover point (where wealth tax equals current federal taxes) is approximately **$1.5-2 million in wealth** for most households.

Below this level, most people pay less under the wealth tax.

Above this level, most people pay more.

How many Americans fall on each side? According to the Federal Reserve's Survey of Consumer Finances, approximately **88-90% of American households** have net wealth below $1.5 million. Roughly **93-95%** fall below $2 million. The median American household controls approximately $190,000 in wealth and would pay about $7,600 in wealth tax, likely less than their current federal tax burden.

This means the wealth tax creates a winning coalition of roughly nine out of ten American households. The system asks the wealthiest 7-12% to pay more, while the vast majority pay less. A structural reform that benefits nine in ten Americans is not a hard sell.

15.5 Special Situations

Primary Residence

Your home is included in wealth and taxed at 4%. As explained at the beginning of this chapter, the **primary residence deferral** allows you to defer taxes on up to $500,000 of home equity (a recommended cap that Congress would set and index to median home prices). Home equity above the cap is taxed normally. This protects ordinary homeowners from cash-flow problems while preventing the wealthy from sheltering mansions.

For working-age homeowners with income, the elimination of income and payroll taxes typically more than offsets the wealth tax on home equity. For retirees, the deferral option ensures no one is forced from their home.

Retirement Accounts

Retirement accounts are included in wealth. The account balance is taxed at 4% annually.

This replaces:

- Income tax on contributions (currently deductible)
- Income tax on withdrawals (currently taxable)
- Required minimum distributions (eliminated)

For retirees, the 4% annual tax on retirement accounts replaces the complex rules around required minimum distributions and taxable withdrawals. Those with large retirement accounts pay more over their lifetime, but they also have large retirement accounts. The primary residence deferral remains available for those whose home equity creates cash-flow challenges.

Small Businesses

See Jake the Plumber and Maya the Contractor above for full worked examples. Business equity is registered using the controller's elected valuation method (Chapter 11 details the menu). Lenders holding standard commercial debt bear duty on those amounts; the owner pays only on equity.

Small business owners at higher wealth levels may pay more than under the current system, but they gain:

- Simplified compliance (no corporate tax returns)
- Predictable liability (no surprise audits)
- Level playing field (competitors can't out-lawyer them)

Inherited Wealth

There is no separate estate tax. Inherited wealth is simply added to the heir's wealth and taxed at 4% going forward.

This eliminates:

- Estate tax planning complexity
- Step-up in basis (gains are never erased)
- Generation-skipping trust games

Inherited wealth is treated like any other wealth. No special rules, no special avoidance strategies.

Charitable Giving, Nonprofit Endowments, and Social Security

These topics are addressed in detail in Appendix H: Policy FAQ. In brief: charitable giving is driven primarily by values, not deductions, and is unlikely to collapse. Nonprofit endowments owe the same 4% rate, which falls within normal endowment spending ranges. Social Security and Medicare benefits continue unchanged, funded from general revenue rather than dedicated payroll taxes.

Racial Wealth Gap

One consequence of shifting from income to wealth taxation demands more than a passing mention. The numbers tell the story.

As Chapter 3 documented, the racial wealth gap is stark: median Black household wealth ($44,100) is roughly one-sixth of median white household wealth ($284,310), per the 2022 Federal Reserve Survey of Consumer Finances.

The current tax system compounds the disparity in ways that are measurable and specific:

Payroll taxes hit hardest where these communities work. Black and Latino workers are disproportionately represented in low-wage service sectors: home health, retail, food service, hospitality. Payroll taxes fall hardest on low-wage workers (the tax applies at 15.3% but disappears above $176,100 in earnings). For a home health aide earning $28,000, the combined burden is $4,284; for a hedge fund manager earning $28 million, the percentage is a fraction of that.

Eliminating payroll taxes delivers the largest proportional benefit to the workers who bear the heaviest proportional burden.

Capital gains preferences deliver almost nothing to these communities. Ninety-two percent of the tax benefit from preferential capital gains rates flows to white families.[2] Eliminating capital gains taxes costs Black and Latino families almost nothing because they have almost no capital gains to begin with. The stepped-up basis, which erases a lifetime of appreciation at death, benefits heirs in proportion to the assets they inherit. For communities systematically excluded from asset accumulation, this provision is irrelevant.

The primary residence deferral matters disproportionately. Black household wealth is approximately 50% concentrated in home equity, compared to roughly 20% for white households. Homeownership rates reflect the legacy of exclusion: 72.4% for white families, 44.7% for Black families, 51% for Hispanic families.[3] For Black families who have managed to build wealth despite generations of barriers, that wealth is overwhelmingly in their homes. The primary residence deferral described at the beginning of this chapter protects this asset specifically. No Black homeowner is forced to sell the home that represents the majority of their family's wealth to pay a tax bill. The deferral accrues at Treasury rates, not the predatory rates that disproportionately target Black and Latino homeowners.

The EITC concern is real and addressed. Twenty-one percent of Black women receive the Earned Income Tax Credit, more than double the 9% of white women.[4] Black and Latino families are disproportionately represented among the 23 million households that receive net transfers through the tax code. As the DeShawn and Keisha example in this chapter demonstrates, the elimination of income taxes without a replacement for these transfers would harm the communities that can least afford it. The direct support program described in Chapter 14 is essential. It replaces hidden transfers with transparent ones and eliminates the filing burden and audit risk that currently fall disproportionately on these families.

The double benefit. For Black and Latino households, the shift from income to wealth taxation delivers gains on both sides of the ledger. On the tax side, eliminated payroll taxes increase take-home pay and create upward wage pressure in the service sectors where these communities are concentrated. The wealth tax on their modest holdings is far below the crossover point: a family with $45,000 in wealth pays $1,800 per year in wealth tax, a fraction of what they currently pay in combined income and payroll taxes. On the transfer side, the direct support program delivers equivalent benefits without requiring families to navigate the tax system to receive them.

A proportional wealth tax does not close the racial wealth gap by itself. Centuries of deliberate exclusion require deliberate remedy. But it stops the current system from *widening* the gap. It does so structurally, through the design of the tax itself, not through targeted programs that can be defunded by the next Congress. Every year the current system operates, it taxes the income that Black and Latino families earn through labor while exempting the wealth that white families accumulated through generations of preferential access. The wealth tax ends that structural injustice.

State and Local Taxes

This proposal affects only federal taxes. State and local taxes (property, state income, sales, state estate) remain unchanged. For most homeowners, the elimination of federal income and payroll taxes more than offsets the 4% wealth tax on home equity even after accounting for local property taxes. See Appendix H: Policy FAQ for detailed treatment of the combined burden, SALT deduction implications, and potential state-level adoption.

15.6 The Simplicity Dividend

Beyond the dollar amounts, consider what you gain in simplicity.

What Disappears

- **Tax returns:** For most people, no annual filing. The ledger knows what you own; the formula calculates what you owe.
- **Withholding:** No more calculating withholding allowances. No more adjusting W-4s.
- **Quarterly estimates:** No more estimated tax payments for the self-employed.
- **Tax planning:** No more timing income and deductions. No more year-end maneuvering.
- **Record keeping:** No more saving receipts for deductions. No more tracking cost basis.

What Remains

- **Ledger maintenance:** Keep your asset declarations current. Update values annually.
- **Payment:** Pay your wealth tax (monthly, quarterly, or annually).

Time Saved

Americans spend an estimated 6 billion hours per year on tax compliance. Much of this disappears under the wealth tax. The time saved has real value: time for family, work, leisure, anything but paperwork.

This simplification has a cost. The tax preparation industry employs hundreds of thousands of people. H&R Block, TurboTax, and thousands of CPA firms have built businesses on complexity. A transition to the wealth tax would significantly reduce demand for tax preparation services. This is a genuine disruption, and the transition plan in Chapter 14 accounts for a phased implementation that gives these industries time to adapt. But the argument that a broken system should be preserved to protect the industry that profits from its brokenness is the same argument that defended telegraph operators against the telephone. The 6 billion hours Americans spend on tax compliance represent real economic waste. Redirecting that labor toward productive work is a net gain, even if the transition is painful for some.

15.7 Summary

The wealth tax affects different people differently:

Most Americans (wealth under $1.5M): Pay less than current federal taxes. The elimination of income and payroll taxes more than offsets the 4% wealth tax.

Upper-middle class ($1.5M-$5M): Mixed results. Some pay more, some pay less, depending on income-to-wealth ratio.

Affluent retirees: Owe more over their lifetime. The primary residence deferral ensures no one is forced from their home. Those with significant liquid assets pay from investment returns.

Wealthy ($5M-$50M): Generally pay more. Accumulated wealth creates significant annual liability. They have the assets to pay.

Ultra-wealthy ($50M+): Pay much more. The buy-borrow-die strategy no longer works. Proportional contribution finally applies.

Billionaires: Pay vastly more. Effective rates rise from near-zero to the proportional rate. This is the point.

Maria keeps more of her paycheck. DeShawn and Keisha build wealth instead of paying for the privilege of earning it. The Johnsons retire without fear of losing their home. David and Victoria pay more, and can afford to. Alexander pays his proportional share for the first time in his life. That is what it means. Not in theory. In dollars.

15.8 Notes

1. For tax year 2025, the EITC for married filing jointly with two qualifying children at $48,000 earned income is approximately $3,460, calculated from the IRS schedule (max credit $7,152, phase-out begins $30,470 MFJ, phase-out rate 21.06%, complete phase-out $64,430). Internal Revenue Service, "Earned Income and EITC Tables," https://www.irs.gov/credits-deductions/individuals/earned-income-tax-credit/earned-income-and-earned-income-tax-credit-eitc-tables; Tax Foundation, "2025 Tax Brackets," Table 5, https://taxfoundation.org/data/all/federal/2025-tax-brackets/.

2. U.S. Department of the Treasury, Office of Tax Analysis, "Disparities in the Benefits of Tax Expenditures by Race and Ethnicity," January 2023, https://home.treasury.gov/news/featured-stories/disparities-in-the-benefits-of-tax-expenditures-by-race-and-ethnicity.

3. U.S. Census Bureau, "Quarterly Residential Vacancies and Homeownership," Current Population Survey/Housing Vacancy Survey, 2023, https://www.census.gov/housing/hvs/.

4. Center on Budget and Policy Priorities, "Policy Basics: The Earned Income Tax Credit," 2024, https://www.cbpp.org/research/policy-basics-the-earned-income-tax-credit.

CHAPTER 16

CONCLUSION

Warren Buffett paid 0.10% on his wealth while a teacher down the street paid 25% of her income. That gap is where this book began. It should be the last number you forget.

You already knew the system was unfair before you picked up this book. What you may not have known is that the unfairness is structural. It is not a flaw in the tax code. It is the tax code. Seventy thousand pages of it, every page a door that someone paid to install and someone else cannot find. The complexity is not a byproduct of governing a modern economy. It is a product. It is sold to the people who can afford it, and the price of admission is more than you will ever earn.

The Sackler family extracted billions through a labyrinth of trusts while hundreds of thousands of Americans died, and by the time anyone looked, the money was gone. The Pentagon operates 208 financial systems that cannot talk to each other and has failed its own audit eight years running. If you earn wages, every dollar you make is reported, tracked, and taxed before it hits your bank account. If you control billions, you live in a different country. Same flag. Different rules.

That is the system we have. This book described a different one.

16.1 What the Numbers Look Like

Here is what changes if this system works as designed.

Maria teaches fourth grade. She makes $58,000 and has scraped together $117,000 in savings. Right now, the federal government takes $13,700 from her. Under the wealth tax, she pays $4,680. She keeps $9,020 more every year. Not because anyone gave her a tax break. Because the system stopped punishing her for working.

DeShawn and Keisha have two kids, two jobs, and $48,000 between them. This book was honest about their situation: a straight swap from income tax to wealth tax would hurt them. So the system includes a direct support program that replaces the transfers currently buried in the tax code. They pay $400. They receive $7,500. They are protected, not harmed. And for the first time, they can see exactly what the government gives them and exactly what it takes, because nothing is hidden behind 70,000 pages anymore.

Victoria controls $70 million and pays an effective rate of 0.23%. She has not earned a traditional paycheck in years. She borrows against her portfolio, spends the loan, and never sells a share. Buy, borrow, die. Under the wealth tax: $2.8 million a year instead of $160,000. The loophole does not close. It ceases to exist.

Alexander controls $8.3 billion. His effective rate is 0.3%. Under the wealth tax: $332 million. His wealth still grows by billions annually. He remains extraordinarily rich, but keeping $8.3 billion now requires deploying $8.3 billion. Deployed capital outpaces the tax. Idle capital does not. Wealth that is not earning is burning. That is the incentive this system installs, and it is the answer to anyone who wants to know why the design leaves Alexander standing.

One tax. One rate. One ledger. The formula fits on a napkin. If you can pledge an asset as collateral, you can value it. If you can value it, you can tax it. If you register it, no one can challenge your claim. If you do not, anyone else can.

Approximate justice is better than precise injustice.

16.2 The Fight

None of this will be easy. Stop nodding. It will be harder than you think.

A constitutional amendment requires two-thirds of Congress and three-quarters of state legislatures. The people who benefit from the current architecture will spend whatever it takes to keep it standing. They will call this socialism. They will call it tyranny. They will predict capital flight, economic collapse, the end of innovation. They will say it has never been done. They will say it cannot be done. They will say it will destroy the economy.

Here is the irony: if you truly believe in capitalism, you should believe that the wealth it creates will outpace the contribution it owes. Capital put to good use in a functioning market economy generates returns that comfortably exceed 3 to 4 percent. The tax does not drain the pool. It skims the overflow. If someone tells you that a 4 percent annual contribution will destroy wealth creation, they are telling you they do not believe capitalism works.

Every one of those objections has been addressed in this book. But answering an objection in a book is not the same as winning a political fight. Books do not pass amendments. People do.

The 16th Amendment did not happen because Congress woke up one morning and decided to tax income. It happened because farmers and workers organized for twenty years, because state legislatures forced the issue, because a political moment arrived and the movement was ready to seize it. The 26th Amendment took 100 days. The 12th took six months. When the moment comes, it moves fast. The slow part is building the understanding that creates the moment.

You now have that understanding.

16.3 What You Know

You know something most people do not. Use it.

When someone says the rich will just leave, tell them about Ingvar Kamprad. The founder of IKEA moved to Switzerland and everyone pointed to him as proof that wealth taxes fail. The real story was transfer pricing. He moved profits through a Dutch foundation and a Liechtenstein trust. He did not flee the tax. He gamed the system. A public ledger makes the game impossible.

When someone says you cannot value private assets, ask them one question: how do banks decide whether to lend against those same assets every single day?

When someone says it is unconstitutional, agree with them. Then remind them the Constitution has been amended twenty-seven times, and one of those amendments was specifically about taxes. The path exists. We have used it before.

You can explain this system in two minutes. Three sentences if you are in a hurry. Here they are.

Warren Buffett pays 0.10 percent on his wealth while a teacher pays 25 percent on her income, because the system taxes the work and protects the wealth. One small tax on the wealth itself, recorded on a public ledger, replaces the seventy thousand pages of code that produced that gap. Almost nine out of ten households pay less, the wealthy pay their actual share, and the Republic stops belonging to its lords.

If you have more than two minutes, fill in the rest. The formula. The ledger. The duty of control. The inversion of incentives: register your wealth and hold the ultimate claim, or leave it for someone else to claim first. You can explain why 88 to 90 percent of American households pay less. You can explain why the remaining 10 to 12 percent can afford to pay more. You can explain it at a dinner party, at a town hall, at a kitchen table.

That is how every major reform in American history started. Not with legislation. With conversation.

16.4 The Choice

Every generation faces a version of this question. Who does the economy serve?

The founding generation broke with hereditary aristocracy. The Civil War generation ended an economic system built on human trafficking. The Progressive generation taxed income, broke the trusts, and told the robber barons that the republic was not for sale. Every one of those fights was ugly. Every one of those fights was called impossible. Every one of those fights was opposed by the people who profited from the status quo, using every tool they had: courts, money, media, and the argument that the current order was natural, inevitable, sacred.

It was none of those things. It was a choice. And it was replaced by a better one.

This generation's version is straightforward. Will wealth remain invisible while work is surveilled? Will the most powerful people in the country continue to contribute the least? Will 70,000 pages of complexity keep protecting the people who can afford to navigate them, and punish everyone who cannot?

The technology to change this exists. Counties have tracked land ownership for centuries. Distributed ledgers have solved the transparency problem. The formula is public. The enforcement is structural. The transition path is mapped.

Maria keeps more of her paycheck. DeShawn and Keisha build wealth instead of paying for the privilege of earning it. The Johnsons retire without fear. Victoria and Alexander pay their share. The Pentagon's books are finally readable. And every citizen can see the formula, check the math, and know that the person next to them is playing by the same rules.

That is what this book described. Not a theory. Not a wish. A system. One that could work.

The Republic belongs to its citizens, not its lords.

The question is whether we are ready to build it.

Three things you can do today. First, go to thelasttax.com and calculate your number. Second, hand this book to someone who disagrees with you about taxes and ask them to read Chapter 15. Third, ask your representative one question: why does a teacher pay more than a billionaire?

End of Main Text
Appendices follow:

- Appendix A: Full Text of Proposed Constitutional Amendment

- Appendix B: Valuation Methods by Asset Class
- Appendix C: Detailed Tax Calculations
- Appendix D: Technical Specifications for the Ledger
- Appendix E: Further Reading
- Appendix F: International Wealth Tax Comparison
- Appendix G: Glossary of Key Terms
- Appendix H: Policy FAQ
- Appendix I: Legal History of Religious Taxation
- Appendix J: Registration and Claims

APPENDIX A

FULL TEXT OF PROPOSED CONSTITUTIONAL AMENDMENT

A.1 The Wealth Tax Amendment

Proposed Amendment to the Constitution of the United States

Section 1. The Sixteenth Amendment is hereby repealed. All federal taxes on income, including but not limited to taxes on wages, salaries, dividends, interest, capital gains, and corporate profits, are hereby abolished in such manner and time as Congress shall prescribe, not to exceed six years after ratification of this Amendment.

Section 2. The total taxes levied upon wealth shall be proportionate to the annual expenditures of the federal government as authorized by Congress. Each person shall be liable for a share of such taxes equal to the proportion and duration of wealth under that person's control as recorded in the public ledger established pursuant to this Amendment.

Section 3. Congress shall establish and maintain a public ledger recording all wealth within the jurisdiction of the United States, the persons controlling such wealth, and the declared value thereof. The public ledger shall be the authoritative record of control over wealth within the jurisdiction of the United States, subject to challenge and amendment only through due process of law.

Section 4. Where control of wealth is subject to revocation, override, or nullification by another, tax liability shall rest upon the person possessing superior authority over such wealth.

Section 5. As used in this Amendment, "person" means a natural person. No entity created by law (corporation, trust, partnership, limited liability company, or otherwise) shall be recorded as a controller of wealth on the public ledger. Government bodies may be recorded as controllers of public assets, but shall bear no tax liability on such assets.

A.2 Section-by-Section Analysis

Section 1: Repeal and Transition

This section accomplishes two things:

Repeals the Sixteenth Amendment. The 16th Amendment, ratified in 1913, gave Congress the power to tax income "from whatever source derived, without apportionment among the several States." This amendment repeals that power, eliminating the constitutional basis for the federal income tax.

Provides up to a six-year transition period. The repeal is not immediate. Congress has up to six years to implement the new wealth tax system before the old taxes are abolished. This ensures continuity of government revenue and allows time for the ledger infrastructure to be built, tested, and validated.

Abolishes all income-based federal taxes. The list is comprehensive: wages, salaries, dividends, interest, capital gains, and corporate profits. This eliminates not just the personal income tax but also:

- Payroll taxes (Social Security and Medicare taxes on wages)
- Corporate income tax
- Capital gains tax
- Estate tax (which taxes the transfer of wealth at death)
- Gift tax

After the transition period, the wealth tax becomes the sole source of federal tax revenue.

Section 2: The Proportional Tax

This section establishes the core formula:

Total taxes equal federal spending. The government collects exactly what it spends. No more, no less. This creates automatic fiscal transparency: every appropriation has a visible cost.

Individual liability is proportional. Your share of the tax equals your share of the nation's wealth. If you control 0.001% of US wealth, you pay 0.001% of federal spending.

Duration matters. Tax liability is proportional to how long you control wealth. Control an asset for half the year, pay half the annual tax on it. This prevents gaming through temporary transfers.

The ledger is authoritative. Only wealth recorded on the public ledger counts for tax purposes. This creates the enforcement mechanism: if you want your wealth to count legally, you must declare it.

Section 3: The Public Ledger

This section mandates the infrastructure and establishes the ledger's authority:

Congress must establish the ledger. This is not optional. The amendment requires Congress to create and maintain the public record of wealth.

The ledger records three things: 1. All wealth within US jurisdiction 2. Who controls that wealth 3. The declared value of that wealth

The ledger is the authoritative record. Registration on the ledger is the definitive assertion of control over wealth. A registered claim is the strongest form of ownership the legal system recognizes: tamper-evident, timestamped, cryptographically verified, and instantly accessible to any court. Anyone can register wealth at any value to gain this superior claim. Congress sets de minimis thresholds above which registration is mandatory; failure to register above the threshold constitutes tax evasion. Below the threshold, registration is voluntary and traditional proof of ownership (receipts, deeds, insurance records) remains sufficient, though the ledger always provides the stronger claim.

Due process governs all challenges. The ledger's authority is not absolute by fiat. Any claim on the ledger can be challenged, and any entry can be amended, but only through due process of law. Competing claims to the same wealth are resolved through the judicial system. This ensures that the ledger settles ownership disputes rather than creating them.

Section 4: The Duty of Control

This section establishes who pays:

Control, not ownership, determines liability. Legal title is irrelevant. Four indicators (use, benefit, exclusion, and transfer) serve as evidence of who controls wealth, but the definitive test is Section 4's superior-authority principle: who can revoke, override, or nullify another's control? That person bears the duty.

Superior authority bears the duty. When control can be revoked by someone else, that someone else is the true controller. This pierces shell companies, trusts, and other structures designed to obscure ownership. Where seizure requires compensating the other party's stake, control is proportional; where it does not, the seizing party bears full duty.

The chain leads to humans. By following the chain of revocable control upward, the system always arrives at a human being who cannot be overridden. That human pays the tax.

Section 5: Natural Person Definition

This section closes a loophole that has plagued American law since *Santa Clara County v. Southern Pacific Railroad* (1886): the treatment of corporations as "persons." Without this clause, "person" in Sections 2 and 4 could be interpreted to include legal entities, allowing a corporation to register as a controller on the ledger, pay the tax through corporate funds, and shield the human behind it from personal accountability. That is exactly what the current system enables.

"Person" means a natural person. A living, breathing human being. Not a corporation, not a trust, not a partnership, not an LLC, not a foundation, not an algorithm. The duty-of-control chain established in Section 4 always terminates at a human. Section 5 ensures the ledger reflects that reality from the start, requiring the human's name at registration rather than accepting layers of legal abstraction.

No legal entity may register as a controller. This is the enforcement of the pass-through principle. A trust holds a building: the trustee or grantor who controls the trust registers as the controller. A corporation holds securities: the shareholders register proportionally. A chain of offshore LLCs holds a penthouse: the human at the top of the chain registers. The entity can appear in the asset description as the vehicle through which control is exercised, but the controller field is always a natural person.

Government bodies are the sole exception. Governments appear on the ledger as controllers of public assets: federal buildings, military installations, national parks, state infrastructure. The rationale is structural: sovereign authority terminates at collective democratic accountability, not at any private individual who captures the value. Taxing government assets would be circular. The government exception also extends to recognized foreign sovereigns holding assets within US jurisdiction, such as foreign embassy properties or sovereign wealth fund investments. However, a purported government entity that is functionally controlled by a private individual (an autocrat's personal fund routed through sovereign machinery) must name the natural person as controller, per Section 4's superior-authority test.

A.3 Comparison to the Sixteenth Amendment

The Sixteenth Amendment (1913)

> "The Congress shall have power to lay and collect taxes on incomes, from whatever source derived, without apportionment among the several States, and without regard to any census or enumeration."

What it did: Overturned the Supreme Court's 1895 Pollock decision, which had struck down a federal income tax as an unconstitutional "direct tax" requiring apportionment among the states.

What it enabled: The modern federal income tax, which has grown from a 1% tax on high incomes to a complex system generating over $2 trillion annually.

The Wealth Tax Amendment

What it does: Replaces income taxation with wealth taxation, fundamentally changing the tax base from flows (income) to stocks (wealth).

What it enables: A simpler, more transparent system where everyone pays proportionally based on what they control, not what they earn.

Key Differences

Feature	16th Amendment	Wealth Tax Amendment
Tax base	Income (flows)	Wealth (stocks)
Complexity	Enables 70,000+ pages of tax code	One formula
Transparency	Opaque; requires professional preparation	Public ledger; anyone can verify
Enforcement	Investigative (IRS must find evasion)	Structural (hiding wealth loses protection)
Evasion strategies	Many (deferral, conversion, offshore)	Few (control always traces to humans)

A.4 Ratification Requirements

Proposal

The amendment must be proposed by either:

- **Two-thirds of both houses of Congress** (290 Representatives, 67 Senators), OR
- **A convention called by two-thirds of state legislatures** (34 states)

All 27 existing amendments were proposed by Congress. The convention method has never been used, though the threat of a convention has sometimes pressured Congress to act.

Ratification

After proposal, the amendment must be ratified by:

- **Three-fourths of state legislatures** (38 states), OR
- **Conventions in three-fourths of states**

Congress chooses which method states must use. All amendments except the 21st (repealing Prohibition) were ratified by state legislatures.

Timeline Precedents

Amendment	Subject	Time from Proposal to Ratification
12th	Electoral College reform	6 months
16th	Income tax	3 years, 7 months
19th	Women's suffrage	1 year, 2 months
20th	Presidential terms	11 months
26th	Voting age to 18	100 days

When political will exists, constitutional amendments can move quickly.

A.5 Implementation Notes

The amendment text is deliberately concise, establishing principles rather than details. Congress retains authority to implement through legislation:

- **Valuation methods** for different asset classes
- **Registration procedures** for the public ledger
- **Enforcement mechanisms** and penalties

- **Citizen enforcement incentives**, including evasion bounty and valuation challenge procedures
- **De minimis thresholds** determining which assets require individual ledger registration and below which traditional proof of ownership remains sufficient
- **Transition rules** during the six-year phase-out
- **Dispute resolution** processes
- **Privacy protections** within the transparency framework

This follows the model of the 16th Amendment, which established Congress's power to tax income but left implementation details to legislation. The wealth tax amendment similarly establishes the framework while preserving legislative flexibility.

This appendix presents illustrative amendment text as discussed in Chapter 10. The actual language would be refined through the legislative process. For detailed analysis of constitutional issues, see Chapter 10: "It's Unconstitutional." For a hypothetical transition timeline, see Chapter 14: "The Transition."

APPENDIX B

VALUATION METHODS BY ASSET CLASS

This appendix provides detailed guidance on how different types of assets would be valued under the wealth tax system. The core principle is simple: **if you can pledge it as collateral, you can value it for taxation.**

B.1 Valuation Principles

The Three-Source Hierarchy

Asset values are determined through a hierarchy of sources, with more objective sources taking precedence:

1. **Market prices**: for publicly traded assets, the market price is definitive
2. **Third-party assessments**: bank appraisals, insurance valuations, audited financial statements
3. **Self-declaration**: owner-declared values, subject to verification and challenge

The "If You Can Pledge It" Principle

Banks value assets every day when making lending decisions. Insurance companies value assets when writing policies. If an asset can be used as collateral or insured, it can be valued for tax purposes.

The wealth tax doesn't require inventing new valuation methods. It applies existing commercial methods consistently.

Verification Mechanisms

Self-declared values are verified through three mechanisms:

1. **Escape assessments**: transactions (sales, loans, insurance) reveal true values
2. **Third-party reporting**: banks, insurers, and auditors report valuations to the ledger

3. **Valuation challenges**: certified appraisers can challenge undervaluations for a share of recovered penalties

---

B.2 Asset Class: Public Securities

Includes: Stocks, bonds, ETFs, mutual funds, and other securities traded on public exchanges

Valuation Method

Market price × shares held

For publicly traded securities, valuation is automatic. The ledger pulls closing prices from exchanges daily. Your holdings are multiplied by the current price.

Valuation Timing

Public securities are priced continuously, so there is no single annual valuation date. The ledger pulls closing prices automatically each trading day, and the duty accrues on the value held across the days you control the position (Chapter 8 explains duration of control). A sale or transfer locks in the value at the transaction date for the outgoing controller; positions still held at year end settle against the December 31 close (or the last trading day if markets are closed). Because this repricing is automated from public market data, it does not trigger per-transaction ledger fees: neither custodians nor controllers are billed for routine daily updates. Filing fees apply only to discrete, controller-initiated actions such as opening or transferring a holding.

Special Considerations

Thinly traded securities: For securities with low trading volume, use the average of the last 30 trading days to smooth volatility.

Foreign securities: Convert to USD using the December 31 exchange rate published by the Federal Reserve.

Restricted stock: Apply a discount for trading restrictions. Standard discounts: - 6-month restriction: 5% discount - 1-year restriction: 10% discount - 2-year restriction: 15% discount

Difficulty Level: Trivial

No disputes expected. Prices are public and verifiable.

B.3 Asset Class: Real Estate

Includes: Residential property, commercial property, land, rental properties, vacation homes

Valuation Method

Comparable sales, professional appraisal, or assessed value
Real estate valuation uses established methods:

1. **Comparable sales approach**: recent sales of similar properties in the same area
2. **Income approach**: for rental properties, capitalized net operating income
3. **Cost approach**: land value plus depreciated replacement cost of improvements

Default Value

If no recent appraisal exists, the **county assessed value** is the default. Owners may challenge this with a professional appraisal.

Escape Assessment Triggers

- Sale or transfer of property
- Refinancing (bank appraisal becomes new value)
- Insurance coverage increase (insured value becomes floor)
- Major improvements (permits trigger reassessment)

Special Considerations

Primary residence deferral: Taxes on the first $500,000 of primary residence equity may be deferred. See Chapter 15 for details.

Illiquid markets: In areas with few comparable sales, use the average of two independent appraisals.

Partial interests: Fractional ownership is valued proportionally, with a 10-20% discount for lack of control.

Difficulty Level: Low

Methods are well-established. Counties have valued real estate for centuries.

B.4 Asset Class: Private Businesses

Includes: Sole proprietorships, partnerships, LLCs, S-corporations, private C-corporations

Valuation Method

Multiple methods, depending on business type and available data:

1. Revenue Multiple

```
Value = Annual Revenue × Industry Multiple
```

Standard multiples by industry:

Industry	Typical Multiple
Professional services	0.5-1.5×
Retail	0.3-0.8×
Manufacturing	0.5-1.0×
Software/SaaS	3-8×
Healthcare	1-2×
Restaurants	0.3-0.5×

2. EBITDA Multiple

```
Value = EBITDA × Industry Multiple
```

EBITDA (Earnings Before Interest, Taxes, Depreciation, and Amortization) multiples typically range from 3-8× depending on industry, growth rate, and size.

3. Book Value

```
Value = Total Assets - Total Liabilities
```

Used for asset-heavy businesses or as a floor value.

4. Recent Transaction

If shares were recently sold or the company raised funding, that transaction price establishes value.

Escape Assessment Triggers

- Sale of any ownership stake
- New investment round
- Bank loan using business as collateral
- Audited financial statements with fair value disclosures

Special Considerations

Minority discounts: Non-controlling stakes receive a 15-25% discount for lack of control.

Marketability discounts: Private company shares receive a 10-20% discount for illiquidity.

Key person risk: Businesses dependent on a single individual may receive additional discounts.

Difficulty Level: Medium

Requires judgment, but methods are standard in M&A, lending, and estate planning.

B.5 Asset Class: Retirement Accounts

Includes: 401(k), 403(b), IRA, Roth IRA, pension plans, deferred compensation

Valuation Method

Account balance as of December 31

Retirement account custodians report balances directly to the ledger. No calculation required.

Special Considerations

Defined benefit pensions: Value equals the present value of expected future payments, calculated using IRS mortality tables and discount rates.

Unvested amounts: Only vested balances are included. Unvested amounts fail the Wealth Test (cannot be separated from employment).

Roth vs. Traditional: Both are valued at face value. The wealth tax replaces income tax, so the traditional/Roth distinction becomes irrelevant.

Difficulty Level: Trivial

Custodians already report balances. No disputes expected.

B.6 Asset Class: Bank Accounts and Cash

Includes: Checking accounts, savings accounts, CDs, money market accounts, cash

Valuation Method

Account balance as of December 31
Banks report balances directly to the ledger.

Special Considerations

Foreign accounts: Converted to USD at December 31 exchange rates. FBAR reporting requirements continue.

Cash holdings: Physical cash above $10,000 must be declared. The ledger cannot verify cash holdings, but unregistered cash sits outside the authoritative record and carries no registered claim.

Cryptocurrency stablecoins: Valued at face value (1 USDC = $1).

Difficulty Level: Trivial

Banks already report this information.

B.7 Asset Class: Vehicles

Includes: Cars, trucks, motorcycles, boats, aircraft, RVs

Valuation Method

Published guide values or recent purchase price

Standard sources: - **Automobiles:** Kelley Blue Book, NADA Guides - **Boats:** NADA Marine - **Aircraft:** Aircraft Bluebook, Vref

For vehicles less than 3 years old, use the higher of guide value or purchase price minus standard depreciation.

Special Considerations

Classic/collector vehicles: Use insurance appraised value or recent auction comparables.

Commercial fleets: May use depreciated book value from business financial statements.

Leased vehicles: Not included in lessee's wealth (lessor owns the asset).

Difficulty Level: Low

Published guides provide objective values for most vehicles.

B.8 Asset Class: Art and Collectibles

Includes: Fine art, antiques, jewelry, wine collections, rare books, sports memorabilia, NFTs

Valuation Method

Insurance value, auction records, or professional appraisal

Hierarchy of sources: 1. **Insurance coverage amount**: if you insure it for $X, it's worth at least $X 2. **Recent auction sales**: comparable works by the same artist/maker 3. **Professional appraisal**: certified appraisers (ASA, AAA accredited)

Escape Assessment Triggers

- Sale or auction
- Insurance policy changes
- Loan using art as collateral
- Donation to museum (appraisal reveals market value)

Special Considerations

Authentication: Value depends on authenticity. Disputed works are valued at zero until authenticated.

Condition: Appraisals must reflect current condition, not theoretical "restored" value.

Collections vs. individual items: Collections may be valued as a unit if typically sold together.

De minimis threshold: Individual items under the de minimis threshold (illustratively $10,000) need not be separately listed on the ledger. Aggregate value of such items should be estimated and reported as a category total. For sub-threshold items, ownership is established through traditional documentation: purchase receipts, insurance riders, appraisals, or photographs with provenance. Controllers who choose to register sub-threshold items receive the full benefit of ledger-based proof: tamper-evident, timestamped, and instantly verifiable by courts and insurers. The threshold applies per item, not per category; a collection of sub-threshold items with meaningful aggregate value must report that aggregate on the ledger.

Difficulty Level: Medium

Subjective, but insurance and auction markets provide anchors.

B.9 Asset Class: Intellectual Property

Includes: Patents, trademarks, copyrights, trade secrets, licensing rights

Valuation Method

Capitalized licensing revenue, acquisition offers, or industry formulas
1. Income Approach

> Value = Annual Licensing Revenue × Capitalization Multiple

Typical multiples: 3-7× depending on remaining life and growth potential.

2. Cost Approach

> Value = Development Cost × Remaining Useful Life Factor

Used when no licensing revenue exists.

3. Market Approach

Recent acquisitions of comparable IP establish value.

Special Considerations

Patents: Value declines as expiration approaches. Apply declining balance based on remaining term.

Trademarks: Can have indefinite life if maintained. Value based on brand recognition and licensing potential.

Copyrights: Value depends on ongoing royalties. Older works with minimal revenue may have negligible value.

Trade secrets: Difficult to value. Use income approach based on competitive advantage.

Difficulty Level: Medium

Requires judgment, but methods exist for M&A and licensing negotiations.

B.10 Asset Class: Cryptocurrency

Includes: Bitcoin, Ethereum, and other digital assets

Valuation Method

Exchange price × holdings

Use the closing price on December 31 from a major exchange (Coinbase, Kraken, Binance US).

Special Considerations

Wallet verification: Holdings must be verifiable through blockchain records or exchange statements.

DeFi positions: Staked assets, liquidity pool positions, and yield farming positions are valued at current withdrawal value.

NFTs: Valued using art/collectibles methods (last sale price, comparable sales, or floor price of collection).

Airdrops and forks: Valued at market price on date of receipt.

Difficulty Level: Low

Blockchain provides transparent records. Exchange prices are public.

B.11 Asset Class: Life Insurance

Includes: Whole life, universal life, variable life policies with cash value

Valuation Method

Cash surrender value as of December 31
Insurance companies report cash values directly.

Special Considerations

Term life: No cash value; not included in wealth.

Policy loans: Outstanding loans reduce the cash value.

Irrevocable life insurance trusts (ILITs): Valued in the trust, with duty of control assigned per trust terms.

Difficulty Level: Trivial

Insurers already calculate and report cash values.

B.12 Asset Class: Trusts and Estates

Includes: Revocable trusts, irrevocable trusts, estates in probate

Valuation Method

Underlying assets valued by their respective methods

The trust itself is not a separate asset class. The assets within the trust are valued according to their type (real estate, securities, etc.).

Duty of Control Assignment

- **Revocable trusts:** Grantor bears full duty (can revoke)
- **Irrevocable trusts:** Duty assigned based on control analysis (see Chapter 6)
- **Estates in probate:** Executor bears duty until distribution

Special Considerations

Spendthrift provisions: Do not affect duty of control. The person who can direct distributions bears duty.

Charitable remainder trusts: Present value of remainder interest is not taxable (charity will receive it). Income interest is valued using IRS actuarial tables.

Difficulty Level: Medium

Requires control analysis, but underlying asset valuation is straightforward.

B.13 Dispute Resolution

Informal Resolution

Most valuation disputes are resolved informally: 1. Owner provides supporting documentation 2. Tax authority reviews and responds 3. Parties agree on adjusted value

Formal Arbitration

If informal resolution fails: 1. Owner and tax authority each select an appraiser 2. The two appraisers select a third (neutral) appraiser 3. Panel determines value by majority vote 4. Decision is binding

Judicial Review

Arbitration decisions may be appealed to Tax Court on questions of law (not valuation judgment).

Valuation Challenges

Certified appraisers may challenge declared values: 1. Challenger files evidence of undervaluation 2. If challenge is accepted, independent panel reviews 3. If undervaluation confirmed: owner pays back taxes + 15% penalty 4. Challenger receives 25% of penalty as bounty 5. If challenge rejected: challenger pays arbitration costs

---

B.14 Payment in Kind: Eligible Assets and Safeguards

During declared economic emergencies (see Chapter 8 for trigger criteria), taxpayers may transfer assets to the government in lieu of cash payment. This section specifies which assets qualify and the protections in place.

Eligible Asset Types

The government prioritizes assets that are liquid, easily valued, and readily administered:

Preferred (high priority): - Public securities (stocks, bonds, ETFs, mutual funds) - Bank deposits and cash equivalents - Cryptocurrency held on major exchanges

Accepted (standard priority): - Real estate (residential and commercial) - Vehicles with published guide values - Life insurance policies (cash surrender value)

Conditional (case-by-case): - Private business interests (requires recent valuation or third-party assessment) - Art and collectibles (requires professional appraisal within 12 months) - Intellectual property (requires income-based valuation)

Excluded: - Retirement accounts (401(k), IRA, Roth IRA, pensions) are protected from payment in kind under all circumstances - Assets with unresolved ownership disputes - Assets subject to existing liens that exceed their declared value

Transfer Valuation

Assets transferred in kind are valued at their current ledger declaration. If the ledger value is more than 12 months old, a fresh valuation using the methods in this appendix is required before transfer.

Safeguards

- **Emergency-only:** Payment in kind is available only during declared economic emergencies, not during normal economic conditions
- **Voluntary:** Taxpayers choose whether to pay in kind or through the standard enforcement process (tax lien certificates)
- **Sovereign wealth fund:** Accepted assets are held in a dedicated fund with a mandate to liquidate over 5-10 years, preventing government fire sales from depressing markets further
- **Proportional acceptance:** The government is not obligated to accept all offered assets; it may prioritize based on liquidity and administrative cost
- **Retirement protection:** Retirement accounts cannot be transferred under any circumstances

---

B.15 Summary Table

Asset Class	Primary Method	Difficulty	Verification
Public securities	Market price	Trivial	Automatic
Real estate	Comparable sales/appraisal	Low	Escape assessments
Private businesses	Revenue/EBITDA multiples	Medium	Third-party reporting
Retirement accounts	Account balance	Trivial	Custodian reporting
Bank accounts	Account balance	Trivial	Bank reporting
Vehicles	Published guides	Low	DMV records
Art/collectibles	Insurance/appraisal	Medium	Valuation challenges
Intellectual property	Capitalized income	Medium	Licensing records
Cryptocurrency	Exchange price	Low	Blockchain records
Life insurance	Cash surrender value	Trivial	Insurer reporting
Trusts	Underlying assets	Medium	Control analysis

This appendix provides general guidance. Congress will establish detailed regulations through implementing legislation. For discussion of valuation principles, see Chapter 11: "You Can't Value Everything."

APPENDIX C

DETAILED TAX CALCULATIONS

This appendix provides worked examples showing how the wealth tax is calculated for households at different wealth levels. All calculations use the formula from Chapter 8. Economic figures are as of FY 2025; the formula self-adjusts as wealth totals and federal spending change.

C.1 The Formula

> `YOUR TAX = (Wealth You Control ÷ Total US Wealth) × Federal Spending`

Using current figures:

- **Total US Wealth (conservative, US households only):** \$175 trillion[1]
- **Total Ledger Wealth (including foreign-controlled US assets):** \$225-250 trillion[2]
- **Federal Spending:** \$7 trillion (FY 2025)

Using the conservative \$175 trillion denominator, this yields an effective rate of approximately **4%** on wealth you control. Once foreign-controlled US assets (~\$70 trillion, see Chapter 8) are captured on the ledger, the rate would fall to approximately **3-3.1%**. All calculations below use the conservative 4% rate.

How Debt Works

Debt is not a "deduction" from your wealth. Instead, debt represents a division of ownership:

- **Your equity** in an asset is the portion you control and pay tax on
- **The lender's claim** (the debt) is wealth the lender controls and pays tax on

For example, if you have a \$350,000 house with a \$120,000 mortgage:

- You control \$230,000 (your equity) → you pay tax on this
- The bank controls \$120,000 (their loan asset) → the bank pays tax on this

The total wealth taxed is still $350,000; it's just split between you and your lender. (See Chapter 8 for the full explanation of how debt divides ownership.)

C.2 Quick Reference Table

Wealth You Control	Annual Wealth Tax	Monthly Equivalent
$50,000	$2,000	$167
$100,000	$4,000	$333
$250,000	$10,000	$833
$500,000	$20,000	$1,667
$750,000	$30,000	$2,500
$1,000,000	$40,000	$3,333
$2,000,000	$80,000	$6,667
$5,000,000	$200,000	$16,667
$10,000,000	$400,000	$33,333
$50,000,000	$2,000,000	$166,667
$100,000,000	$4,000,000	$333,333
$1,000,000,000	$40,000,000	$3,333,333

C.3 Effective Rate Under Behavioral Response

If behavioral responses shrink the wealth recorded on the ledger, the formula raises the rate to meet spending; revenue is matched by definition (see Chapter 8). The table shows the effective rate at several levels of response, assuming $7 trillion in federal spending:

Scenario	Ledger Wealth	Effective Rate
Full capture including foreign wealth	$245 trillion	2.9%
Conservative estimate (this book's baseline)	$175 trillion	4.0%
5% of wealth exits the ledger	$166 trillion	4.2%
15% of wealth exits the ledger	$149 trillion	4.7%

The first two rows show the range this book considers most likely. The bottom two show what happens if behavioral responses are larger than expected. Even a 15% reduction in the denominator, far beyond what the empirical literature suggests for a system without exemptions or jurisdiction shopping, produces only a 4.7% rate, within the range of long-term equity returns and below the combined federal burden most workers pay today.

C.4 Non-Profit and Institutional Controller Calculations

Chapter 6 establishes that board members and directors of non-profit entities bear duty on the institutional wealth they control. The following worked examples show how the duty is distributed and funded.

Church with a $2 Million Building

- **Asset:** Church building valued at $2 million
- **Controllers:** 5 board members with equal authority
- **Each member's share:** $2,000,000 / 5 = $400,000
- **Annual duty per member:** $400,000 x 4% = **$16,000**
- **Total institutional duty:** $80,000 per year
- **Funded by:** Church operating budget (donations), the same way the church currently covers insurance, utilities, and maintenance

Charity with a $50 Million Endowment

- **Asset:** $50 million endowment
- **Controllers:** 7 board members with equal authority
- **Each member's share:** $50,000,000 / 7 = ~$7,143,000
- **Annual duty per member:** ~$7,143,000 x 4% = **~$285,700**
- **Total institutional duty:** $2,000,000 per year
- **Funded by:** Endowment returns (historically 5-7% annually for well-managed funds) more than cover the 4% duty, leaving 1-3% for operations and growth

Foundation with a $1 Billion Endowment

- **Asset:** $1 billion endowment
- **Controllers:** 10 board members with equal authority

- **Each member's share:** $1,000,000,000 / 10 = $100,000,000
- **Annual duty per member:** $100,000,000 x 4% = **$4,000,000**
- **Total institutional duty:** $40,000,000 per year
- **Funded by:** Foundation investment returns, which at historical averages produce $50-70 million annually

In each case, the duty falls on the controllers personally, but they command the entity's resources to pay it. A board member does not write a personal check from household savings. They direct the institution's funds to cover the obligation.

C.5 Detailed Persona Calculations

For full persona profiles with detailed asset tables, narrative explanations, and current-vs-proposed comparisons, see **Chapter 15: What It Means for You**. Chapter 15 covers Maria the Teacher, DeShawn and Keisha (working family), Jake the Plumber, the Johnsons, the Carters (first-generation wealth builders), Maya the Contractor, the Heberts (cattle ranchers), Bill the TV Star, David the Entrepreneur, the Hendersons, Victoria the Investor, and Alexander the Billionaire. Jennifer the Retiree appears in the primary residence deferral discussion.

This appendix provides the full Jennifer the Retiree worked-math calculation as a complement to the deferral example in Chapter 15, plus a summary comparison table.

Jennifer the Retiree

Profile:

- Age: 72, widow
- Occupation: Retired
- Annual income: $48,000 (Social Security + pension)

Wealth Jennifer Controls:

Asset	Value
Home (paid off)	$400,000
Retirement savings	$50,000
Total Wealth	**$450,000**

Note: Jennifer has no debt. She controls all of her assets outright.

Wealth Tax Calculation:

```
$450,000 × 4% = $18,000 per year
```

Current Federal Tax Burden:

Tax Type	Amount
Federal income tax	$3,200
Social Security taxation	$1,800
Total Federal Burden	**$5,000**

Comparison (without deferral):

```
Current system:   $5,000
Wealth tax:      $18,000
Annual increase: $13,000
```

With Primary Residence Deferral:

Jennifer can defer taxes on up to $500,000 of primary residence equity. Her home equity is $400,000 (fully paid off).

```
Deferrable amount: $400,000 × 4% = $16,000
Remaining tax due: $50,000 × 4% = $2,000
```

Comparison (with deferral):

```
Current system:         $5,000
Wealth tax (cash due): $2,000
Annual savings:         $3,000
```

The $16,000 deferred amount accrues as a lien on her home at Treasury rate + 1% (~5%). When the home is eventually sold or transferred, the accumulated taxes are paid from proceeds.

Result: With deferral, Jennifer pays $2,000 annually in cash (60% reduction), with $16,000 deferred against her home equity.

All Personas: Summary Comparison

Persona	Total Wealth	Current Federal Tax	Wealth Tax (4%)	Change
Maria the Teacher	$117,000	$13,700	$4,680	Saves $9,020 (66%)
The Johnsons	$738,000	$52,000	$29,520	Saves $22,480 (43%)
Jennifer the Retiree	$450,000	$5,000	$2,000 (with deferral)	Saves $3,000 (60%)
Bill the TV Star	$15,000,000	$1,958,000	$600,000	Saves $1,358,000 (69%)
David the Entrepreneur	$11,600,000	$300,000	$464,000	Pays $164,000 more (55%)
The Hendersons	$4,350,000	$43,000	$154,000 (with deferral)	Pays $111,000 more
Victoria the Investor	$70,000,000	$160,000	$2,800,000	Pays $2,640,000 more
Alexander the Billionaire	$8,300,000,000	$25,000,000	$332,000,000	Pays $307,000,000 more

For full asset breakdowns, narrative explanations, and affordability analysis for each persona, see Chapter 15.

C.6 The Crossover Point

The crossover point (where wealth tax equals current federal taxes) depends on the ratio of income to wealth.

General Guidelines:

Income-to-Wealth Ratio	Crossover Point
High income, low wealth (young professionals)	Pay less under wealth tax

Income-to-Wealth Ratio	Crossover Point
Moderate income, moderate wealth (middle class)	Pay less under wealth tax
Low income, high wealth (retirees, investors)	Pay more under wealth tax
Very low income, very high wealth (billionaires)	Pay much more under wealth tax

Approximate Crossover:
For a household with typical income-to-wealth ratios, the crossover point is approximately **$1.5-2 million in wealth**.

- Below $1.5 million: Most households pay less
- $1.5-2 million: Mixed results depending on income
- Above $2 million: Most households pay more

Methodology: How "88 to 90 Percent of Households Pay Less" Is Derived

The headline claim that approximately 88 to 90 percent of American households pay less under the wealth tax than under the current federal system is derived from the following sources and calculations.

Data sources:

- Federal Reserve *Survey of Consumer Finances*, 2022 wave (released October 2023). Provides household net-worth distribution by percentile.
- Federal Reserve *Distributional Financial Accounts*, Q3 2025 release. Confirms the wealth distribution has not shifted materially since the SCF release; the top 1 percent share continues to climb (31.7 percent of all household wealth as of Q3 2025).
- Congressional Budget Office distributional analyses of effective federal tax rates by income quintile, used to estimate current federal burden per household.

Net-worth percentile thresholds (2023 SCF):

Percentile	Net Worth Threshold
50th (median)	$192,000
75th	$658,000
90th	$1,921,000

Percentile	Net Worth Threshold
95th	$3,780,000
99th	$13,667,000

The crossover calculation:

For each percentile bracket, two numbers are compared. The current federal burden is the household's federal income tax plus the employee share of payroll tax plus the employer share of payroll tax (economically borne by workers through reduced wages, see Chapter 2) plus an estimated labor incidence of the corporate income tax. This produces an effective federal burden of roughly 22 to 28 percent of total compensation for typical wage-earning households, rising with income.

The wealth tax burden is 4 percent of household net worth, with deferral available for primary-residence equity up to $500,000.

Wealth Percentile	Net Worth	Typical Income	Current Federal Burden	Wealth Tax (4%)	Result
50th (median)	$192,000	~$80,000	~$18,000-20,000	$7,683	Saves ~$11,000
75th	$658,000	~$130,000	~$30,000-35,000	$26,334	Saves ~$5,000-9,000
90th	$1,921,000	~$220,000	~$55,000-65,000	$76,830	Pays ~$12,000-22,000 more

The crossover lands between the 88th and 90th percentile, depending on assumptions about labor incidence of corporate tax and on whether primary-residence deferral is included. Households below this range save under the wealth tax. Households above it pay more, often substantially more, with the largest increases concentrated in the top 1 percent where current effective federal rates fall below 1 percent of wealth.

The published claim "approximately 88 to 90 percent of households pay less" reflects the range produced by these assumptions. The lower bound (88 percent) is the conservative case that excludes deferral and uses lower assumptions about indirect corporate-tax incidence. The upper bound (90 percent) includes deferral and higher incidence assumptions. Both fall within what the available data supports.

A note on individual variation: Percentile-level math hides household-level variation. A household at the 80th percentile by wealth with high income (a high-earning professional with modest accumulated savings) saves the most under the system. A household at the same percentile with low income (a retiree on fixed income with a paid-off home) may pay more in cash terms before applying primary-residence deferral. Chapter 15 walks through individual cases. The methodology above describes the population-level result.

C.7 Payment Options

Annual Payment with Early Discounts

The wealth tax is payable on a descending early-payment discount schedule modeled on Florida's property tax system (Florida Statutes section 197.162). The earlier you pay within the November-to-February window, the larger the discount; across all taxpayers this staggers payment dates so that simultaneous asset sales cannot move markets.

Payment Month	Discount
November	4%
December	3%
January	2%
February	1%
March (gross amount due)	0%

Example: $100,000 wealth tax - Pay in November: $96,000 (save $4,000) - Pay at gross in March: $100,000

Monthly Payment Option

Pay 1/12 of estimated annual tax each month, with a year-end true-up once the December 31 valuation is final.

Quarterly Payment Option

Pay 1/4 of estimated annual tax each quarter. 1% discount for full quarterly prepayment.

Primary Residence Deferral

Taxes on up to $500,000 of primary residence equity may be deferred. Deferred amounts accrue as a lien at Treasury rate + 1% (~5%), payable when the home is sold or transferred.

C.8 Summary: Who Pays More, Who Pays Less

Category	Typical Outcome
Workers with modest savings	Pay significantly less
Young professionals (high income, low wealth)	Pay less
Middle-class homeowners	Pay less
Upper-middle class ($1-3M wealth)	Mixed results
Affluent retirees ($3-10M wealth)	Pay more (deferral available)
Wealthy investors ($10-50M)	Pay more
Ultra-wealthy ($50M+)	Pay much more
Billionaires	Pay vastly more

The system shifts the tax burden from income (which penalizes work) to wealth (which reflects accumulated resources and power).

For discussion of the formula and its implications, see Chapter 8. For full persona profiles with detailed asset tables and narrative explanations, see Chapter 15.

C.9 Notes

1. Board of Governors of the Federal Reserve System, *Financial Accounts of the United States* (Z.1), Q4 2025 release (March 19, 2026), https://www.federalreserve.gov/releases/z1/.

2. U.S. Bureau of Economic Analysis, *U.S. International Investment Position*, year-end 2025 release, https://www.bea.gov/data/intl-trade-investment/international-investment-position.

APPENDIX D

TECHNICAL SPECIFICATIONS FOR THE LEDGER

This appendix provides technical details on the public ledger system that would enforce the wealth tax. It is aimed at people with a technical background or policy specialists who want to evaluate the system's feasibility in detail. Everyone else can safely skip this appendix; the key concepts are explained in accessible terms in Chapters 7 and 15. The specifications represent one viable architecture; Congress determines final implementation through a competitive design process.

D.1 System Overview

Purpose

The public ledger is the authoritative record of:

1. All wealth within US jurisdiction
2. The identity of controllers (real names, publicly searchable)
3. Declared values of assets (aggregated by category for public view, itemized for government)
4. Transfer and change history (government access only)
5. Tax compliance status

Design Principles

- **Transparency:** All records publicly verifiable
- **Tamper-evidence:** Any alteration is detectable
- **Record integrity, not content correctness:** The architecture guarantees that records are tamper-evident and verifiable, not that they are true. Content correctness is addressed through the hybrid input mechanism (see Data Inputs)
- **Redundancy:** Multiple independent copies prevent data loss
- **Accessibility:** Citizens can verify their own records
- **Transparency-first:** Real names with asset categories balance accountability and security

---

D.2 Architecture

Three-Layer Structure

```
┌──────────────────────────────────────────────────────────┐
│                    CANONICAL LEDGER                      │
│        (Government-maintained, authoritative)            │
└──────────────────────────────────────────────────────────┘
                             │
                             ↓
┌──────────────────────────────────────────────────────────┐
│                   DISTRIBUTED MIRRORS                    │
│   (Universities, watchdogs, international bodies)        │
└──────────────────────────────────────────────────────────┘
                             │
                             ↓
┌──────────────────────────────────────────────────────────┐
│                    PUBLIC INTERFACE                      │
│         (Aggregate data, verification tools)             │
└──────────────────────────────────────────────────────────┘
```

Layer 1: Canonical Ledger

The government maintains the authoritative record with legal force.
Characteristics:

- Single source of truth for legal purposes
- Courts recognize canonical entries as proof of ownership
- Tax calculations based on canonical values
- Maintained by federal agency (new or existing, e.g., IRS)

Technical Requirements:

- High availability (99.99% uptime target)
- Strong access controls for write operations
- Complete audit trail of all changes
- Cryptographic signing of all entries

Layer 2: Distributed Mirrors

Independent institutions maintain synchronized copies.

Mirror Operators:

- Major universities (MIT, Stanford, etc.)
- News organizations (AP, Reuters, etc.)
- International bodies (OECD, World Bank)
- Civic watchdog organizations
- State governments

Purpose:

- Detect tampering with canonical ledger
- Provide redundancy against data loss
- Enable independent verification
- Prevent political manipulation

Synchronization:

- Real-time replication from canonical ledger
- Cryptographic verification of each block
- Divergence alerts if mirrors disagree
- Public dashboard showing mirror status

Layer 3: Public Interface

Citizens interact through user-friendly tools.
Features:

- Aggregate statistics (wealth distribution, compliance rates)
- Personal record verification (with authentication)
- Tax calculation tools
- Filing and declaration portals

D.3 Data Model

Asset Record Structure

Each asset record exists only in the government's Tier 2 database. Individual assets are not visible in the public Tier 1 view; they are aggregated into categories on the controller's public record.

```
{
  "asset_id": "UUID-128bit",
  "asset_type": "real_estate | securities | vehicle | ...",
  "aggregation_category": "real_property | financial_securities |
     business_interests | other_assets",
  "description": "Detailed description (Tier 2 only)",
  "declared_value": 500000,
  "valuation_date": "2026-12-31",
  "valuation_method": "comparable_sales",
  "controller_id": "UUID-128bit",
  "controller_name": "Jane Rodriguez",
  "control_type": "direct | delegated | shared",
  "control_vehicle": "direct | trust | corporate | partnership | estate",
  "control_percentage": 100,
  "control_start_date": "2020-06-15",
  "jurisdiction": "US",
  "location": "Detailed location (Tier 2 only)",
  "encumbrances": ["lien_id_1", "lien_id_2"],
  "compliance_status": "current | delinquent | disputed",
  "last_updated": "2026-12-31T23:59:59Z",
  "signature": "cryptographic_signature"
}
```

Controller Record Structure

Each controller (natural person, or government body for public assets) has two views: a public view (Tier 1) and a government view (Tier 2). Per the Amendment's Section 5, only natural persons and government bodies may be registered as controllers. Legal entities (corporations, trusts, partnerships, estates) are recorded as the *control vehicle* on the asset record, not as controllers themselves.

Public View (Tier 1, searchable by name):

```
{
  "controller_name": "Jane Rodriguez",
  "controller_type": "natural_person | government",
  "total_declared_wealth": 5550000,
  "compliance_status": "current",
  "tax_year_2026": {
    "assessed_wealth": 5550000,
    "tax_due": 222000,
    "tax_paid": 222000
  },
  "category_totals": {
    "real_property": 1200000,
    "financial_securities": 3400000,
```

```
    "business_interests": 800000,
    "other_assets": 150000
  },
  "signature": "cryptographic_signature"
}
```

Government View (Tier 2, confidential, full itemization):

```
{
  "controller_id": "UUID-128bit",
  "controller_name": "Jane Rodriguez",
  "controller_type": "natural_person",
  "registration_date": "2020-01-15",
  "total_declared_wealth": 5550000,
  "asset_count": 12,
  "compliance_status": "current",
  "tax_year_2026": {
    "assessed_wealth": 5550000,
    "tax_due": 222000,
    "tax_paid": 222000,
    "payment_date": "2027-01-15"
  },
  "identity_verification": {
    "ssn_hash": "SHA256_HASH",
    "verification_level": 3,
    "kyc_date": "2020-01-15"
  },
  "asset_refs": ["asset_id_1", "asset_id_2", "..."],
  "signature": "cryptographic_signature"
}
```

Transaction Record Structure

Every change is recorded:

```
{
  "transaction_id": "UUID-128bit",
  "transaction_type": "registration | transfer | valuation_update | ...",
  "timestamp": "2026-06-15T14:30:00Z",
  "asset_id": "UUID-128bit",
  "from_controller": "UUID-128bit",
  "to_controller": "UUID-128bit",
  "value_before": 450000,
  "value_after": 500000,
  "notary_id": "NOTARY-ID",
  "filing_fee_paid": 50,
  "signature": "cryptographic_signature"
```

```
}
```

D.4 Identity Management

Real-Name Registration

Controllers are identified by real name on the public ledger.
How It Works:

1. Individual registers with government (KYC verification)
2. Government creates controller record with verified real name
3. Real name appears on the public ledger (Tier 1); records of the top 10% of wealth holders and public officials are searchable by name, while all other records are reachable only by the controller's Ledger ID
4. Government maintains full identity details (SSN, address, contact) in Tier 2 only
5. Lookup notifications: any search of a controller's record triggers a notification to that controller identifying who searched

Transparency Properties:

- Public can look up a record and see total wealth, tax burden, compliance status, and asset categories; name search is limited to the top 10% of wealth holders and public officials, while everyone else is reachable only by Ledger ID
- Public cannot see individual asset details, transaction history, or personal identifiers (SSN, address)
- Government has full itemized records for tax administration and enforcement
- Individual assets are revealed only by voluntary consent or judicial order (Tier 3)

Identity Verification Levels

Level	Verification	Capabilities
Level 1	Email + phone	View own records
Level 2	Government ID	File declarations, make payments
Level 3	In-person or notarized	Transfer high-value assets
Level 4	Biometric + multi-factor	Administrative functions

D.5 Data Inputs: The Hybrid Mechanism

The ledger's cryptographic guarantees apply to the record, not to the reality the record describes. An entry cannot be silently altered after it is written, and the chain of entries cannot be silently rewritten. Neither property constrains the correctness of the data at the moment of entry. The distinction between immutability of the record and correctness of the content is sometimes called the oracle problem, and it is the system's most important design constraint.

The system addresses this constraint through a hybrid input mechanism. Data enters the ledger through three pathways, each with different integrity properties.

Self-declaration. The controller reports the asset and its declared value directly. Self-declaration is the default pathway for assets that have no natural third-party reporter: operating businesses below regulatory thresholds, privately held intellectual property, personal art collections, and miscellaneous tangible property above the de minimis threshold. Integrity depends on the controller's exposure to downstream liability. A false declaration is tax evasion on the same footing as falsifying a Form 1040.

Compelled third-party reporting. A party other than the controller reports the asset's existence, controllership, or value because that party already possesses the information as a condition of its own business operations. This pathway covers:

- Custodial brokerage accounts (custodians report position holdings at declared custodial value, using the same mechanism as existing IRS Form 1099-B)
- Deposit accounts at banks and credit unions (institutions report balances using existing US and international reporting frameworks)
- Real property (county recorders report deed filings at the same moment the deed is recorded)
- Vehicle titles (state DMVs report at the moment of title transfer)

- Insured tangible property above a Congressional threshold (insurers report covered items and declared coverage values)
- Pledged loan collateral (lenders report collateral assignments at the moment the security interest is perfected)
- Licensed intellectual property (licensees report the commercial terms that establish a market value)

Third-party reporting is more reliable than self-declaration because the reporter has no incentive to inflate or deflate the reported value, and because the report duplicates information the reporter already captures for its own purposes. Extending existing reporting duties is administratively cheaper than creating new ones.

Transaction triggers. Certain events automatically establish a new value without requiring either self-declaration or compelled reporting, because the event itself generates a verified market price. Transaction triggers include arm's-length sales, auction results, capital raises with priced rounds, and court-ordered valuations in divorce, bankruptcy, or estate proceedings.

The boundary question. The exact boundary between self-declaration and compelled reporting is a live design question that this appendix does not resolve, and that this book does not pretend to resolve. The tradeoffs are substantive.

Extending compelled reporting reduces reliance on controller honesty, at the cost of imposing administrative duties on third parties who may object to the burden. Every expansion of compelled reporting is a political negotiation with the affected industry.

Restricting compelled reporting preserves regulatory restraint and protects business relationships between controllers and their bankers, brokers, insurers, and appraisers, at the cost of widening the aperture for under-declaration. Restraint is cheaper to enact but produces a weaker system.

A middle path couples compelled reporting to verification events rather than annual reports. Under this approach, third parties report only when they are already generating a valuation for their own purposes: a bank reports collateral value when it books a loan, not annually; an insurer reports coverage value when it underwrites a policy, not annually. This minimizes administrative burden while catching the moments when values are being independently verified anyway.

Congress and the implementing agency resolve this boundary through rulemaking, industry consultation, and iteration. The architecture supports all three positions. The choice is policy, not technology.

D.6 Transaction Processing

Registration Flow

```
1. DECLARATION
   └─> Controller submits asset details via portal or notary

2. VALIDATION
   └─> System checks: completeness, format, controller authority

3. AUTHENTICATION
   └─> Controller identity verified (Level 2+)
   └─> Transaction digitally signed

4. NOTARIZATION
   └─> Authorized notary reviews and co-signs
   └─> Filing fee collected

5. RECORDING
   └─> Transaction added to pending block
   └─> Block finalized at regular interval (hourly)

6. REPLICATION
   └─> Block propagated to all mirrors
   └─> Mirrors verify and acknowledge

7. CONFIRMATION
   └─> Controller receives confirmation
   └─> Asset appears on ledger
```

Transfer Flow

```
1. INITIATION
   └─> Seller initiates transfer request

2. ACCEPTANCE
   └─> Buyer accepts and provides controller ID

3. VERIFICATION
```

```
   └> System verifies: seller controls asset, no blocking liens

4. AUTHENTICATION
   └> Both parties authenticate (Level 2+)
   └> Both sign transaction

5. NOTARIZATION
   └> Notary verifies identities and intent
   └> Filing fee collected

6. RECORDING
   └> Control transferred on ledger
   └> Tax liability transfers with control

7. CONFIRMATION
   └> Both parties receive confirmation
```

D.7 Reassessment Triggers

Once an asset is on the ledger, its declared value is not updated on a schedule. Updates occur when a triggering event establishes a new value, and between events the prior value stands. This design keeps administrative cost bounded and limits the surface area for manipulation. A controller cannot opportunistically re-value an asset year to year, and the system does not force reassessment when no new information exists.

Arm's-length sale. The sale price becomes the new ledger value effective the transaction date. Both parties are reported on the transaction record.

Pledge as collateral. When an asset is pledged against a loan, the lender's appraisal becomes the new ledger value. Lenders have a direct financial incentive to appraise accurately, which makes the pledged value one of the most reliable inputs available to the system.

Capital raise with priced round. For equity stakes in private businesses, a priced investment round establishes a new valuation for the entity and, by extension, for all outstanding equity. The lead investor's price becomes the new ledger value for all equity holders until the next triggering event.

Insurance coverage. When an asset is insured against loss, the insurer's declared coverage value becomes the new ledger value. Coverage-based valuations are conservative, since insurers tend to underwrite replacement rather than appreciation, but they are independent of the controller's declaration.

Licensing revenue. For intellectual property, the commercial terms of a licensing agreement establish a new value based on the income stream the IP generates. Revenue multiples or discounted cash flow methods are applied per the controller's elected valuation method.

Court-ordered valuation. Any judicial proceeding that produces a valuation (divorce, bankruptcy, probate, civil judgment) generates a new ledger entry. Courts already value assets for these proceedings, and the ledger entry is an additional output of work the judiciary already performs.

Declared impairment by the controller. A controller can declare that an asset's value has fallen: a business revenue decline, a damaged physical asset, a lapsed patent, a tenant default. The declaration is accepted at face value and takes effect immediately, with one consequence. The declaration is publicly visible and subject to challenge. A false impairment declaration exposes the controller to tax evasion liability if the asset's true value is subsequently revealed by any other trigger.

Audit challenge. A challenge by the tax authority, a third party, or another controller can force reassessment. Challenge processes are described in Chapter 11.

Between-trigger behavior. In any given tax year, assets without a triggering event retain their prior-year value. Controllers are not required to refresh valuations on assets that have not transacted, been pledged, been licensed, been insured, or been impaired. The ledger grows by events, not by schedule.

D.8 Security Architecture

Cryptographic Foundations

Hash Function: SHA-3-256 for all integrity checks

Digital Signatures: Ed25519 for transaction signing

Encryption: AES-256-GCM for sensitive data at rest

Key Management: Hardware security modules (HSMs) for government keys

Block Structure

Transactions are grouped into blocks for efficiency and integrity:

```
┌──────────────────────────────────────────┐
│ BLOCK HEADER                             │
│ ├─ Block number: 1,234,567               │
│ ├─ Timestamp: 2026-12-31T12:00:00Z       │
│ ├─ Previous block hash: 0x7f3a...        │
│ ├─ Merkle root: 0x9b2c...                │
│ └─ Government signature: 0x4d1e...       │
├──────────────────────────────────────────┤
│ TRANSACTIONS                             │
│ ├─ Transaction 1                         │
│ ├─ Transaction 2                         │
│ ├─ ...                                   │
│ └─ Transaction N                         │
├──────────────────────────────────────────┤
│ BLOCK FOOTER                             │
│ ├─ Transaction count: N                  │
│ ├─ Total fees: $X                        │
│ └─ Block hash: 0x8c4f...                 │
└──────────────────────────────────────────┘
```

Tamper Detection

Merkle Trees: Each block contains a Merkle root summarizing all transactions. Any change to any transaction changes the root.

Hash Chains: Each block references the previous block's hash. Altering any historical block breaks the chain.

Mirror Consensus: Mirrors continuously verify their copies match. Divergence triggers alerts.

Public Verification: Anyone can download the ledger and verify the hash chain.

DDoS Mitigation

The public-facing ledger is read-heavy by design: millions of Tier 1 lookups per day, with write operations limited to registered controllers and authorized notaries. This asymmetry enables aggressive caching and distribution.

Traffic distribution. Public read endpoints are served through a content delivery network (CDN) with geographically distributed edge nodes. Tier 1 records are cached at the edge and refreshed on a fixed interval (hourly during normal operations, daily during surge conditions). An attacker attempting to overwhelm the system with read requests hits the CDN, not the canonical ledger.

Rate limiting. API endpoints enforce per-source rate limits. Authenticated queries (controllers accessing their own records, government users performing Tier 2 lookups) receive higher thresholds than anonymous public queries. Graduated throttling slows suspicious traffic before it reaches saturation.

Write-path isolation. Transaction submission endpoints are physically separated from public read infrastructure. A volumetric attack against the public interface does not affect the ability to process registrations, transfers, or tax payments. The write path is accessible only through authenticated channels with mutual TLS.

Upstream filtering. Transit providers and peering partners apply volumetric filtering at the network edge, dropping malformed packets and known attack signatures before they enter the ledger's network perimeter. This follows the model used by major financial infrastructure (SWIFT, Fedwire) and critical government systems.

Zero-Day Response Protocol

No system is immune to undiscovered vulnerabilities. A rehearsed response limits the damage; an improvised one compounds it.

Coordinated vulnerability disclosure. The ledger operates a public vulnerability disclosure program modeled on DOD's "Hack the Pentagon" bug bounty (operational since 2016, thousands of vulnerabilities identified and patched). Security researchers who discover vulnerabilities receive structured reporting channels, defined response timelines (acknowledgment within 48 hours, patch deployment within 30 days for critical issues), and financial rewards scaled to severity.

Automated patch pipeline. Security patches follow a staged deployment process: development, automated testing against a full ledger replica, canary deployment to a subset of mirror nodes, and progressive rollout. Critical patches (actively exploited vulnerabilities) follow an accelerated timeline with manual authorization gates.

Key rotation. Government signing keys stored in hardware security modules (HSMs) are rotated on a fixed schedule (quarterly for operational keys, annually for root keys). Emergency rotation procedures allow compromised keys to be revoked and replaced within hours. All historical signatures remain verifiable through the key chain of custody.

Rollback capability. If a vulnerability compromises block integrity, the system can roll back to the last verified-good state using mirror consensus. Because 50+ independent mirrors maintain cryptographically verified copies, the correct state is always recoverable by majority agreement. Transactions processed during the compromised window enter a dispute resolution queue with extended review periods.

Federated Verification Network

The Distributed Mirrors section in Architecture introduced the mirror network as a tamper-detection layer. The same mirrors also provide resilience against single points of failure, including failure of the canonical ledger itself. This section describes those additional resilience properties.

Independent implementations. Mirror operators are encouraged to use independently developed software for ledger verification. A zero-day vulnerability in one implementation does not compromise mirrors running different codebases. This diversity-of-implementation principle follows the approach used in aviation (independent flight control computers) and nuclear safety systems (diverse redundancy).

Asynchronous transaction queuing. If the canonical ledger becomes unavailable, authorized submission endpoints queue incoming transactions with cryptographic timestamps. When service resumes, queued transactions are processed in timestamp order. No transaction is lost. Tax deadlines extend automatically by the duration of any outage (as specified in the Downtime Contingencies section).

Federated read access. During a canonical ledger outage, designated mirrors (those maintained by federal agencies and tier-one institutional partners) serve read-only access to the public. Citizens can verify their records, law enforcement can check compliance status, and courts can access Tier 2 data through established judicial channels. The system degrades gracefully: reduced write capability, full read capability.

Consensus-based recovery. When the canonical ledger recovers from an outage or compromise, it re-synchronizes by comparing its state against the mirror network. If the canonical copy diverges from mirror consensus, the mirrors are authoritative. This prevents a compromised canonical instance from propagating corrupted data to the broader network.

Air-Gapped Recovery

For catastrophic scenarios (sustained nation-state cyberattack, simultaneous compromise of canonical ledger and multiple mirrors, or infrastructure destruction), the system maintains offline recovery capability.

Offline backup ledger. Complete ledger snapshots are written to air-gapped storage (physically disconnected from any network) at geographically distributed secure facilities. These facilities follow the model established by FEMA's continuity-of-government infrastructure: hardened sites, independent power, and physical access controls.

Backup frequency. Offline snapshots are updated daily under normal operations. During elevated threat conditions, snapshot frequency increases to every four hours. The maximum data loss in a total-destruction scenario is bounded by the snapshot interval.

Recovery procedure. In a catastrophic recovery scenario, the most recent verified offline snapshot becomes the new canonical ledger. Transactions between the snapshot and the failure point are reconstructed from mirror copies, queued submissions, and third-party records (bank confirmations, notary logs). A dedicated reconciliation period allows controllers to verify their records and flag discrepancies.

D.9 Capacity and Performance

Scale Requirements

Metric	Estimate
Total assets	500-700 million
Total controllers	150-180 million
Daily transactions (steady state)	2-5 million
Peak transactions (tax season)	10-20 million/day
Annual data growth	5-10 TB
Total ledger size (10 years)	50-100 TB

Performance Targets

Operation	Target Latency
Read (single record)	< 100ms
Write (transaction submission)	< 1 second
Block finalization	1 hour
Mirror synchronization	< 5 minutes
Full ledger verification	< 24 hours

Comparison to Existing Systems

Technology metrics below are illustrative and change as underlying systems evolve. The comparison demonstrates relative scale, not exact current figures.

System	Daily Transactions	Data Size
Visa	~700 million[1]	N/A
Bitcoin	~500,000	~730 GB
Ethereum	~1.5 million	~1.3 TB
NYSE	~1.5 billion (shares)	N/A
Wealth Ledger	**2-5 million**	**50-100 TB**

The wealth ledger's requirements are well within current technical capabilities.

D.10 Privacy and Transparency Architecture

Three-Tier Information Model

Tier	Who Sees It	What They See
Tier 1a: Public (Name-Searchable)	Any citizen; applies to top 10% by wealth + public officials	Real name, total declared wealth, tax burden, compliance status, asset categories with category totals
Tier 1b: Public (ID-Accessible)	Anyone with the controller's Ledger ID	Same fields as above; record is not discoverable by name search
Tier 2: Government	Tax authority, law enforcement (with warrant)	Full itemized records: individual assets, values, locations, transaction history, audit trail

Tier	Who Sees It	What They See
Tier 3: Individual Disclosure	Specific parties (by consent or court order)	Individual asset details individually disclosed from categories

Ledger ID System

Every controller receives a unique Ledger ID at registration: a 32-character alphanumeric identifier (e.g., `WL-7K9F-3M2X-P8R4-N6T1-Q5W2-J4H8-V9C3`) generated cryptographically and not derivable from the controller's name or other personal information.

Name-searchable threshold. The system maintains a percentile-based threshold (initially the 90th percentile of declared wealth). Controllers whose total declared wealth exceeds this threshold, and all controllers flagged as elected or appointed public officials, have records indexed by name in the public search interface. The threshold is recalculated quarterly based on current ledger data.

Ledger ID lookup. Controllers below the threshold have records accessible only through their Ledger ID. The public search interface does not return results for name queries against these records. Controllers can share their Ledger ID voluntarily (for loan applications, insurance, verification) and revoke shared access at any time.

Threshold transitions. When a controller's wealth crosses the threshold (in either direction), their searchability status updates at the next quarterly recalculation. Controllers approaching the threshold receive advance notification. The transition is automatic and does not require action by the controller.

Public official flagging. Elected and appointed officials are flagged as name-searchable upon taking office and remain flagged for the duration of their service plus a defined post-service period (initially five years). Flagging is triggered by cross-reference with the Office of Government Ethics and state-level equivalents.

Asset Aggregation Categories

The public-facing Tier 1 view is computed from the government's Tier 2 records by aggregating individual assets into broad categories:

Aggregation Category	Included Asset Types
Real Property	Residential, commercial, and agricultural real estate

Aggregation Category	Included Asset Types
Financial Securities	Stocks, bonds, mutual funds, ETFs, and other market instruments
Business Interests	Ownership stakes in private companies, partnerships, sole proprietorships
Other Assets	Cash, bank deposits, money market accounts, certificates of deposit, art, collectibles, vehicles, intellectual property, cryptocurrency, other tangible/intangible property

The aggregation is a simple summation: individual asset values within each category are summed to produce the category total. No individual asset details (identity, location, specific value) are exposed in the public view. Cash and equivalents fold into "Other Assets" rather than appearing as their own category, to prevent the public view from exposing a controller's liquid-asset position.

Lookup Notification System

Every search of a Tier 1 record generates a notification to the record's controller:

- Notification includes: searcher's identity (authenticated), timestamp, and access type
- Notifications are logged and auditable
- Notification delivery is near-real-time (within minutes)
- Searchers must authenticate before searching (no anonymous lookups)

This system, modeled on Norway's 2014 reform, reportedly reduced frivolous searches by approximately 90% while maintaining full public access.

Tier 3 Selective Disclosure

Individual asset details are disclosed from categories through two mechanisms:

Consent-based: Controller authorizes disclosure of a specific asset to a specific party (e.g., bank, insurer). Authorization is recorded on the ledger with expiration date and scope limits.

Court-ordered: Judiciary issues an order for disclosure of specific assets through existing court rules for financial discovery. Orders are processed through the judicial branch, not the tax authority, maintaining separation of powers.

Protected Information

The following data exists only in Tier 2 (government) records and is never exposed publicly:

- Social Security numbers and taxpayer identification numbers
- Home addresses and contact information
- Individual asset identities, locations, and specific values
- Transaction history (dates, counterparties, amounts)
- Bank account and brokerage account numbers
- Valuation methodology details

D.11 Disaster Recovery and Catastrophic Event Protocols

Note: This section is aimed at a technical and policy-specialist audience. It provides the detailed resilience specifications referenced in Chapter 14.

Any system this critical needs contingency plans. Servers crash. Networks go down. Cyberattacks happen. Natural disasters destroy data centers. A wealth tax system that depends on a functioning ledger needs protocols for when that ledger is unavailable.

Redundancy

- Primary data center + hot standby
- Geographic distribution (East Coast, West Coast, Central)
- Mirror copies at 50+ independent institutions
- Offline backups updated daily

Recovery Objectives

Metric	Target
Recovery Point Objective (RPO)	< 1 hour
Recovery Time Objective (RTO)	< 24 hours
Maximum tolerable downtime	72 hours

Circuit Breakers

Like stock market circuit breakers that halt trading during extreme volatility, the wealth ledger includes automatic pauses:

Integrity Circuit Breaker: If the system detects data inconsistencies between the canonical ledger and mirrors, new transactions are paused until the discrepancy is resolved. This prevents corrupted data from propagating.

Load Circuit Breaker: If transaction volume exceeds system capacity, new non-essential transactions are queued. Essential transactions (tax payments, ownership transfers for sales) get priority.

Security Circuit Breaker: If a cyberattack is detected, the system enters read-only mode. Existing records remain accessible, but no new entries are accepted until the threat is neutralized.

Downtime Contingencies

Short-term outage (hours to days):

- Tax deadlines automatically extend by the duration of the outage
- Transactions queue and process when service resumes
- No penalties for missed deadlines during outage periods

Medium-term outage (days to weeks):

- Fallback to paper/electronic filing with manual reconciliation
- Temporary acceptance of third-party records (bank statements, brokerage reports) as proof of holdings
- Expedited processing when service resumes

Long-term outage (weeks to months):

- Reversion to prior-year valuations for tax calculation
- Emergency authorization for alternative record-keeping
- Congressional notification and oversight

Mirror Redundancy

Geographic distribution. Mirrors are located across multiple regions, countries, and continents. A disaster affecting one region does not affect others.

Institutional diversity. Mirrors are maintained by different types of institutions (universities, news organizations, international bodies, private watchdogs). No single point of failure.

Automatic failover. If the canonical ledger becomes unavailable, authorized mirrors can serve read-only access. Citizens can still verify their records even if they cannot update them.

Recovery Procedures

Data recovery. The canonical ledger is backed up continuously to geographically distributed storage. Recovery point objective: less than 1 hour of data loss in worst case.

Service recovery. Hot standby systems can assume primary role within hours. Recovery time objective: less than 24 hours for full service restoration.

Dispute resolution. Any transactions that occurred during an outage or recovery period receive extended dispute windows. No one is penalized for system failures.

Lessons from Existing Systems

Cryptocurrency exchanges have developed proven practices for handling outages. Huobi's circuit breakers pause trading during extreme volatility to prevent cascade failures. Major exchanges maintain hot and cold wallet separation to limit damage from security breaches. Decentralized protocols like ERC-7265 implement "speed bumps" that slow suspicious transactions without halting the entire system. The wealth ledger incorporates these lessons: circuit breakers for extreme conditions, separation of critical functions, and graceful degradation rather than catastrophic failure.

D.12 Funding Model

Transaction Fees

Transaction Type	Fee
Initial asset registration	\$5-\$50
Annual valuation update	\$1-\$10
Control transfer (title change)	\$10-\$100

Transaction Type	Fee
Dispute filing	\$50-\$500

Fees scale with asset value and complexity. Additional fee categories (lien recording, compliance certificates, and similar technical transactions) may be defined by Congress within the same cost-recovery framework. These figures match Chapter 7's fee schedule.

Revenue Projection

Item	Annual Estimate
Registration fees	\$200-400 million
Transfer fees	\$300-500 million
Update fees	\$100-200 million
Other fees	\$50-100 million
Total	**\$650M - \$1.2B**

This covers estimated operating costs of \$500M - \$1B annually, making the system self-sustaining.

Fee Distribution

- 60% - System operations and maintenance
- 20% - Mirror operator compensation
- 15% - Development and improvements
- 5% - Reserve fund

D.13 Implementation Timeline

Phase 1: Foundation (Year 1)

- Architecture design and vendor selection
- Core infrastructure deployment
- Security certification
- Pilot with federal agencies

Phase 2: Limited Deployment (Year 2)

- Public securities integration
- Bank account integration
- Voluntary registration opens
- Mirror network established

Phase 3: Expansion (Year 3)

- Real estate integration
- Vehicle integration
- Mandatory registration begins
- Full mirror synchronization

Phase 4: Full Operation (Year 4+)

- All asset classes integrated
- Legacy systems retired
- Continuous improvement
- International coordination

D.14 Technology Options

Ledger Architecture Options

Option	Pros	Cons
Permissioned blockchain (Hyperledger Fabric)	Proven, scalable, controllable	Requires trust in operators
Hybrid blockchain	Combines public verification with private control	More complex
Distributed database (CockroachDB, Spanner)	High performance, mature	Less tamper-evident
Custom solution	Optimized for requirements	Development risk

Recommendation: Permissioned blockchain with public verification layer.

Existing Precedents

Estonia's KSI Blockchain: Hash-linked timestamping technology ("blockchain-style" by Estonia's own description) that protects critical government records, including health and judicial files, against tampering. Estonia separately operates X-Road, a non-blockchain data-exchange backbone connecting government services for 1.3 million citizens.

Sweden's Lantmäteriet: Blockchain-based land registry pilot. Demonstrated feasibility for property records.

DTCC's Project Ion: Distributed ledger for securities settlement. DTCC settles trillions in daily dollar value across all systems; Project Ion specifically processes over 100,000 bilateral equity transactions daily.

D.15 Design Decisions for the Competitive Process

The following parameters are resolved during the competitive design process, where competing implementations demonstrate their approach to each:

1. **Block interval:** Hourly? Daily? Real-time with batching?
2. **Mirror requirements:** Minimum number? Geographic distribution?
3. **Identity verification:** Government-issued digital ID? Third-party providers?
4. **International interoperability:** Standards for cross-border asset tracking?
5. **Legacy integration:** How to import existing records (county, DMV, SEC)?
6. **Dispute resolution:** On-chain or off-chain arbitration?

This appendix provides technical context for the ledger system described in Chapter 7. Final specifications would be determined through the competitive design process authorized by Congress.

D.16 Notes

1. Visa processed approximately 257.5 billion transactions in fiscal 2025, or roughly 705 million daily. Wikipedia, "Visa Inc.," https://en.wikipedia.org/wiki/Visa_Inc.

FURTHER READING

This appendix lists books, reports, and resources that go beyond the citations in the main text. For sources cited in chapter footnotes, see the Bibliography. The list below is curated for readers who want to dig deeper into the topics this book covers.

E.1 Further Reading by Topic

On Wealth Inequality

- Piketty, Thomas. *Capital in the Twenty-First Century.* Harvard University Press, 2014.
- Stiglitz, Joseph. *The Price of Inequality.* W.W. Norton, 2012.
- Reich, Robert. *The System: Who Rigged It, How We Fix It.* Knopf, 2020.
- Saez, Emmanuel, and Gabriel Zucman. *The Triumph of Injustice: How the Rich Dodge Taxes and How to Make Them Pay.* W.W. Norton, 2019.
- Madoff, Ray D. *The Second Estate: How the Tax Code Made an American Aristocracy.* University of Chicago Press, 2025.

On Tax Policy

- Slemrod, Joel, and Jon Bakija. *Taxing Ourselves.* 5th ed. MIT Press, 2017.
- Graetz, Michael. *100 Million Unnecessary Returns: A Simple, Fair, and Competitive Tax Plan for the United States.* Yale University Press, 2008.
- Kleinbard, Edward. *We Are Better Than This.* Oxford University Press, 2014.
- Saez, Emmanuel, and Gabriel Zucman. "Progressive Wealth Taxation." *Brookings Papers on Economic Activity*, 2019.
- Summers, Lawrence, and Natasha Sarin. "A Wealth Tax Presents Problems." *Washington Post*, 2019.
- Perret, Sarah. "Why Did Other Wealth Taxes Fail?" *Tax Notes International*, 2020.

- OECD. *The Role and Design of Net Wealth Taxes in the OECD.* 2018. https://www.oecd.org/tax/tax-policy/role-and-design-of-net-wealth-taxes-in-the-OECD.htm.

On American Tax History

- Mehrotra, Ajay K. *Making the Modern American Fiscal State.* Cambridge University Press, 2013.
- Weisman, Steven R. *The Great Tax Wars.* Simon & Schuster, 2002.

On Constitutional Reform

- Levinson, Sanford. *Our Undemocratic Constitution.* Oxford University Press, 2006.
- Sabato, Larry. *A More Perfect Constitution.* Walker & Company, 2007.
- Kyvig, David E. *Explicit and Authentic Acts.* University Press of Kansas, 1996.
- Amar, Akhil Reed. *America's Constitution: A Biography.* Random House, 2005.

On Blockchain and Government

- Nakamoto, Satoshi. *Bitcoin: A Peer-to-Peer Electronic Cash System.* 2008. https://bitcoin.org/bitcoin.pdf.
- Tapscott, Don, and Alex Tapscott. *Blockchain Revolution.* Portfolio, 2016.
- Werbach, Kevin. *The Blockchain and the New Architecture of Trust.* MIT Press, 2018.

On Property Rights and Ownership

- Pipes, Richard. *Property and Freedom.* Vintage, 2000.
- De Soto, Hernando. *The Mystery of Capital.* Basic Books, 2000.

On Valuation Methods

- Damodaran, Aswath. *Investment Valuation.* 3rd ed. Wiley, 2012.
- Appraisal Institute. *The Appraisal of Real Estate.* 15th ed. 2020.

E.2 Online Resources

Government Sources

- IRS: https://www.irs.gov/
- Federal Reserve: https://www.federalreserve.gov/
- Congressional Budget Office: https://www.cbo.gov/
- Treasury Department: https://home.treasury.gov/
- Census Bureau: https://www.census.gov/

Research Organizations

- Tax Policy Center: https://www.taxpolicycenter.org/
- Tax Foundation: https://taxfoundation.org/
- Institute on Taxation and Economic Policy: https://itep.org/
- Brookings Institution: https://www.brookings.edu/
- National Bureau of Economic Research: https://www.nber.org/
- Lincoln Institute of Land Policy: https://www.lincolninst.edu/

Advocacy Organizations

- Americans for Tax Fairness: https://americansfortaxfairness.org/
- Patriotic Millionaires: https://patrioticmillionaires.org/
- Tax Justice Network: https://taxjustice.net/

Implementation References

- Hyperledger Fabric Documentation: https://hyperledger-fabric.readthedocs.io/
- Estonia's X-Road: https://e-estonia.com/solutions/interoperability-services/x-road/
- Florida Department of Revenue Tax Certificate Program: https://floridarevenue.com/property/

E.3 A Note on Perspectives

The list above includes both supportive and skeptical perspectives on wealth taxation. Consult multiple viewpoints and form your own conclusions.

Supportive of wealth taxation: Saez and Zucman, ProPublica investigations, Tax Justice Network.

Skeptical of wealth taxation: Tax Foundation, Summers and Sarin, some OECD analyses.

This book attempts to address the major objections fairly. The strongest arguments deserve the strongest counterarguments.

APPENDIX F

INTERNATIONAL WEALTH TAX COMPARISON

This appendix examines wealth taxes implemented in other countries, what we can learn from their successes and failures, and how the design described here addresses the problems they encountered.

F.1 Overview

Wealth taxes are not new. At least a dozen countries have implemented some form of annual wealth tax over the past century. Some succeeded; many failed. Understanding why requires examining each case carefully. Tax rates and thresholds below are as of 2025 unless otherwise noted; these change with legislation.

Country	Status	Years Active	Peak Rate	Outcome
France	Modified	1982-1986, 1989-present	1.5% (ISF)	Narrowed to real estate (IFI) in 2018
Norway	Active	1892-present	0.85%	Functioning, recently increased
Switzerland	Active	Varies by canton	0.3-1.0%	Functioning, cantonal variation
Spain	Active (restored)	1977-2008, 2011-present	3.5%	Repealed then restored
Sweden	Repealed	1911-2007	1.5%	Repealed after capital flight
Germany	Suspended	1952-1996 collected	1.0%	Suspended after 1995 court ruling on valuation inequality
Netherlands	Modified	2001-present	~1.2% effective	Shifted to presumed return model

Country	Status	Years Active	Peak Rate	Outcome
Italy	One-off levy	1992 only	0.6% (one-time)	Emergency measure on bank deposits, not a recurring wealth tax
Argentina	Active	1973-present	2.25%	High evasion, enforcement challenges
Colombia	Active	2023-present	1.5%	Permanently reintroduced under Law 2277 of 2022

F.2 France: The Cautionary Tale

History

France's wealth tax, the *Impôt de solidarité sur la fortune* (ISF), is the most frequently cited example of wealth tax failure. Understanding what actually happened is essential.

1982-1986: First attempt. President Mitterrand's socialist government introduced the *Impôt sur les grandes fortunes* (IGF), targeting wealth above 3 million francs. It was repealed in 1986 when the right won parliamentary elections.

1989-2017: ISF era. The wealth tax returned under Mitterrand in 1989 as the ISF. It applied to net assets above approximately €800,000 (threshold varied over time), with rates from 0.5% to 1.5%.

2017: Repeal. President Macron replaced the ISF with a tax on real estate wealth only (IFI), exempting financial assets.

What Went Wrong

Narrow base, high rates. The ISF applied only to households above the threshold, creating a cliff effect. Households just above the threshold faced significant tax; those just below paid nothing. This created strong incentives to restructure wealth to stay below the threshold.

Exemptions and loopholes. The ISF exempted: - Business assets (if the owner was actively involved) - Art and antiques - Intellectual property - Forestry investments

These exemptions created obvious avoidance strategies. Wealthy French invested in exempt categories, restructured businesses to qualify for exemptions, and shifted assets into art collections.

Valuation disputes. Without a public ledger, valuation was contentious. Taxpayers had incentives to undervalue; the tax authority had to challenge valuations case by case. Litigation was expensive and time-consuming.

No exit controls. France had weak exit tax provisions until 2011. Wealthy French could relocate to Belgium, Switzerland, or Monaco and escape the tax entirely. An estimated 10,000 wealthy households left France over the ISF's three decades, though the actual revenue impact is disputed.

Political vulnerability. The ISF was a political football, expanded by the left, contracted by the right. This instability made long-term planning difficult and encouraged temporary relocation during left-wing governments.

Revenue and Impact

The ISF raised approximately €5 billion annually at its peak, about 1.5% of total tax revenue. Critics argued the revenue was offset by capital flight; supporters argued the flight was exaggerated.

Studies of the ISF's impact are contested: - A 2019 study estimated 10,000 taxpayers left France due to the ISF, costing €7 billion in capital flight - Other economists argue the departures were overstated and many "departures" were paper relocations while actual residency continued in France

Lessons for This Design

France's Problem	This Design's Solution
Narrow base with threshold cliff	Universal application, no threshold
Extensive exemptions	Minimal exemptions (Wealth Test applies to all assets)
Valuation disputes	Public ledger with self-declaration and market verification
Weak exit controls	Strengthened exit tax with clawback provisions
Addition to existing taxes	Replacement of all federal taxes
Political instability	Constitutional amendment (harder to repeal)

The ISF failed not because wealth taxes cannot work, but because of specific design flaws that this design avoids.

F.3 Norway: The Success Story

History

Norway has maintained a wealth tax continuously since 1892, making it one of the longest-running wealth taxes in the world.

Current structure: - Threshold: NOK 1.7 million (~$170,000) for individuals - Rate: 1.0% (increased from 0.85% in 2022) - Base: Net wealth including real estate, securities, bank deposits, and business assets - Valuation: Listed securities at market value; real estate at assessed value (typically below market)

What Works

Broad base, moderate rate. Norway taxes most forms of wealth at a relatively low rate. The broad base means fewer avoidance opportunities; the moderate rate means the incentive to evade is limited.

Integration with income tax. Norway's wealth tax is part of a comprehensive tax system. It's not an add-on but an integral component. This integration reduces arbitrage opportunities.

Cultural acceptance. Norwegian society has high trust in government and strong norms of tax compliance. The wealth tax is seen as legitimate, not punitive.

Transparent society. Norway publishes tax returns publicly. Anyone can look up anyone else's income and wealth. This transparency reduces evasion and increases social pressure for compliance.

Challenges

Valuation inconsistencies. Real estate is assessed at roughly 25% of market value for primary residences, creating a preference for real estate over financial assets. This distorts investment decisions.

Business asset treatment. Business assets are valued at a discount, creating incentives to hold wealth in business form rather than personal form.

Capital flight concerns. Some wealthy Norwegians have relocated to Switzerland or other low-tax jurisdictions. The most famous case is Kjell Inge

Røkke, who moved to Switzerland in 2022 citing tax burden. However, most wealthy Norwegians remain.

Lessons for This Design

Norway's Strength	Application to This Design
Broad base	Wealth Test ensures comprehensive coverage
Moderate rate	~3-4% (conservative estimate) is higher but replaces all other taxes
Transparency	Public ledger institutionalizes transparency
Cultural acceptance	Requires building political support

Norway's Weakness	This Design's Solution
Valuation inconsistencies	Market-based valuation with escape assessments
Business asset discounts	No discounts; Duty of Control applies equally
Some capital flight	Strengthened exit tax; wealth-based not citizenship-based

---

F.4 Switzerland: Cantonal Variation

History

Switzerland has no federal wealth tax, but all 26 cantons impose wealth taxes with varying rates and structures.

Current structure: - Rates: 0.3% to 1.0% depending on canton - Base: Net wealth including real estate, securities, vehicles, and other assets - Thresholds: Vary by canton; typically CHF 50,000-100,000 - Valuation: Cantonal tax authorities assess; real estate often below market

What Works

Competition and experimentation. Cantonal variation allows experimentation. Cantons compete for wealthy residents, but all maintain some wealth tax. This suggests wealth taxes are compatible with attracting wealth.

Integration with other taxes. Swiss wealth taxes are part of a comprehensive system including income taxes and property taxes. The total burden is considered, not just the wealth tax in isolation.

Strong enforcement. Swiss tax authorities have broad powers and high compliance rates. The culture of compliance is strong.

Challenges

Race to the bottom. Cantons compete by lowering rates, potentially eroding the tax base. Some cantons (Zug, Schwyz) have very low rates to attract wealthy residents.

Valuation complexity. Each canton has its own valuation methods, creating inconsistency and arbitrage opportunities.

Secrecy concerns. Switzerland's banking secrecy tradition conflicts with transparency goals, though this has eroded significantly under international pressure.

Lessons for This Design

Switzerland's Strength	Application to This Design
Proven compatibility with wealth attraction	Demonstrates wealth taxes don't necessarily cause flight
Strong enforcement culture	Ledger-based enforcement even stronger
Integration with other taxes	Full replacement even more integrated

Switzerland's Weakness	This Design's Solution
Race to the bottom	Federal system, no state competition
Valuation inconsistency	Uniform federal standards
Secrecy tradition	Public ledger eliminates secrecy

F.5 Sweden: The Repeal

History

Sweden maintained a wealth tax from 1911 to 2007, when it was repealed by a center-right government.

Structure before repeal: - Threshold: SEK 1.5 million (~$200,000) - Rate: 1.5% - Base: Net wealth including real estate, securities, and other assets

Why It Was Repealed

Capital flight. Sweden experienced significant capital flight, most famously IKEA founder Ingvar Kamprad, who relocated to Switzerland in 1973 and didn't return until 2014 (after the wealth tax was repealed). Chapter 12 tells the fuller story, including the transfer-pricing restructuring that mattered more than his personal departure. Other prominent Swedes, including members of the Wallenberg family, also relocated.

Narrow base. Extensive exemptions (pension assets, business assets, primary residence partially) narrowed the base and created avoidance opportunities.

Administrative burden. Valuation disputes were common and expensive to resolve.

Political shift. The 2006 election brought a center-right coalition that had campaigned on tax reduction. The wealth tax was an easy target.

Post-Repeal Assessment

Studies of Sweden's repeal show mixed results: - Some wealthy Swedes returned after repeal - Revenue loss was partially offset by increased income tax compliance (less incentive to hide income when wealth wasn't taxed) - Wealth inequality increased after repeal

Lessons for This Design

Sweden's Problem	This Design's Solution
Narrow base with exemptions	Comprehensive Wealth Test
Weak exit controls	Strengthened exit tax
Political vulnerability	Constitutional amendment
Administrative burden	Ledger-based self-declaration

F.6 Germany: Constitutional Failure

History

Germany maintained a wealth tax (*Vermögensteuer*) from 1952 until it was suspended in 1997.

The ruling: In 1995, the Federal Constitutional Court (*Bundesverfassungsgericht*) found that the wealth tax, combined with income taxes, could result in confiscatory taxation (total burden exceeding 100% of income in some cases). The court didn't rule wealth taxes unconstitutional per se, but required that total taxation not exceed roughly 50% of income. The legislature was given a deadline to reform the tax.

Post-ruling: The legislature failed to act by the deadline, and the tax was suspended from January 1, 1997. Attempts to revive it have failed politically.

Lessons for This Design

Germany's Problem	This Design's Solution
Interaction with income tax created confiscatory rates	Wealth tax replaces income tax entirely
Constitutional vulnerability	Explicit constitutional amendment
Political difficulty of redesign	Clean-slate design, not retrofit

Germany's experience actually supports this design's approach: replacing income taxes with wealth taxes avoids the confiscation problem entirely.

F.7 Spain: Repeal and Restoration

History

Spain introduced a wealth tax in 1977, suspended it in 2008 during the financial crisis (by setting the rate to 0%), and restored it in 2011.

Current structure: - Threshold: €700,000 (plus €300,000 primary residence exemption) - Rates: 0.2% to 3.5% (progressive) - Regional variation: Some autonomous communities (Madrid) have effectively eliminated it through 100% rebates

What This Shows

Wealth taxes can be restored. Once repealed, wealth taxes are not gone forever. Political conditions change.

Regional competition is problematic. Madrid's effective elimination of the wealth tax has attracted wealthy Spaniards from other regions, creating internal capital flight.

High top rates create avoidance incentives. Spain's 3.5% national top rate (on wealth above €10.7 million) is among the highest in the world, creating strong incentives for avoidance.

Lessons for This Design

Spain's Experience	Application to This Design
Restoration is possible	Political will can overcome opposition
Regional competition problematic	Federal system prevents internal flight
High progressive rates create avoidance	Flat ~3-4% rate, simpler compliance

---

F.8 Argentina and Colombia: Emerging Market Challenges

Argentina

Argentina has maintained various forms of wealth tax since 1973, currently the *Impuesto sobre los Bienes Personales*.

Challenges: - High inflation makes valuation difficult - Weak enforcement infrastructure - Extensive informal economy - History of economic instability undermines compliance

Lessons: Argentina's difficulties confirm two prerequisites: institutional stability and enforcement capacity. The ledger system provides enforcement. The United States already has institutional stability. Argentina's failure is a case study in why the ledger matters, not an argument against wealth taxation.

Colombia

Colombia introduced a wealth tax in 2019 as part of broader tax reform.

Structure: - Threshold: COP 5 billion (~$1.3 million) - Rate: 1.0-1.5% - Temporary: Originally set to expire in 2021, extended

Early experience: Too early to assess fully, but implementation has been smoother than Argentina's due to stronger institutions.

F.9 Common Patterns Across Countries

Why Wealth Taxes Fail

1. **Narrow base with extensive exemptions.** Every exemption creates an avoidance opportunity. France's art exemption, Sweden's pension exemption, and Germany's business asset treatment all became avoidance vehicles.

2. **Addition to existing taxes.** When wealth taxes are added on top of income taxes, the combined burden can become confiscatory, creating both legal challenges (Germany) and political opposition.

3. **Weak exit controls.** Without strong exit taxes, the wealthy can simply leave. France and Sweden both experienced significant departures.

4. **Valuation disputes.** Without transparent, market-based valuation, every assessment becomes a negotiation. Administrative costs mount; compliance suffers.

5. **Political vulnerability.** Wealth taxes imposed by statute can be repealed by statute. Changes in government lead to changes in policy.

Why Wealth Taxes Succeed

1. **Broad base with few exemptions.** Norway and Switzerland tax most forms of wealth, reducing avoidance opportunities.

2. **Moderate rates.** Lower rates reduce the incentive to evade or relocate.

3. **Strong enforcement.** Countries with high compliance cultures and strong tax authorities have better outcomes.

4. **Transparency.** Norway's public tax returns create social pressure for compliance.

5. **Integration with overall tax system.** Wealth taxes work best as part of a coherent system, not as an add-on.

F.10 How This Design Learns From History

Historical Problem	This Design's Solution
Narrow base, extensive exemptions	Wealth Test applies to all exchangeable, assessable, separable assets
Addition to existing taxes	Complete replacement of all federal taxes
Weak exit controls	Strengthened exit tax with clawback; wealth-based not citizenship-based
Valuation disputes	Public ledger with self-declaration, escape assessments, and valuation challenges
Political vulnerability	Constitutional amendment (requires supermajority to repeal)
Administrative burden	Ledger-based system with automated compliance
Lack of transparency	Public ledger makes all wealth visible

This design incorporates lessons from every major wealth tax experiment:

- **From France:** Avoid exemptions; strengthen exit controls; constitutional foundation
- **From Norway:** Broad base works; transparency aids compliance
- **From Switzerland:** Wealth taxes are compatible with attracting wealth
- **From Sweden:** Exit controls matter; political stability matters
- **From Germany:** Don't add to income tax; replace it
- **From Spain:** Federal uniformity prevents internal flight

The international experience doesn't show that wealth taxes can't work. It shows that *poorly designed* wealth taxes fail, while *well-designed* wealth taxes can succeed. This design is built to succeed.

F.11 Summary Table: Learning From International Experience

Country	Key Lesson	How This Design Applies It
France	Exemptions kill wealth taxes	Minimal exemptions via Wealth Test

Country	Key Lesson	How This Design Applies It
France	Exit controls essential	Strengthened exit tax
Norway	Broad base + moderate rate works	Universal application
Norway	Transparency aids compliance	Public ledger
Switzerland	Wealth taxes compatible with prosperity	Demonstrates feasibility
Sweden	Political stability matters	Constitutional foundation
Germany	Don't stack on income tax	Complete replacement
Spain	Regional competition problematic	Federal uniformity

The wealth tax described in this book is not an untested experiment. It builds on over a century of international experience, incorporating the lessons of both success and failure.

F.12 International Coordination Architecture

Chapter 12 makes the case that the core enforcement of the wealth tax works unilaterally: US-situs wealth cannot physically leave, and the owner's address is irrelevant. That is the core argument. But a second question remains: what does cross-border coordination add, and how is it built? This section walks through the institutional detail that Chapter 12 summarizes in two paragraphs.

The short version is that the diplomatic template already exists, and the infrastructure is already built. The US has spent the last fifteen years, through FATCA, the OECD, and the tax treaty network, constructing exactly the kind of cross-border reporting system a wealth tax needs. The work is not to invent it. The work is to extend it.

OECD Initiatives

The Organisation for Economic Co-operation and Development has led efforts to increase tax transparency:

Common Reporting Standard (CRS): Over 100 countries automatically exchange financial account information. Hiding assets abroad is increasingly difficult.

Base Erosion and Profit Shifting (BEPS): International efforts to prevent corporations from shifting profits to tax havens.

Global Minimum Tax: Agreement among major economies for a 15% minimum corporate tax rate, reducing the benefit of profit shifting.

The Race to the Bottom Is Slowing

For decades, countries competed to attract capital by lowering taxes. This "race to the bottom" eroded tax bases worldwide.

That race is slowing. Countries recognize that tax competition is collectively self-defeating. International coordination is increasing. The environment for tax havens is becoming less hospitable.

US Leadership

The US, as the world's largest economy, can accelerate this trend. US adoption of a wealth tax with strong enforcement would pressure other countries to cooperate. Tax havens that refuse to share information could face consequences: restricted access to US markets, exclusion from US banking, diplomatic pressure.

The US doesn't need to wait for international consensus. But international trends are moving in a favorable direction.

FATCA as Precedent

The diplomatic template already exists. The Foreign Account Tax Compliance Act (FATCA), enacted in 2010, requires foreign financial institutions to report accounts held by US persons or face a 30% withholding tax on US-source payments. As of 2025, more than 100 countries have signed intergovernmental agreements (IGAs) to implement FATCA reporting. Foreign banks comply because the cost of exclusion from US financial markets is unacceptable.

FATCA proves three things. First, the US has the leverage to compel foreign cooperation on tax transparency. Second, countries will sign bilateral agreements rather than lose access to US capital markets. Third, the compliance infrastructure (reporting systems, data exchange protocols, legal frameworks) already exists in over 100 countries.

The wealth tax extends this model. Instead of reporting only financial accounts held by US persons abroad, the framework expands to include reporting on nationals who control US assets. The mechanism is the same: report, or face withholding and market restrictions. The infrastructure is already built.

Joining the Common Reporting Standard

There is an irony in the current system that the wealth tax resolves. The US championed FATCA and pressured the world to adopt tax transparency. Then, when the OECD built the Common Reporting Standard (CRS) as a multilateral version of the same idea, the US declined to join. Over 100 countries automatically exchange financial account information with each other. The US demands incoming reports from all of them. It sends nothing back.

This has made the United States one of the world's largest tax havens. Foreign nationals can park money in US banks, trusts, and shell companies with limited reporting to their home countries. States like South Dakota, Nevada, and Delaware actively market their secrecy protections to foreign wealth.

The wealth tax changes the calculus. A system that requires every controller of US wealth to register by name, regardless of nationality, eliminates the secrecy that makes the US attractive as a haven. Joining CRS becomes not a concession but a natural extension of the ledger's transparency principle. The US gains moral authority to demand cooperation because it is finally offering reciprocity.

Bilateral Enforcement Treaties

For enforcement against assets controlled by non-cooperative foreign nationals, the US can build on existing treaty infrastructure.

Mutual Legal Assistance Treaties (MLATs). The US maintains MLATs with over 70 countries, providing for cross-border evidence gathering, asset tracing, and legal cooperation. These treaties already cover tax fraud. Extending them to cover wealth tax compliance requires amendment, not reinvention.

Tax treaties. The US has income tax treaties with approximately 65 countries. These treaties include provisions for information exchange, mutual assistance in collection, and dispute resolution. A new "Wealth Transparency Agreement" (WTA) template, modeled on existing tax treaty structures, could provide for: reciprocal asset reporting, joint audit authority for cross-border control chains, agreed valuation standards for assets that span jurisdictions, and enforcement cooperation including mutual recognition of liens.

Trade agreement integration. Future trade agreements can include wealth transparency provisions, just as recent agreements have incorporated labor standards, environmental protections, and intellectual property rules. Countries seeking preferential trade access agree to reciprocal asset reporting. This is not unprecedented: the EU already conditions market access on anti-money-laundering compliance.

Arbitration Offramps

International disputes are inevitable. A sovereign wealth fund will contest its controller classification. A foreign government will claim diplomatic immunity for assets that look commercial. A country will refuse to comply with reporting requests. These disputes need a resolution mechanism that does not default to confrontation.

Standing arbitration panel. The design calls for a permanent international panel for wealth tax disputes, modeled on existing institutions. The World Trade Organization's dispute resolution mechanism handles trade conflicts between nations through structured proceedings with binding outcomes. The International Centre for Settlement of Investment Disputes (ICSID), a World Bank institution, resolves disputes between governments and foreign investors. Both demonstrate that international arbitration works for complex economic disputes.

The wealth tax arbitration panel would handle three categories of disputes:

Controller classification. When a foreign government claims that an entity is sovereign (and therefore exempt) while the US contends it is privately controlled, the panel reviews the control chain and applies the amendment's superior-authority test. "Sovereign wealth fund" is not a magic label. Norway's Government Pension Fund, managed under parliamentary oversight, registers as a government entity. A Gulf state vehicle controlled by a single royal family member registers that person as controller. If one person directs the investments, captures the returns, and treats the fund as a private account routed through sovereign machinery, the natural-person rule applies.

Diplomatic immunity boundaries. Embassy properties are exempt under the Vienna Convention. Commercial real estate held by a foreign government for investment purposes is not. The panel draws the line in contested cases.

Enforcement cooperation. When a country refuses to comply with information requests or enforce liens against assets held within its borders, the panel determines whether the refusal is justified (legitimate sovereignty concerns) or obstructive (deliberate shielding of non-compliant controllers). Obstructive refusals trigger the graduated enforcement sequence described below.

Graduated Enforcement for Non-Cooperative Jurisdictions

Rather than immediate economic confrontation, the system provides escalating responses with offramps at every stage:

1. **Information request.** Formal diplomatic request for controller identification and asset reporting. Most countries comply at this stage, as they already do under FATCA and CRS.
2. **Withholding.** Non-responsive jurisdictions face the FATCA-model withholding described above, creating domestic pressure from their own banking sector to cooperate.
3. **Restricted market access.** Continued non-cooperation triggers restrictions on access to US capital markets, government procurement, and financial services.
4. **Arbitration referral.** The dispute is referred to the standing arbitration panel for binding resolution. Both parties present their case. The panel's determination is enforceable through existing international legal frameworks.

At each stage, compliance ends the escalation. The goal is cooperation, not punishment. Countries that engage in good faith, even if slowly, are treated differently from those that deliberately obstruct.

End of Appendix F

APPENDIX G

GLOSSARY OF KEY TERMS

Asset Aggregation Categories: The four broad groupings into which individual assets are combined for public display on the Tier 1 ledger: Real Property, Financial Securities, Business Interests, and Other Assets. The government's Tier 2 database contains full itemization; the public Tier 1 view aggregates individual asset values into category totals. Cash and equivalents fold into "Other Assets" so the public display does not expose a controller's liquid-asset position. Not to be confused with lien bundling (see Chapter 9). See Chapter 13 and Appendix D.

Asset Class: A category of wealth the system tracks and values together. Five broad classes cover almost all wealth: real estate, financial securities (stocks, bonds, funds), business interests (private companies and partnerships), cash and equivalents (deposits, money market accounts), and other assets (art, vehicles, intellectual property, cryptocurrency, and other tangible or intangible property). Each class has its own valuation method. For public display on the Tier 1 ledger, cash and equivalents fold into "Other Assets" to avoid exposing controllers' liquid-asset positions, so the public sees four categories rather than five (see "Asset Aggregation Categories"). See Chapter 11 and Appendix B.

Buy-Borrow-Die: The wealth preservation strategy described in Chapter 2: accumulate appreciating assets, borrow against them tax-free, and hold until death erases all unrealized gains through stepped-up basis. See Chapter 2 for the full mechanics.

Circuit Breaker: A mechanism that uses a three-year rolling average of total ledger wealth as the tax formula's denominator, preventing sharp market declines from causing a destabilizing spike in effective tax rates. See Chapter 8.

Crossover Point: The wealth level (approximately $1.5-2 million) at which a household's wealth tax liability equals their current federal tax burden. Below this point, most households pay less. Above it, most pay more. See Chapter 15.

De Minimis Threshold: The per-item value above which individual ledger registration is required. Congress sets this threshold through implementing legislation (illustratively $10,000 per item). Above the threshold, failure to register is tax evasion, because the controller has a duty to declare. Below the threshold, registration is voluntary; traditional proof of ownership (receipts, titles, insurance documents, photographs) remains legally sufficient, though ledger registration is always available and provides the strongest claim. The threshold applies to individual items, not aggregate value; a controller with meaningful total personal effects still reports the aggregate as a category total on the ledger. See Chapter 7, Chapter 11, and Appendix B.

Duty of Control: The principle that tax liability follows control of wealth, not nominal ownership. Four indicators (use, benefit, exclusion, and transfer) serve as evidence of control, but the definitive test is seizure power: who can reclaim the asset and on what terms? Where control can be revoked by a higher authority, that authority bears the duty. Where seizure requires compensating the other party's stake, control is proportional; where the seizing party can take everything, control is total. See Chapter 6.

Effective Tax Rate: The actual percentage of income or wealth paid in taxes, as opposed to the statutory rate. Because of deductions, credits, and avoidance strategies, effective rates are often far lower than statutory rates. Under the current system, a billionaire's effective rate on total wealth can be below 1%. See Chapters 2 and 3.

Escape Assessment: A market-based verification mechanism. When a controller transacts with third parties (banks, insurers, buyers), any valuation discrepancy between the ledger declaration and the transaction value triggers review. See Chapter 9.

Evasion Bounty: A financial reward paid to whistleblowers who provide evidence of wealth concealed from the public ledger or declarations so fraudulent they constitute deliberate evasion. Funded from poundage collected on delinquent accounts. The whistleblower files a formal claim with the tax authority, which investigates using Tier 2 access; if evasion is confirmed, the whistleblower receives 15-30% of recovered taxes. See Chapter 9.

Ledger (Public Ledger): The comprehensive, tamper-evident record of all wealth within US jurisdiction, and the authoritative record of control. Registration on the ledger is the definitive assertion of ownership; a registered claim supersedes competing paper claims. The government maintains the canonical copy; independent institutions maintain mirrors for verification. See Chapter 7.

Lien Bundling: The practice of packaging tax lien certificates on mixed liquid and illiquid assets into diversified bundles for sale to private investors, minimizing the need for government purchase of illiquid assets. The liquid assets (real estate, securities) make the bundle attractive; the illiquid ones (art, collectibles, minority stakes) come along. See Chapter 9.

Natural Person Rule: The ledger design constraint that only natural persons (and government bodies for public assets) may be recorded as controllers on the public ledger. No corporation, trust, LLC, partnership, foundation, or other legal entity can sign the ledger. The human who controls the entity registers under their own name; the entity appears as the control vehicle in the asset description.

The sole exception is government bodies, which appear as controllers of public assets because sovereign authority cannot be traced further to a private individual. Codified in Section 5 of the proposed Amendment. See Chapter 6 and Appendix A.

Pass-Through Principle: The principle that entities do not bear tax duty; the humans who control them do. For for-profit entities, duty passes through to equity holders (shareholders, owners) and debt holders (creditors, lenders). For non-profits, duty passes through to the board members, directors, or trustees who control the entity's assets. The entity is the vehicle; the human controller is the taxpayer. The natural person rule enforces this on the ledger: the human must be named as controller at registration, not the entity. See Chapter 6.

Payment in Kind: An emergency safety valve allowing taxpayers to transfer assets to the government in lieu of cash payment during declared economic crises. See Chapter 8 and Appendix B.

Poundage: Fees, interest, and enforcement costs assessed on delinquent wealth tax accounts, analogous to penalties in property tax enforcement. See Chapter 9.

Primary Residence Deferral: A protection allowing homeowners to defer wealth taxes on up to $500,000 of primary residence equity. The deferred amount accrues as a lien at Treasury rate + 1%, payable when the home is sold or transferred. See Chapter 15.

Proportional Tax: The wealth tax formula: Your Tax = (Your Wealth / Total Ledger Wealth) x Federal Spending. Using the conservative $175 trillion denominator, this yields an effective rate of approximately 4%. See Chapter 8.

Shell Company/Structure: A legal entity (corporation, LLC, trust, or partnership) that exists primarily to hold assets or obscure the identity of the true owner rather than to conduct active business. Shell structures layered across multiple jurisdictions are a primary tool for hiding wealth from tax authorities. The public ledger's duty-of-control principle pierces these structures by tracing control to the human beneficiary. A shell company cannot appear as a controller on the public ledger; the natural person behind it must. See Chapters 4 and 6.

Stepped-Up Basis: A provision in current tax law that resets the cost basis of inherited assets to their market value at the time of the owner's death, effectively erasing all unrealized capital gains accumulated during the owner's lifetime. This is the "die" step of buy-borrow-die and the single largest wealth-tax-avoidance mechanism in the current code. See Chapter 2.

Tax Gap: The difference between the total taxes legally owed and the total taxes actually collected. The IRS estimates the annual gross federal tax gap at $696 billion (roughly $606 billion after enforcement), representing revenue lost to evasion, avoidance, and non-filing. See Chapters 1 and 4.

Three-Tier Information Model: The privacy architecture for the public ledger. Tier 1 (public): names, total wealth, compliance status, asset categories. Tier 1 has two sub-modes: Tier 1a (name-searchable) for the top 10% of wealth holders and public officials, and Tier 1b (ID-accessible) for everyone else, where the same record exists but is reachable only via the controller's Ledger ID rather than by name search. Tier 2 (government): full itemized records. Tier 3 (individual disclosure): specific asset details by consent or court order. See Chapter 13 and Appendix D.

Transfer Pricing: The practice of setting prices for transactions between related entities (such as subsidiaries of the same multinational corporation) to shift profits to low-tax jurisdictions. A common strategy for reducing taxable income across borders. The wealth tax eliminates the incentive for transfer pricing by taxing wealth directly rather than income. See Chapter 12.

Valuation Challenge: A formal dispute process in which a certified appraiser challenges a controller's declared asset value as significantly below market value. An independent arbitration panel reviews the evidence; if the challenge is upheld, the controller pays back taxes plus a 15% penalty, and the challenger receives 25% of the penalty as a bounty. If the challenge is rejected, the challenger pays arbitration costs. One of the three pillars of market verification alongside escape assessments and third-party reporting. See Chapter 11 and Appendix B.

Wealth Test: The three-part test determining what counts as taxable wealth. An asset must be exchangeable (can be traded), assessable (can be valued), and separable (can be transferred while remaining what it is). See Chapter 5.

Whistleblower: A person who files an evasion bounty claim, providing evidence that wealth has been concealed from the public ledger or that declarations constitute deliberate fraud. Any person may serve as a whistleblower; no professional certification is required. See Chapter 9.

Zero-Knowledge Proof: A cryptographic technique allowing one party to prove a statement is true without revealing the underlying data. Used in the ledger's classified spending tier to verify that spending falls within authorized limits without revealing what was purchased. See Chapter 14.

APPENDIX H

POLICY FAQ

This appendix addresses frequently asked questions about how the wealth tax interacts with charitable giving, nonprofit institutions, Social Security, and state and local taxes. For the core design, see Part II (Chapters 5-9). For persona profiles and worked examples, see Chapter 15.

H.1 What the Duty Protects

What does paying the duty actually protect me from?

A registered, duty-paying stake gets three layers of protection. Against private claimants, no one can displace your stake without going through due process before the Judgment Layer; the earlier filing holds while the dispute is heard. Against the government taking property for public use, the 5th Amendment's Takings Clause requires equitable compensation, and your registered stake is exactly the kind of property the clause was written to protect. Against enforcement for nonpayment, the protection falls away by your own choice; the lien-and-auction track that follows is the same machinery that resolves an unpaid property tax today, applied uniformly across asset classes.

Chapter 10 develops the constitutional grounding.

H.2 Charitable Giving

Under the current system, charitable donations are tax-deductible, creating the perception that deductions drive giving. The evidence suggests otherwise. Research consistently shows that the tax deduction is a secondary motivation for charitable giving; personal values, religious commitment, and community connection are the primary drivers. Studies of countries that have reduced or eliminated charitable deductions (including the UK's periodic adjustments) show modest effects on total giving, typically reductions of 5-15%, not collapse.

Under the wealth tax, there are no deductions of any kind. But there are also no income taxes, payroll taxes, or capital gains taxes. For the roughly 90% of Americans who would pay less under the wealth tax, the increase in disposable income could more than offset any reduction in deduction-motivated giving. The wealthiest donors, who benefit most from deductions, give for reasons that have little to do with tax savings: legacy, influence, institutional commitment, and genuine philanthropy. Giving may change in composition. It is unlikely to disappear.

Consider the numbers. In 2023, Americans gave approximately $557 billion to charity.[1] The tax deduction's value depends on the donor's marginal rate. A household in the 24% bracket that donates $10,000 saves $2,400 in taxes. Under the wealth tax, that $2,400 subsidy disappears, but so does the household's entire federal income tax bill. If the household's total wealth is under $1.5 million, they pay less overall. The net effect: more money in the donor's pocket, even without the deduction.

For ultra-wealthy donors, the calculus is different but the conclusion is similar. A billionaire currently donating $100 million per year captures a $37 million deduction (at 37% marginal rate). Under the wealth tax, that deduction vanishes, but the donation also reduces the donor's taxable wealth by $100 million, saving $4 million in annual wealth tax. The subsidy is smaller, but the motivation for giving at this scale was never primarily about tax savings.

H.3 Nonprofit Endowments

Large institutional endowments (university funds, hospital foundations, charitable trusts) would owe the same 4% on assets they control. A $50 billion university endowment would owe $2 billion annually. This is a significant obligation, but consider the context: most large endowments already target 5% annual spending rates and earn 7-10% on diversified portfolios over the long term. The wealth tax replaces the existing (modest) excise tax on investment income and operates within the range of normal endowment distribution.

Institutions would need to adjust spending and investment strategies, but the 4% rate is below long-term portfolio returns. The more important point: wealth controlled by institutions is still wealth. Exempting endowments would create the largest tax shelter in American history. If the principle is that all wealth on the ledger is taxed equally, exceptions undermine the system's integrity. The duty of control (Chapter 6) applies to the board members who direct institutional assets, just as it applies to individuals who direct personal assets.

What about smaller nonprofits? A community food bank with $500,000 in assets owes $20,000 annually. A local church with a $1 million building owes $40,000. These are real obligations, but they replace the organization's current share of economic friction from the tax system: the payroll taxes on their employees, the compliance costs of maintaining tax-exempt status, and the indirect burden of operating in an economy distorted by 70,000 pages of tax code. Most small nonprofits would find the transition manageable. Those that cannot sustain operations under the wealth tax face the same question any organization faces: is the institution deploying its resources effectively?

H.4 Social Security and Medicare

The current system funds Social Security and Medicare through dedicated payroll taxes. Under the wealth tax, payroll taxes are eliminated. Social Security and Medicare benefits continue unchanged, funded from general revenue (the wealth tax).

This is not unprecedented. Social Security already receives significant general revenue transfers. The shift simply makes explicit what is already partially true: these programs are funded by the federal government, and the federal government's revenue comes from taxation.

Benefit levels, eligibility rules, and program structure are unaffected. The only change is the funding source.

What about the Social Security trust fund? The trust fund is an accounting mechanism, not a separate pool of money. It holds Treasury securities, which are claims on future general revenue. Whether the revenue comes from payroll taxes or a wealth tax, the trust fund's ability to pay benefits depends on the federal government's overall fiscal capacity. A wealth tax that generates sufficient revenue strengthens rather than weakens that capacity.

What about the regressive nature of payroll taxes? The current payroll tax is the most regressive federal tax: it applies at a flat 15.3% (including the employer share) on the first $176,100 of wages (2025), then drops to 2.9% above that. Someone earning $50,000 pays a higher effective payroll rate than someone earning $500,000. Someone living on investment income pays nothing. Replacing this with a proportional wealth tax eliminates one of the most regressive features of the current system.

Critics will argue that severing the payroll-tax-to-Social-Security link weakens the program's political protection. There is truth to this concern. The dedicated payroll tax has historically made Social Security the "third rail" of American politics, because every worker can say "I paid into this." However, the wealth tax creates an even broader constituency: 90% of Americans paying less in total taxes means 90% of Americans with a direct stake in protecting the system that funds their benefits. The political protection shifts from "I paid into this" to "this system saves me money." Both are powerful motivations. The wealth tax does not weaken Social Security; it changes the source of its political armor.

H.5 State and Local Taxes

The wealth tax affects only federal taxes. State and local taxes remain unchanged.

You will still pay:

- **State income taxes** (in states that have them)
- **Property taxes** (to your county or municipality)
- **Sales taxes** (where applicable)
- **State estate or inheritance taxes** (in states that have them)

The federal wealth tax replaces federal income tax, federal payroll taxes, federal corporate tax, federal capital gains tax, and federal estate tax. It does not touch state or local revenue systems.

What about the combined burden? For homeowners in high-property-tax areas, the combined federal wealth tax and local property tax on a home can feel significant. However, remember that the wealth tax replaces all federal income and payroll taxes. A homeowner earning $80,000 currently pays roughly $18,000 in federal taxes. If their home equity is $300,000, the wealth tax on the home portion is $12,000, less than their eliminated federal income tax alone. For most homeowners, the math still favors the wealth tax even after adding property taxes. The crossover point analysis in Chapter 8 accounts for total wealth including home equity.

Why not replace state taxes too? This is a federal constitutional amendment. States retain their sovereign authority to tax as they choose. Some states may eventually adopt similar wealth-based systems; others may not. That's federalism working as designed.

What about state income tax deductions? Currently, you can deduct state and local taxes (SALT) from your federal income tax, subject to caps. Under the wealth tax, there is no federal income tax to deduct from. State taxes become a separate, standalone obligation. For most people, the elimination of federal income tax more than compensates for losing the SALT deduction. A family in New Jersey paying $15,000 in state and local taxes currently deducts $10,000 (the SALT cap), saving roughly $2,200 in federal taxes. Under the wealth tax, that $2,200 deduction disappears, but so does their entire federal income and payroll tax bill.

Will states change their systems? Possibly. If the federal government successfully implements a wealth-based system, some states may follow. Others may see an opportunity to attract residents by keeping income-based systems that favor the wealthy. That's federalism working as designed; states can experiment with different approaches.

Does the wealth tax interact with property taxes? Both are taxes on assets, but they operate independently. Your local property tax applies to real estate assessed values. The federal wealth tax applies to total net wealth. A homeowner pays both, but the federal wealth tax replaces federal income and payroll taxes that were often a larger burden. Chapter 15's persona profiles (particularly Maria the Teacher and Jennifer the Retiree) show the combined math for typical homeowners.

H.6 Progressive Surtaxes for Special Projects

Can Congress add a progressive rate on top of the wealth tax?

Not as permanent brackets. As a time-limited, special-purpose surtax for a named project, yes. The four percent floor is the constitutional duty. Anything above it is statutory, scoped, dated, and disclosed on the same public ledger that holds the base rate.

The distinction matters. Permanent progressive brackets are what failed in the income tax: they created a permanent incentive to restructure wealth into whichever bracket-friendly form the latest amendment overlooked, and they grew an industry of advisors paid to play the seam. A surtax that funds a transcontinental rail line and expires the day the line is paid off is a different instrument. It does not invite a permanent avoidance industry because it is not permanent.

In wartime and other extraordinary circumstance, this is more than permission. Those who control the most wealth have the most to lose if the Republic falls. A temporary progressive surtax in such moments is not a gift to the public. It is the wealthy paying for the survival of the system that protects their wealth.

The Rising Tide logic in Chapter 8 still governs. An infrastructure surtax that grows national wealth by compounding prosperity and opportunity for its citizens lowers everyone's effective rate over time, including the rate of those who paid the surtax. The flat floor exists because the floor must be sound. The system does not require, and does not forbid, the body politic from building above the floor when a generational project warrants it.

See Chapter 8, A Floor Not a Ceiling, for the canonical statement of this doctrine.

H.7 Notes

1. Giving USA Foundation, *Giving USA 2024: The Annual Report on Philanthropy for the Year 2023*, researched and written by the Indiana University Lilly Family School of Philanthropy (Chicago: Giving USA Foundation, 2024), https://givingusa.org/.

APPENDIX I

LEGAL HISTORY OF RELIGIOUS TAXATION

This appendix develops the legal and historical case referenced in Chapter 6's treatment of non-profits, charities, and churches. The chapter's core argument is that the federal government's current practice of exempting religious institutions from taxation is a policy choice, not a constitutional requirement, and that the duty-of-control framework does not cross any new line that the federal government has not already crossed. This appendix walks through the four pieces that support that argument: the feudal origins of the exemption, Madison's 1785 Memorial and Remonstrance, Grant's 1875 proposal, and the Supreme Court's treatment in Walz v. Tax Commission.

I.1 The Feudal Inheritance

The practice of exempting religious institutions from taxation is not American in origin. It traces back to medieval England, where the Crown did not tax the Church because the Church was a parallel sovereign. Bishops held land as peers of the realm. Monasteries operated as semi-autonomous economic units. The Church had its own courts, its own tax-collection mechanism (the tithe), and its own diplomatic relationships with foreign powers. The Crown's jurisdiction reached where the Church's did not, and vice versa. Taxing the Church would have been roughly equivalent to taxing a foreign state.

When the American colonies and then the Republic inherited English common law, they inherited this arrangement alongside everything else. By the time the First Amendment was written, the exemption had been in place for centuries and was treated as a background assumption rather than a policy choice. It was never re-examined on its merits. The constitutional debates at the founding did not address whether the Church-as-sovereign logic still applied in a republic that had formally rejected established churches. The exemption simply persisted. The 1954 addition of 501(c)(3) status under the Internal Revenue Code extended the same logic to all non-profit entities, transforming a historical accommodation for religious institutions into a general policy of non-profit tax exemption.

The relevant point for this book: the current exemption is not a principled policy choice grounded in First Amendment theory. It is a historical artifact carried forward from a political arrangement the United States formally rejected at its founding. Congress can reconsider it without disturbing any constitutional commitment.

I.2 Madison's Memorial and Remonstrance (1785)

James Madison, the principal author of the First Amendment, argued forcefully against state financial entanglement with religion in his 1785 *Memorial and Remonstrance Against Religious Assessments*. The occasion was a Virginia proposal to use tax revenue to support "teachers of the Christian religion," a general religious assessment that would have funded Christian ministers with public money.

Madison's core argument was that government financial entanglement with religion corrupts both. When the state taxes its citizens to fund religious institutions, the state inherits authority over which religious institutions qualify. That authority is inherently corrupting: it creates winners and losers among denominations, it politicizes religious leadership, and it makes the church dependent on the state's continued favor. The *Memorial and Remonstrance* persuaded the Virginia legislature to defeat the assessment bill and instead pass Jefferson's Virginia Statute for Religious Freedom, which became one of the direct antecedents of the First Amendment.

The relevant point for this book: Madison's argument runs against state *support* for religion, not against state *taxation* of religious institutions. These are different things. A government that taxes religious institutions uniformly, as one category of controller among many, is not picking winners among denominations. It is treating them the same. Madison's actual argument, carefully read, does not support the exemption. It supports the opposite: that any arrangement which makes religious institutions financially dependent on the state corrupts religion, and unconditional tax exemption is exactly such an arrangement. The church that pays the same civic obligation as every other controller of wealth is a church whose religious independence the state has no financial lever to erode.

I.3 Grant's 1875 Address to Congress

On December 7, 1875, President Ulysses S. Grant delivered his seventh annual message to Congress and proposed a constitutional amendment requiring "the taxation of all property equally, whether church or corporation, exempting only the last resting place of the dead."

Grant's motivation was practical. He noted that untaxed church property in the United States had grown from about $83 million in 1850 to over $1 billion by 1875, a twelvefold increase in twenty-five years during a period when the total wealth of the country had grown at a much slower rate. He warned that if the trend continued, religious institutions would eventually dominate a large share of the tax base and put the United States in the same position as medieval Europe, where vast religious holdings operated outside the civic economy. He called for taxing all property equally, church or corporation.

Grant's proposal failed. Congress declined to take up the amendment, and the exemption persisted. The trend Grant warned about continued. Church property in the United States today is worth hundreds of billions of dollars by conservative estimate, and much of it is concentrated in a small number of large institutions. The principle Grant proposed is now 150 years overdue.

I.4 Walz v. Tax Commission (1970)

The Supreme Court's most significant modern ruling on religious taxation is *Walz v. Tax Commission of the City of New York*, 397 U.S. 664 (1970). The case was brought by a New York taxpayer who argued that New York City's property tax exemption for religious institutions violated the Establishment Clause by providing indirect financial support to religion. The Court ruled 7-1 against him.

What the Court actually held: the property tax exemption is *permitted* under the Establishment Clause. It is constitutional for a state to exempt religious property from taxation without thereby establishing religion.

What the Court did *not* hold: that exempting religious property is *required*. The Court's opinion, written by Chief Justice Burger, was explicit about this distinction. The Court found the exemption constitutionally permissible. It did not find the exemption constitutionally mandated. Congress, or a state legislature, remains free to tax religious property if it chooses to.

The Court introduced the concept of "excessive entanglement" in *Walz* and refined it in subsequent cases. The concept has since been used to evaluate Establishment Clause challenges to various government-church interactions. The test is whether a specific program creates entanglement beyond what is already tolerated. It is not a general rule that any contact between government and religious institutions is forbidden.

I.5 Existing Entanglement

The federal government already has substantial and tolerated entanglement with religious institutions.

IRS definitions. The IRS maintains a fourteen-factor test for what qualifies as a "church" under the Internal Revenue Code for purposes of 501(c)(3) status, employment tax rules, and exemption from certain information-reporting requirements. The test requires the government to evaluate religious organizations on factors that include "a distinct religious history," "a literature of its own," "established places of worship," and "regular religious services."

The Johnson Amendment. 26 U.S.C. § 501(c)(3) prohibits tax-exempt religious organizations from intervening in political campaigns on behalf of candidates. The IRS has enforced this rule against churches whose clergy endorse political candidates from the pulpit. This is a direct federal regulation of the content of religious speech, and it has been repeatedly upheld.

Payroll taxes. Churches pay Social Security and Medicare taxes on their lay employees under the Federal Insurance Contributions Act. Clergy pay self-employment tax on their ministerial income under the Self-Employment Contributions Act. These are direct federal tax obligations imposed on religious institutions and their workers.

Workplace safety and labor relations. The Department of Labor enforces workplace safety laws at religious schools and religious workplaces. The National Labor Relations Board has jurisdiction over labor relations at religious institutions in certain contexts, subject to the ministerial exception.

None of these entanglements have been found to violate the Establishment Clause. A wealth duty on the humans who control religious property is, under this existing framework, unremarkable. It asks religious institutions to comply with the same rule that governs every other controller of wealth. It does not require the government to make any religious judgment, evaluate any theological position, or favor any denomination. It is a civically neutral rule of general applicability.

I.6 The Theological Objection

The theological objection most often raised against taxing religious institutions has an internal tradition running the other way. In Matthew 22, Jesus is asked whether it is lawful to pay taxes to Caesar. His answer is to render unto Caesar what is Caesar's and unto God what is God's. That is not an argument against taxation. It is an argument that civic and religious obligations are different categories, and both are real. The duty-of-control framework asks religious institutions to render the same civic obligation as every other controller of wealth. No more, no less.

I.7 The Bottom Line

The Supreme Court has never ruled that taxing religious institutions is unconstitutional. Congress has had 150 years of notice that the current exemption is a policy choice, not a legal requirement. The historical case for the exemption rests on a feudal arrangement the United States formally rejected at its founding. Madison's actual argument runs against state support for religion, not against state taxation of religious institutions. Grant's proposal to tax all property equally was sound in 1875 and remains sound now.

The wealth tax does not require any new constitutional theory. It requires Congress to make a different choice within the range of choices the Constitution already permits.

APPENDIX J

REGISTRATION AND CLAIMS, HOW DUTY OF CONTROL RESOLVES IN PRACTICE

The duty of control is one sentence: whoever holds seizure power over wealth bears the duty to pay. The arrangements people build over wealth are not. This appendix shows how that one sentence resolves into a working analysis for the structural patterns that hold most wealth in the United States.

It is a starting point, not a verdict. Two trusts with identical names can have opposite controllers depending on what their documents say. Two pension funds can produce different registrants depending on what oversight the participants actually have. The seizure-power test does not run on labels. It runs on the specific terms of the specific agreement. This appendix gives the templates. The agreement gives the answer.

J.1 Why Terms Matter

The diagnostic is the same one that produces the headlines every year.

A foundation receives three hundred million dollars from its founder, sets up a board, hires staff, files its annual returns. Five years later, the founder's children are board members, the founder's spouse is the executive director drawing a salary, and the foundation's investments are routed through entities the family also owns. Legally, the foundation is a separate institution with an independent board. Practically, it is the family's wealth wearing a different jacket. The Trump Foundation was dissolved by New York court order in 2018 with exactly this pattern. It was not unique. Every year another case surfaces.

A pension fund holds two billion dollars for thirty thousand participants. The trustees are nominally fiduciaries. The investment manager is paid a percentage of assets. Over a decade, the manager directs investments toward funds the manager partly owns, charges layered fees, accepts kickbacks dressed as research credits. Participants see lower returns. The manager extracts the difference. Detroit's pension trustees lived through their version of this story. Central States Teamsters lived through another. The participants were the nominal beneficiaries. The seizure power was elsewhere.

A donor-advised fund agreement says the sponsoring charity has "ultimate discretion" over the assets and the donor's role is "advisory only." Across the entire industry over decades, the rate at which sponsoring charities have refused donor advice for reasons other than fraud or terrorism approaches zero. The legal form says the charity controls. The conduct says the donor controls. Both parties have agreed to leave the fiction undisturbed because the fiction lets the donor park wealth indefinitely without paying tax on a foundation's payout requirement.

These are not aberrations. They are evidence that nominal control and actual control diverge whenever the terms of an arrangement let them. The duty of control framework asks the question the current system avoids: whose wealth can be taken from them, and who can do the taking? The taker is the controller. The person whose wealth can be taken holds a derivative position, valuable to the extent the terms protect it from seizure.

That is the principle. The patterns below show how the analysis runs.

J.2 The Four Patterns

Every legal claim over wealth in the United States is an instance of one of four patterns.

Direct

One person holds the wealth and no other party has a claim to seize. Sole owner of a house. Single-member LLC. Sole proprietor. Individually titled brokerage account.

The titled party is the controller. They register. There is no further analysis.

Layered

A structure stands between the wealth and the human. Trusts, corporations, partnerships, holding companies, funds, foundations, foreign shells, decentralized autonomous organizations, and any other arrangement where wealth sits inside a legal vehicle rather than directly in a person's name.

The analysis runs upstream by asking, at each level, who can override the level below. The chain terminates at the human or humans whose seizure power cannot be overridden by anyone. They are the controllers and they register. If the chain does not terminate at an identifiable human, the wealth becomes Open.

This is the largest pattern in practice. Most wealth above modest household levels is held through some layered structure, and the seizure analysis is the lens that sees through it.

Shared

Multiple parties hold mutually independent rights against portions of the same wealth, and each party's stake is protected from seizure by the others under specific terms. The standard mortgage is the canonical case. The lender can foreclose, but must sell at fair market value and return any surplus above the debt. The borrower's equity is protected from seizure. Both parties have genuine control over their respective portions.

Each party registers what their agreement protects from seizure by the others, and no more. Joint tenants register their respective shares. Partners register what their partnership agreement preserves to them. A pension participant in a properly governed plan registers their accrued benefit. A bondholder registers the principal and accrued interest secured by the bond's terms.

Where the agreement does not protect a stake, the party has no genuine control and registers nothing. The other party registers the full value.

Open

No human can be identified as a controller through any of the analyses above. The wealth sits unregistered on the ledger.

Any person who can demonstrate practical control may register, take the duty, and hold the authoritative claim. This is the enforcement backstop. It applies to foreign-structured wealth on US soil where the chain of control has been deliberately obscured, decentralized organizations without identifiable participants, abandoned accounts past statutory escheat periods, trusts with no traceable controller after death of the grantor and dispersal of the protective layer, and any arrangement where the structure itself prevents identification of a human seizure-holder.

The pattern closes the shell game. A structure can refuse to identify its controller, but it cannot prevent someone else from claiming the wealth and the authority that comes with it.

J.3 The Three Questions

Applied to any arrangement, in this order:

1. Who can take this wealth from its current holder?

That party has seizure power. They are the candidate controller. If the answer is "no one," go to question 3.

2. If the taker takes, must they compensate any other party's stake?

If yes, the arrangement is Shared. Each party registers what their agreement protects.

If no, the arrangement is Layered or Direct. The taker registers the full value, regardless of who currently holds title.

3. If no taker can be identified, who has demonstrable practical control?

If a person can be identified through documented decision-making, beneficial use, or any other observable exercise of control, that person is the controller. The legal form does not matter; conduct does.

If no person can be identified at all, the wealth is Open. Anyone with a credible claim of control may register and take both the duty and the authority.

The questions are deliberately blunt. They cut through every label by asking only about the mechanics of seizure and protection.

J.4 Reference Table

Most arrangements fit a row in this table without re-running the full analysis.

Structure	Pattern	Default registrant under standard terms
Sole ownership, single-member LLC	Direct	Titled party
Joint tenancy, community property	Shared	Each tenant by titled share
Standard mortgage with surplus protection	Shared	Borrower on equity, lender on lien
Predatory loan with no surplus protection	Layered	Lender, full value
Public corporation shares	Layered	Each shareholder, their own shares
Closely held LLC, partnership, S-corp	Layered	Each owner by economic share, with substance override

Structure	Pattern	Default registrant under standard terms
Holding company, subsidiary chain	Layered	Trace to the parent's controllers
Mutual fund, ETF, pooled investment	Layered	Each investor, their own stake
Defined-contribution pension, IRA, 401(k)	Shared	Each participant, their own account
Defined-benefit pension with real oversight	Shared	Each participant, accrued benefit
Defined-benefit pension where managers can self-deal	Layered	Managers as controllers
Revocable trust	Layered	Grantor
Irrevocable trust with retained settlor power	Layered	Settlor
Irrevocable trust with trust protector replacement	Layered	Trust protector, or whoever appointed them
Fully discretionary trust, no protector, no modification rights	Layered	Trustee (rare; usually variants apply)
Donor-advised fund where charity follows advice	Layered	Donor or successor advisor
Foundation with independent board	Layered	Board members collectively
Foundation with family-dominated board	Layered	Family under shell-game analysis
Independent congregational church	Shared	Members collectively, by participation
Church with diocesan or conference authority	Layered	Diocese or conference controllers
Foreign entity with traceable US controller	Layered	The US controller
Foreign entity, no traceable controller, US-situs assets	Open	Anyone with demonstrated control
Decentralized organization with identifiable participants	Layered	Each participant, their stake
Decentralized organization with no identifiable participants	Open	Anyone with demonstrated control
Decedent's estate during probate	Court-controlled	Resolves to heirs on distribution
Government-held public assets	Sovereign	Government, no duty

The table is a starting point. The real test for any specific arrangement is the seizure-power analysis applied to the actual terms of the actual document.

J.5 Three Worked Examples

Example 1: A discretionary irrevocable trust (Layered)

Wealthy Grandparent funded a one hundred million dollar dynasty trust in 2010. The trust document names an independent professional trustee with full discretion. Beneficiaries are Grandparent's three children and any issue. A trust protector named in the document holds the power to replace the trustee for cause. The protector is Grandparent's longtime estate attorney, who consults with the children on matters of trust administration.

Question 1: who can take this wealth?

Not the trustee. The trustee is bound by the document and can be replaced by the protector for cause. Not the trustee's institution; same constraint.

The trust protector can take. They can replace the trustee with another trustee who reaches different conclusions about distributions. The protector's power is upstream of the trustee's discretion.

Can anyone replace the protector? The document allows the children, acting unanimously, to replace the protector. The children's collective authority is upstream of the protector's authority. Their collective authority is upstream of everything in the structure.

Question 2: must the takers compensate any other party? No. The children acting collectively can redirect the entire corpus toward themselves and their issue.

Result: the three children are the collective controllers. Each registers a share consistent with their reasonably expected entitlement. If distributions over the trust's history have been roughly even, each registers one third. The trust protector and the trustee are delegates and bear no duty.

Variants change the analysis. If the document had named the children as primary beneficiaries with vested remainders rather than as discretionary beneficiaries, each child would register their vested share directly. If the document had named no protector and no modification mechanism, the trustee would be the genuine controller and would register as a natural person, not as a fiduciary of the trust. If Grandparent had retained a substitution power, Grandparent would be the controller through the same grantor-trust analysis used elsewhere in this book, and the rest of the structure would be irrelevant.

The label "discretionary irrevocable trust" did not settle the analysis. The terms did.

Example 2: A family farm with a mortgage (Shared)

The Okafor family farm is held by Okafor Family LLC, of which Grace Okafor is sole member. The farm assets total two million dollars: land, equipment, livestock, structures. The farm carries a five hundred thousand dollar mortgage with a regional bank. The mortgage is a standard commercial loan: on default, the bank may foreclose, must sell at fair market value, and must return any surplus to Grace.

Question 1: who can take this wealth?

Grace can dispose of the farm at any time, subject to satisfying the mortgage. The bank can take the farm on default, but only by paying off Grace's equity stake from the proceeds.

Question 2: must the takers compensate the other party?

Yes, in both directions. Grace's equity is protected from bank seizure by the surplus-return provision. The bank's lien is protected from Grace's disposition by the requirement to satisfy the mortgage on sale.

Result: Shared pattern. Grace registers one and a half million dollars of equity on her household ledger. The bank registers a five hundred thousand dollar lien on its institutional ledger, and the bank's controllers (its shareholders, in standard form) bear duty on that lien through their share registrations.

Variant: if the mortgage were a predatory title-loan-style instrument with no surplus protection, the bank could take everything on default. Grace would register nothing; the bank would register the full two million. Grace would be a tenant in fact, even though she holds the title.

The Okafor farm is a Shared arrangement because the mortgage terms preserve Grace's stake. A different loan with worse terms would convert it to a Layered arrangement and Grace would be on the wrong side of the seizure question.

Example 3: A foreign shell holding a Manhattan penthouse (Layered, then Open)

A forty million dollar penthouse is titled to Sunshine Holdings LLC, a Cayman Islands entity. Sunshine Holdings is wholly owned by Beach House Trust, a Cook Islands asset-protection trust. The settlor of Beach House Trust is Jane Owner, a US citizen and resident. The trust's grantor retained no formal control powers. The trustee has full discretion among Jane, her three children, and "any persons the trustee deems appropriate."

Question 1: who can take this wealth?

Trace the chain. The trustee can act, but who appointed the trustee, and who can replace them? The trust document allows replacement by a protector named in an appointment letter; the letter names Jane's longtime advisor, who acts in concert with Jane on trust matters. Jane funded the trust. Jane is a beneficiary. Jane's family receives all distributions. The structure exists primarily to hold a single asset Jane uses as her residence when in New York.

Under the shell-game analysis, Jane is the controller. The chain of nominal control terminates at her practical authority. The intermediate entities are metadata.

Question 2: must Jane compensate any other party? No. The structure has no other genuine claimant. The trustee, the protector, and the LLC manager are all delegates of Jane's authority.

Result: Jane registers the full forty million on her household ledger. Sunshine Holdings and Beach House Trust appear in the asset description as the vehicles through which the title is held, but the controller field reads "Jane Owner."

Now the variant Chapter 12 contemplates: Jane refuses to register.

The penthouse sits on the ledger with no registered controller. Three claim paths open.

First, family-internal claim. Jane's adult children, the trust protector, or any beneficiary can step up, register, bear the duty, and take the authoritative claim. Whoever registers becomes the legally recognized controller of the penthouse. Jane's title through the entity chain is unenforceable against a registered claim.

Second, third-party claim. Anyone who can demonstrate practical control of the property may register. A documented agent with direction-from-Jane records, a property manager whose authority is on file with the building, an ex-spouse with a settlement agreement referencing the property. The claimant takes the duty and the wealth.

Third, the lien-and-auction process from Chapter 9. If no one claims the penthouse and the wealth tax goes unpaid, the ordinary process runs. The penthouse is liened, auctioned, and proceeds satisfy the duty plus poundage. Surplus, if any, escheats after a statutory period.

Chapter 12's point that the owner can leave but the wealth cannot is the consequence of all three paths working together. The asset is on US soil. The system does not need Jane's cooperation to extract value from it.

J.6 Connection to the Rest of the Framework

The patterns above produce registrations. Registrations are the foundation of everything else.

Chapter 7 describes how registrations enter the ledger and how third-party reporting feeds them automatically for the common cases (deeds, brokerage positions, business registrations, probate valuations). Chapter 9 describes what happens when registered duty goes unpaid, and how unregistered wealth becomes vulnerable to claim. Chapter 11 describes the Judgment Layer that resolves contested valuations and competing claims.

Appendix A Section 4 establishes the constitutional rule that "where control of wealth is subject to revocation, override, or nullification by another, tax liability shall rest upon the person possessing superior authority over such wealth." That is the seizure-power principle in constitutional language. Section 5 adds that only natural persons and governments register. Together they are the constitutional foundation that this appendix turns into operational analysis.

The four patterns and three questions are the bridge between the principle and the implementing statute Congress will eventually write. Congress writes the attribution rules for thousands of specific agreement patterns; this appendix shows the framework Congress works in. The patterns do not change with the statute. The statute fills in the details that practical administration requires.

The diagnostic survives every variation. Who can take the wealth, must they compensate the other party, and if no one can be identified, who has demonstrable control. Three questions. Four patterns. One principle. Every claim over wealth in the United States resolves through this analysis, regardless of the label the parties have agreed to attach to their arrangement.

BIBLIOGRAPHY

Sources cited in this book are listed below in alphabetical order. Chapter footnotes use Chicago Notes form; full citations appear here in Chicago Bibliography form. Court cases sort by case name, with the *v.* word ignored.

Aladangady, Aditya, Jesse Bricker, Andrew C. Chang, Sarena Goodman, Jacob Krimmel, Kevin B. Moore, Sarah Reber, Alice Henriques Volz, and Richard A. Windle. "Changes in U.S. Family Finances from 2019 to 2022: Evidence from the Survey of Consumer Finances." *Federal Reserve Bulletin* 109, no. 6 (October 2023). https://www.federalreserve.gov/publications/files/scf23.pdf.

Board of Governors of the Federal Reserve System. "Distributional Financial Accounts." Q3 2025 release. https://www.federalreserve.gov/releases/z1/dataviz/dfa/.

Board of Governors of the Federal Reserve System. *Financial Accounts of the United States* (Z.1). Q4 2025 release (March 19, 2026). https://www.federalreserve.gov/releases/z1/.

Board of Governors of the Federal Reserve System. *Survey of Consumer Finances*. 2022 data, released October 2023. https://www.federalreserve.gov/econres/scfindex.htm.

Brownlee, W. Elliot. *Federal Taxation in America: A History*. 3rd ed. Cambridge: Cambridge University Press, 2016.

Brushaber v. Union Pacific Railroad, 240 U.S. 1 (1916).

Bundesverfassungsgericht (German Federal Constitutional Court). 2 BvL 37/91. June 22, 1995.

Burwell v. Hobby Lobby Stores, Inc., 573 U.S. 682 (2014).

California Employment Development Department. "Contribution Rates, Withholding Schedules, and Meals and Lodging Values." https://edd.ca.gov/en/payroll_taxes/rates_and_withholding/. See also California Senate Bill 951 (2022), which eliminated the State Disability Insurance wage cap effective January 1, 2024.

Capaccio, Anthony. "Pentagon Racks Up $35 Trillion in Accounting Changes in One Year." *Bloomberg*, January 22, 2020. https://www.bloomberg.com/news/articles/2020-01-22/pentagon-racks-up-35-trillion-in-accounting-changes-in-one-year.

Center on Budget and Policy Priorities. "Policy Basics: The Earned Income Tax Credit." 2024. https://www.cbpp.org/research/policy-basics-the-earned-income-tax-credit.

Centers for Disease Control and Prevention. "Drug Overdose Deaths." https://www.cdc.gov/overdose-prevention/data-research/facts-stats/.

Committee for a Responsible Federal Budget. "CBO Estimates 2025 Deficit Totaled $1.8 Trillion." October 2025. https://www.crfb.org/blogs/cbo-estimates-2025-deficit-totaled-18-trillion.

Congressional Budget Office. "Monthly Budget Review: Summary for Fiscal Year 2025." 2025. https://www.cbo.gov/publication/61307.

Congressional Budget Office. "Revisiting the Extent to Which Payroll Taxes Are Passed Through to Employees." Working Paper 2021-06, June 2021. https://www.cbo.gov/publication/57089.

e-Estonia. "KSI Blockchain." https://e-estonia.com/solutions/cyber-security/ksi-blockchain/.

Economist/YouGov. "Majorities of Americans Say Wealth Inequality Is a Problem and Want Government Intervention." Poll, January 2-5, 2026. https://today.yougov.com/politics/articles/53821-majorities-americans-say-wealth-inequality-is-problem-want-government-intervention-january-2-5-2026-economist-yougov-poll.

Eisinger, Jesse, Jeff Ernsthausen, and Paul Kiel. "The Secret IRS Files: Trove of Never-Before-Seen Records Reveal How the Wealthiest Avoid Income Tax." *ProPublica*, June 8, 2021. https://www.propublica.org/article/the-secret-irs-files-trove-of-never-before-seen-records-reveal-how-the-wealthiest-avoid-income-tax.

Florida Statutes § 197.162. https://www.flsenate.gov/Laws/Statutes/2024/197.162.

Giving USA Foundation. *Giving USA 2024: The Annual Report on Philanthropy for the Year 2023*. Researched and written by the Indiana University Lilly Family School of Philanthropy. Chicago: Giving USA Foundation, 2024. https://givingusa.org/.

Henry, James S. *The Price of Offshore Revisited: New Estimates for "Missing" Global Private Wealth, Income, Inequality, and Lost Taxes*. Tax Justice Network, July 2012. https://www.taxjustice.net/cms/upload/pdf/Price_of_Offshore_Revisited_120722.pdf.

Internal Revenue Service. "Earned Income and EITC Tables." https://www.irs.gov/credits-deductions/individuals/earned-income-tax-credit/earned-income-and-earned-income-tax-credit-eitc-tables.

Internal Revenue Service. *Internal Revenue Service Data Book, 2024*. Publication 55B. Washington, DC: U.S. Department of the Treasury, 2024. https://www.irs.gov/pub/irs-pdf/p55b.pdf.

Internal Revenue Service. *Statistics of Income, Individual Income Tax Returns, Tax Year 2022*. Washington, DC: Internal Revenue Service, 2024. https://www.irs.gov/statistics.

Internal Revenue Service. "Tax Gap Projections for Tax Years 2021 and 2022." October 2024. https://www.irs.gov/newsroom/the-tax-gap.

Navigator Research. "Four in Five Americans Support Raising Taxes on the Rich and Corporations to Reduce the Deficit." January 2026. https://navigatorresearch.org/four-in-five-americans-support-raising-taxes-on-the-rich-and-corporations-to-reduce-the-deficit/.

NPR. "Purdue Pharma, Sacklers Reach New $7.4 Billion Opioid Settlement." June 16, 2025. https://www.npr.org/2025/06/16/nx-s1-5435318/purdue-pharma-sacklers-reach-new-7-4-billion-opioid-settlement.

People of the State of New York v. Donald J. Trump et al. New York Attorney General filings, 2022. https://ag.ny.gov/sites/default/files/tto_release_properties_addendum_-_final.pdf. Civil fraud judgment of approximately $464 million entered February 2024 and vacated on Eighth Amendment grounds by the Appellate Division, First Department, August 21, 2025. See NBC News, https://www.nbcnews.com/politics/donald-trump/judgment-trump-civil-fraud-case-officially-entered-464-million-rcna140256, and *The D&O Diary*, https://www.dandodiary.com/2025/08/articles/director-and-officer-liability/ny-court-affirms-trump-civil-fraud-ruling-vacates-massive-damages/.

Pichet, Eric. "The Consequences of the French Wealth Tax: An Empirical Analysis." Summarized in Tyler Cowen, "The Economic Consequences of the French Wealth Tax," *Marginal Revolution*, September 2024. https://marginalrevolution.com/marginalrevolution/2024/09/the-economic-consequences-of-the-french-wealth-tax.html.

Pollock v. Farmers' Loan & Trust Co., 157 U.S. 429 (1895).

Rothstein, Richard. *The Color of Law: A Forgotten History of How Our Government Segregated America*. New York: Liveright, 2017.

Santa Clara County v. Southern Pacific Railroad, 118 U.S. 394 (1886).

Tax Foundation. "2025 Tax Brackets." https://taxfoundation.org/data/all/federal/2025-tax-brackets/.

Tax Justice Network. *The State of Tax Justice 2024*. November 2024. https://taxjustice.net/reports/the-state-of-tax-justice-2024/.

Tax Policy Center. "Who Will Pay No Federal Individual Income Tax in 2025?" Urban-Brookings Tax Policy Center, 2025. https://taxpolicycenter.org/fiscal-facts/who-will-pay-no-federal-individual-income-tax-2025.

Tyler v. Hennepin County, 598 U.S. 631 (2023).

U.S. Bureau of Economic Analysis. *U.S. International Investment Position*. Year-end 2025 release. https://www.bea.gov/data/intl-trade-investment/international-investment-position.

U.S. Census Bureau. "Quarterly Residential Vacancies and Homeownership." Current Population Survey/Housing Vacancy Survey, 2023. https://www.census.gov/housing/hvs/.

U.S. Department of the Treasury, Office of Tax Analysis. "Disparities in the Benefits of Tax Expenditures by Race and Ethnicity." January 2023. https://home.treasury.gov/news/featured-stories/disparities-in-the-benefits-of-tax-expenditures-by-race-and-ethnicity.

U.S. Government Accountability Office. *Department of Defense: Actions Needed to Reduce Accounting Adjustments*. GAO-20-96. January 2020. https://www.gao.gov/products/gao-20-96.

U.S. Government Accountability Office. *F-35 Program: DOD Needs Better Accountability for Global Spare Parts and Reporting of Losses Worth Millions*. GAO-23-106098. May 2023. https://www.gao.gov/products/gao-23-106098.

U.S. Government Accountability Office. *Financial Management: DOD Needs to Improve System Oversight*. GAO-23-104539. March 2023. https://www.gao.gov/products/gao-23-104539.

Walz v. Tax Commission of the City of New York, 397 U.S. 664 (1970).

Wikipedia. "Deepwater Horizon oil spill." https://en.wikipedia.org/wiki/Deepwater_Horizon_oil_spill.

Wikipedia. "Visa Inc." https://en.wikipedia.org/wiki/Visa_Inc.

ABOUT THE AUTHOR

Dan Shaffer is a data engineer and founder of 4D4 Labs, a boutique data engineering studio in Cleveland, Ohio. Over fifteen years, he has designed data pipelines, automation systems, and analytics platforms across healthcare, finance, ecommerce, and government-facing systems. His work exposed him to the machinery behind property taxation, public records, assessments, and government data workflows. Before that, he managed a Domino's Pizza in Ohio, where he learned what it feels like to work for a paycheck the tax system reaches before you do. *The Last Tax* began as an engineering question: if counties can track every acre of land, and banks can value every asset they lend against, why does the federal tax system pretend it cannot see wealth?

www.ingramcontent.com/pod-product-compliance
Ingram Content Group UK Ltd.
Pitfield, Milton Keynes, MK11 3LW, UK
UKHW020201290926
15471UKWH00005B/1000